International Journal for Theory and Analysis of Literature and Communication

Volume 43, Number 2   June 2022

Critical Approaches to the Storytelling Boom

Maria Mäkelä
Tampere University

Hanna Meretoja
University of Turku

Abstract   The proponents of the contemporary storytelling boom, such as professional business storytellers and self-help coaches, urge individuals, groups, institutions, and corporations alike to find and tell their story. Social media as the
predominant narrative environment for contemporary storytellers promotes the
instrumentalization and commodification of stories of personal experience. Literary fiction as the primary locus for narrative experimentation finds itself conditioned and challenged by the story logic of social media, but it also possesses unique
affordances for a critical engagement with the current celebration of narrative. How
should a narrative theorist position oneself vis-à-vis these developments that are
currently changing the public notions of what narratives are and what they can do?
By drawing from narrative hermeneutics and cognitive and rhetorical narratology,
this article outlines a "story-critical" approach to the current storytelling boom and
provides examples of how to bring narrative-theoretical findings to bear on public and professional nonacademic storytalk. The article focuses particularly on a
critical analysis of storytelling consultancy, provides an overview of antinarrativist
approaches and recent criticism of the storytelling boom in narrative studies, analyzes the story logic of social media, discusses the critical potential of contemporary
"metanarrative" forms of fiction, and proposes narrative hermeneutics as one pos-

This article was written in the context of the consortium project "Instrumental Narratives: The Limits of Storytelling and New Story-Critical Narrative Theory," funded by the
Academy of Finland (grant nos. 314768 and 314769).

Poetics Today 43:2 (June 2022)   DOI 10.1215/03335372-9642567

sible paradigm for the critical examination of storytelling cultures. It concludes by
envisioning future forms of public critical engagement for narrative theorists. Popular notions of narrative tend to celebrate the cognitive and moral benefits of storytelling while downplaying the limits of narrative understanding and popular story
formulas; this article thus identifies the dissemination of tools for a critical narrative analysis among various audiences as an important task for narrative scholars.

Keywords   storytelling boom, story-critical narrative theory, social media storytelling, narrative hermeneutics, metanarrative fiction, storytelling consultancy

"Narratives are everywhere" was once the triumphant slogan of narrative
scholars, but now we are starting to realize that this pervasiveness might in
fact be a problem. In contemporary social media-induced narrative environments, stories of personal change and disruptive experience often end
up dominating over scientific knowledge or discussion of structural social
issues. As scholar of social politics Sujatha Fernandes (2017) has argued,
the contemporary storytelling boom is, in essence, inextricable from the
neoliberal doctrine that highlights the upward mobility of an individual,
while downplaying supra-individual societal structures and processes. Narrative has, indeed, a unique capacity to capture and convey human experience—what it feels like to be this particular person living through these
particular events (e.g., Bruner 1991; Herman 2009). This affordance of narrative is now widely mobilized across spheres of life: storytelling consultancy thrives; economists talk about "narrative economics" (Shiller 2019),
and practices ranging from personal branding (see Salmon 2010) to sociopolitical activism (see Polletta 2006; Fernandes 2017) increasingly draw
from a narrative repertoire. What has not received much scholarly attention are the possible downsides of these engaging narratives that everyone
should allegedly be crafting in today's story economy. While Western literary and philosophical traditions have their own strong *story-critical* cur-
rents, contemporary practices of storytelling have been, for the most part,
uncritically celebrated. We have organized this special issue according to
the premise that this wholehearted embrace of storytelling is something
that ought to be challenged by narratologists as well as philosophically,
sociologically, and psychologically oriented narrative scholars.

Many contemporary researchers in literary studies, psychology, and
philosophy like to claim that engaging with narratives enhances our mind-
reading ability, or cognitive empathy, and that such skills play a crucial
role in social interaction and moral development (see, e.g., Keen 2007;
Kidd and Castano 2013; Nussbaum 2010). It is no wonder, then, that narrative is touted as the miracle cure for a wide variety of individual and
social ills. Many narrative studies approaches lend generous support to

the instrumentalization of narrative form, and storytelling consultants and manuals eagerly repeat more or less streamlined versions of recent studies on narrative and empathy (see, e.g., Peterson 2017). Yet narrative may just as easily be put to uses that are dubious, if not dangerous. The widespread, uncritical use of narratives of personal experience in journalism and social media may have large-scale consequences that are neither intended nor anticipated. Experientiality may come at the cost of informativeness or of understanding complex phenomena, while the narrative form as such tends to complicate the distinction between factual and fictional rhetoric (see Björninen 2019) in contemporary storytelling environments. Self-fashioning through cultural narratives adopted from self-help literature is not without its risks either. While narratives are ideally suited to conveying human experiences, they may simplify and misrepresent—or simply fail to depict—complex social interactions or material processes that have a timescale that goes beyond an individual lifetime, such as climate change (see, e.g., Raipola 2019; Caracciolo 2021). Consequently, pertinent tasks for contemporary narrative scholars are to highlight not only the affordances but also the epistemic, cognitive, and ethical limitations of narrative forms and, in particular, to articulate the specific elements of narrative that function as such limitations (Mäkelä 2018; Mäkelä et al. 2021; Meretoja 2018; Meretoja and Davis 2018).

This special issue of *Poetics Today*, entitled "Critical Approaches to the Storytelling Boom," seeks to redefine the role of narrative theorists and analysts in the contemporary storytelling boom. If research on the benefits of storytelling has caught on in the public imagination and various professional practices, we should be in a position to disseminate *critical practices* for the analysis of the forms and contexts of storytelling, as well. In this special issue, narrative scholars across disciplines analyze and critique different aspects of the storytelling boom and discuss contemporary narrative instrumentalization by various actors ranging from antifeminists and storytelling consultants to reading groups. In this introduction, we seek to briefly recontextualize the features of the storytelling boom within contemporary narrative scholarship as well as within some earlier forms of "story-criticism" in Western philosophical thought and literary tradition. We will also propose new theoretical and pragmatic narrative studies approaches to the storytelling boom that provide a critical edge and resist easy amalgamation with the general storytalk and the commodification of storytelling. Our primary goal here is to look for and suggest societally sustainable and methodologically productive forms of scholarly engagement with the storytelling boom.

The special issue does not rely on one, fixed definition of narrative, but rather attempts a pragmatic approach to contemporary notions of "stories" and "narratives" dominating the public sphere. The starting-point for this exploration is the instrumentalization of narrative in various spheres of life, and in relation to this social phenomenon, the notions of narrative as a cognitive sense-making tool, a culturally mediated hermeneutic practice of shaping experience, and a rhetorical strategy to capture the attention of audiences amid the information overload are highlighted instead of a more traditional, structural understanding of "narrative" as a mere causal-temporal ordering of events. A particularly exciting tension emerges between social media and literary understandings of narrative. Social media storytelling may consist of a simple "share" or foreground the uneventfulness of one's everyday life in ways that would not be tellable in any other storytelling context. Literary fiction, in turn, attempts to redefine and regain its role as artistic storytelling amid the explosion of instrumental narratives, both conforming to and challenging the success of "true stories" and social media authenticity.

Inside Looking Out or Outside Looking In? Narrative Studies and the Storytelling Boom

At best, a narrative-theoretical intervention in the business- and self-help-led storytelling boom would support the development of new, socially, culturally, and ecologically sustainable narrative practices in different spheres of life. The more sophisticated the commercially and politically motivated use of narrative becomes, the greater is the need for tools of critical narrative analysis among various societal and professional groups and the general audience. Yet the task is not simple, as both public discourses and collective imaginaries are saturated by storytalk coming from various actors attempting to make a profit and gain visibility with storytelling. The task of narrative scholars is made even more difficult by the fact that the storytelling boom has selectively adopted concepts and empirical findings from narrative studies, thus integrating scholarly discourse into the neoliberal aims and rhetoric of the "story business."

The contemporary profit-driven storyteller's stock response to critique is to refer to our allegedly universal need for narratives. The public discourse around storytelling is permeated by a "campfire rhetoric" that associates even the most commodified use of narratives with the elementary role that storytelling has played in human culture and evolution through the ages, thus echoing the twenty-first-century cognitive-evolutionary approaches to narrative (e.g., Boyd 2009). This is emblematically expressed in the marketing guru Jonah Sachs's (2012: 44) acclaimed *Winning the Story Wars: Why*

Those Who Tell—and Live—the Best Stories Will Rule the Future: "Great stories are universal because at their core, humans have more in common with each other than the pseudo-science of demographic slicing has led us to believe. Great brands and campaigns are sensitive to the preferences of different types of audiences, but the core stories and the values they represent can be appreciated by anyone. Universality is the opposite of insincerity." Short as it is, this quotation contains several keywords and associations of the storytelling boom: universality, values, sincerity.

While celebrating the universal value and stock of narratives, today's most popular storytelling manuals feature lists of necessary and avoidable narrative elements for storytellers. In his recent best-selling manual *Storyworthy: Engage, Teach, Persuade, and Change Your Life Through the Power of Storytelling*, for example, Matthew Dicks (2018: 26) proclaims a recognizable "change"—even a personal epiphany—to be necessary for successful storytelling: "You must start out as one version of yourself and end as something new." In fact, for Dicks, *storytelling* denotes primarily (if not exclusively) *personal storytelling*: "There is power in personal storytelling that folktales and fables will never possess" (25). Sachs calls for an "update" and "enactment" of myths as the most efficient marketing tool in today's "story wars." For decades, one of the darling theories of story consultancy has been Joseph Campbell's (1949) *Hero's Journey* or the *monomyth*, which argues for the universal story model of an archetypal hero triumphing over supernatural powers and emerging as an exemplary individual who is able to benefit his entire community. Sachs follows suit: "In my experience, the more of [Campbell's] insights you use [in training marketers], the more likely your audiences are to say, 'Aha! This my story!'" (147). None of the storytelling manuals and trainings that we have seen using Campbell's theory acknowledges, much less engages with, the long line of criticism against Campbell's ahistorical, universalizing Jungian presumptions, stretching from poststructuralist problematization of a collective unconscious to recent feminist interventions in the public sphere such as *The Heroine Journeys* project.[1] As Brian Attebery (2014: 119), among others, asserts, Campbell bends his evidence to fit the monomyth, while his theory "rests on shaky folkloristic and ethnographic grounds."

Either derived from the universal stock of stories or rooted in one's personal experience, the "compelling story" of the contemporary storytelling boom can thus be conceptualized as a successful amalgamation of the particular and the universal. The experiential truth conveyed by storytelling is commodified, and rather than treated as an intersubjective act, it is con-

---

1. See *The Heroine Journeys* project, heroinejourneys.com.

sidered an asset in the attention economy. In the words of storyteller Matthew Dicks (2018: 26): "We tell stories to express our hardest, best, most authentic truths. . . . They [people] want the real deal. They want the kind of stories that just might make them fall in love with the storyteller."

Professional storytellers clearly favor cognitive, psychological, and anthropological or folkloristic theories of narrative. For example, the amateur definitions of narrative by the storytelling consultants often look like smart adaptations of cognitive-narratological prototype definitions (Mäkelä et al. 2021: 142; Mäkelä 2021: 50). Dicks's foregrounding of *personal experience* is a case in point, as it resonates with the emphasis of cognitive narratologists on narrative as *mediated experientiality* (Fludernik 1996; Herman 2009). Or consider the definition by Sachs (2012: 20–21): "Stories are how we humans arrange and recount our experiences of the world so that others will want to listen to and learn from them. They allow us to create order out of the chaotic, otherwise meaningless experience of our senses by editing out irrelevant details, defining a cause for each effect and providing meaning in the string of things we have seen, felt or even just imagined." By emphasizing the ordering of lived experience, immersive storyworld details, and a recognizable "breach" (Bruner 1991) or "storyworld disruption" (Herman 2009), these storytelling consultants superficially align themselves with hermeneutic approaches which emphasize narrative as the human mode of experiencing time (Ricoeur 1983) and with the cognitive approaches that see it as a tool for "coming to terms with time, process, and change" (Herman, Jahn, and Ryan 2005: iv).

Moreover, the storytelling business has been eager to adopt the recently widely popularized studies on the links connecting narrative, reading, and empathy. Both cognitive-narratological approaches to readerly immersion (e.g., Ryan 2001) and experimental psychological studies of how reading literary narratives enhances empathy (see, e.g., Kidd and Castano 2013) have been translated and commercialized into training material for individuals and organizations. An illuminating example can be found within the web materials of "storyteller" and "coach" Katja Alanne who heads a storytelling training for organizations by the in-service training program at the University of Helsinki, Finland. What follows are fragments of a story allegedly told by a business manager encountering change resistance in her customer services team. This team was supposed to launch a new chat service until workers resisted. The sustained conflict culminated in an encounter between an employee and the manager:

> So, one day Mirja came and talked to me and told me straightforwardly that "Listen Liisa, you're not going to make this change happen by lecturing about

its benefits. You need to think about ways of helping us with this. This is not a piece of cake, and every one of us will need personal support from you."

I went speechless and then hugged her suddenly. She went totally speechless too. . . .

And just guess if the chat thing took off after that. It sure did.

The storytelling trainer continues:

Didn't the story sweep you off your feet? Feeling anxious about Liisa's challenge and being relieved at the end by how all turned out so well. You were swept away and immersed by this story. According to research a story activates not only the linguistic but also the kinetic faculties of your brain. The latter occurred when you read about Liisa hugging Mirja. (Alanne 2019)

Enactivist second-wave cognitive narratologists will recognize the arguments as their own, as their recent research has emphasized the readerly enactment of the embodied actions represented in narratives (e.g., Kuzmičová 2014). Yet the ways in which these arguments are being watered down and bluntly instrumentalized may not exactly fit academics' idea of a successful dissemination of research results among the nonacademic audiences. Enactivist narratology does not assume a simple causality between narrative enactment and empathy or any other fixed rhetorical function or ethical effect. The theoretically and methodologically problematic equation between theory of mind and moral agency which does have supporters in narrative studies (for criticism, see, e.g., Gallagher and Hutto 2008; Zahavi 2014; Meretoja 2018: 3–5) results in the context of storytelling consultancy in a deliberatively backward reasoning where immersion in a compelling story (such as the one quoted above) in a workshop is believed to make us more ethical and hence more efficient team workers in the future.

A reliance on discourses of the cognitive and evolutionary "naturalness" of storytelling thus efficiently and cleverly highlights the shared cognitive-emotional ground created by compelling narratives while downplaying the instrumentalization of storytelling in specific contexts. Such "campfire rhetoric" pitches storytelling as a "natural" part of our brain architecture dating back to ancient tribal settings and therefore somehow stripped off of manipulative uses. This naturalizing is particularly apparent in narrative environments that are saturated with conflicts of interest and of ideology, such as political debate and activism. While cognitive narrative studies as such cannot be blamed for promoting any particular ideology, its vocabulary lends itself easily to idealizing and naturalizing discourse in which politicians or advertisers sell ideas in the package of an emotionally appealing story that focuses on individual experience. The cognitive narrative prototype, the recounting of disruptive individual experience with immersive storyworld detail, thrives in the contemporary story economy as "compelling stories" highlighting the upward mobility of the neoliberal subject. Maria Mäkelä has identified as one such recurring masterplot (cf. Abbott 2008) what she coins the "conversion story of the wellness entrepreneur," the story formula where "getting off the hamster wheel" and the experience of burnout lead to new, transformative business ideas (Mäkelä 2018; Mäkelä 2020).

From the point of view of narrative theory, this curious yet strategically beneficial relationship between the naturalness of storytelling and its conspicuously manipulative uses can be conceptualized as an intentional collapsing of the cognitive and the rhetorical: storytelling is marketed with the cognitive vocabulary of essentiality, universality, embodiment, naturalness, and empathy, and yet it is precisely these features that are considered efficient rhetorical tools, or even weapons in the "story wars." Such neoliberal, streamlined interpretation of the cognitive rhetoric is effective in effacing socioeconomic and cultural backgrounds of storytellers and audiences.

Antinarrativist Approaches and Recent Criticism
of the Storytelling Boom in Narrative Studies

This is not to say that narrative scholarship has not provided *any* resistance. In narrative theory and philosophy of narrative, story-critical views emerged at the same time as the so-called narrative turn. Among the first to argue that narratives impose a false, coherent order on events and experiences were philosophers of history who, from the 1960s onward, drew attention to how historians retrospectively narrativize the past. Such scholars emphasized that narrative is not inherent to historical events but rather something that historians project onto them. Louis Mink wrote in 1970: "Stories are not lived but told" (557). Similarly, Hayden White (1981: 4) argued that human reality is fundamentally nonnarrative and it is problematic to narrativize it: "Real events should simply be; . . . they should not pose as the *tellers* of a narrative."[2]

In the 1970s and 1980s, the claim that narratives are not only essential to the ways in which human beings make sense of their being in the world but also inherently beneficial, particularly in terms of moral integrity, became increasingly popular. Alasdair MacIntyre (1984: 219), for example, argued that moral accountability requires "the unity of a narrative embodied in a single life," that a good life has the form of a narrative "quest," and that

2. This section's account of the antinarrativist approaches draws on Meretoja 2014, 2018.

"the only criteria for success or failure in a human life as a whole are the criteria of success or failure in a narrated or to-be-narrated quest."

Since then, such positions have been fiercely attacked by several thinkers (e.g., Strawson 2004; Sartwell 2000; Currie 2010). The strong antinarrativist view is most famously articulated by the philosopher Galen Strawson (2004), who focuses on refuting two "narrativist" theses.[3] First, what he calls the "psychological Narrativity thesis" is "a descriptive, empirical thesis about the nature of ordinary human experience," one that argues that "human beings typically see or live or experience their lives as a narrative or story of some sort" (428). Second, what he calls the "ethical Narrativity thesis" is a normative claim which asserts that "experiencing or conceiving one's life as a narrative is a good thing . . . essential to a well-lived life" (428). Strawson draws attention to different ways in which individuals experience their existence in time. While "Diachronics"[4] consider the self "as something that was there in the (further) past and will be there in the (further) future," "Episodics" have little or no sense of having a self that "persists over a long stretch of time" (430). He argues that "the fundamentals of temporal temperament are genetically determined" and neither "time-style" is "an essentially inferior form of human life" (431). However, Strawson then goes on to insist that the Episodic disposition is ultimately morally superior to the Diachronic one: "The best lives almost never involve this kind of self-telling" characteristic of the Diachronic disposition (437). For him, narrative self-reflection is inherently harmful: "My guess is that it almost always does more harm than good—that the Narrative tendency to look for story or narrative coherence in one's life is, in general, a gross hindrance to self-understanding: to a just, general, practically real sense . . . of one's *nature*. . . . The more you recall, retell, narrate yourself, the further you risk moving away from accurate self-understanding, from the *truth of your being*" (447; emphasis added).

Strawson's antinarrativist position relies on the notion that narratives falsify our self-understanding by projecting a false idea of a unified self. According to his "realistic materialism," the self ultimately exists only during an "uninterrupted or hiatus-free period of consciousness" (Strawson 1999a: 7, 21) so that a duration of "up to three seconds" is "the normal duration of human selves" (Strawson 1999b: 111). He calls this the "Pearl view," because "it suggests that many mental selves exist, one at a time

3. For criticism of Strawson's position, see, e.g., Battersby 2006; Eakin 2006; Schechtman 2007; Ritivoi 2009; Meretoja 2014, 2018.
4. Presumably Strawson uses capitalization to emphasize that he takes these to be stable (genetically determined) "time-styles."

and one after another, like pearls on a string," in the life of a human being (1999a: 20). Underlying such strong antinarrativist positions is the tacit assumption that the world is given to us in raw, unmediated experiences, which narratives falsify and distort by imposing order on them, and that these raw, disconnected units of experience are more real than experiences that are narratively interpreted or remembered (Meretoja 2018: 57). However, this assumption rests upon the problematic empiricist-positivistic notion of "pure experience," immediately given here and now, a kind of "myth of the given" (Sellars 1963: 127–96; see also Freeman 2015: 239). Most thinkers who emphasize the ethical questionability of narrative see the relationship between experience and narrative as one of *imposition*—of imposing order, meaning, and structure on something that inherently lacks it. They tend to see life as a temporal process, flow, or flux, and they regard this imposition as problematic on both ontological and ethical grounds (Meretoja 2018: 56–57). There is a need for story-critical approaches that do not rely on such totalizing views of narrative as inherently ontologically or ethically questionable but which, rather, analyze different uses of narrative in social contexts. Such contributions can be found in narrative hermeneutics and sociologically oriented narrative studies.[5]

Some of the most influential recent critical indictments of the storytelling boom within narrative studies have targeted the use of political storytelling or "curated" narratives in the context of human rights activism. Anthropologist Amy Shuman writes in her *Other People's Stories* (2005) on the self-congratulatory attitude with which other people's personal narratives are being adopted to promote "good causes" and on the ethical problems in promoting stories of personal experience as representative of a collective or a cause. In Shuman's (2005: 5) memorable words: "The appropriation of stories can create voyeurs rather than witnesses and can foreclose meaning rather than open lines of inquiry and understanding. Appropriation can use one person's tragedy to serve as another's inspiration and preserve, rather than subvert, oppressive situations."

A related critique of emancipatory storytelling can be found in sociologist Francesca Polletta's *It Was Like A Fever* (2006). Challenging the storytelling consultants' urge to look for the *hero's journey* stories that rearticulate myths and invite clear moral positioning, Polletta argues for the political effectiveness of complex and even morally ambivalent narratives. Fernandes's *Curated Stories* (2017) continues in a similar vein by critically analyzing the organized production and circulation of touching real-life stories

---

5. See, e.g., Meretoja 2018; Meretoja and Davis 2018; Schiff et al. 2017. We discuss narrative hermeneutics later on.

and the consequent attempt at "giving voice" to the oppressed by political and charitable campaign organizations. Fernandes traces the emergence of the storytelling boom (or what she calls "storytelling turn") to the rise of personal storytelling in the civil rights movements in the 1960s and feminism in the 1970s. She makes a strong claim that these emancipatory movements and their storytelling practices were already usurped by the neoliberal policies of the ensuing decades as the telling of one's story was made a spectacle and thus divorced from political concerns, particularly from matters of class (Fernandes 2017: 17). Fernandes also discusses other evident precursors of the storytelling boom such as the "therapeutic turn" with its self-help discourses (21–23). According to Fernandes, the new millennium finally saw the configuration of storytelling on the model of the market:

> Nonprofit storytelling and advocacy storytelling are increasingly defined by a business model that emphasizes stories as an investment that can increase competition positioning, help to build the organization's portfolio, and activate target audiences. . . . Narrating one's story is also a process of neoliberal subject-making, as actors learn how to be entrepreneurial, self-reliant actors who seek upward mobility rather than building class consciousness. (18)

Yet another forerunner in the criticism of the storytelling boom is Christian Salmon, whose *Storytelling: Bewitching the Modern Mind* (2010; the French original is *Storytelling: La machine à fabriquer des histoires et à formater les esprits*, 2007) appears to be the academic "story-critical" monograph most widely read and circulated outside of academia. Salmon's (2010: 7–10) synthetic approach to the storytelling boom conceived as a proliferation in the "instrumental use of narrative"—recognizes the concurrence of the "narrativist turn" in social sciences and the "Internet explosion" in the mid-1990s (6). Of particular relevance is Salmon's genealogy of the storytelling boom within US politics, management training, and advertising. Moreover, following narrative theorist Peter Brooks's concern that "the very promiscuity of the idea of narrative may have rendered the concept useless" (Brooks 2001; cited in Salmon 2010: 7), Salmon scrutinizes the expansion of the use of "story" as a buzzword in various spheres of life from international politics to corporate strategies. Ultimately, Salmon (2010: 10) is concerned by how instrumentalized storytelling transforms the sharing and accumulation of collective experience into a unidirectional act of control:

> The great narratives that punctuate human history—from Homer to Tolstoy and from Sophocles to Shakespeare—told of universal myths and transmitted the lessons learned by past generations. They passed on lessons in wisdom that

were the fruit of cumulative experience. Storytelling goes in the opposite direction: it tacks artificial narratives on to reality, blocks exchanges, and saturates symbolic space with its series and stories. It does not talk about past experience. It shapes behaviors and channels flows of emotion. Far from being the "course of recognition" that Paul Ricoeur detected in narrative activity, storytelling establishes narrative systems that lead individuals to identify with models and to conform to protocols.

While we share some of Salmon's concerns, his idealization of the "campfire" of myths and the Western cultural (male) canon as conveyors of universal truths, as well as his demonization of the contemporary storytelling business—which, indeed, feeds on the idea of the neoliberal individual as a disciple of the storytelling industry—is unnecessarily black-and-white. Our notion of "wisdom" is and must be changing, and one of the driving forces not yet discussed by Salmon's 2007 book is social media platforms that paradoxically both multiply and delimit the possibilities for collective (narrative) truth formation. Moreover, the contemporary literary sphere is far from being immune to the doctrines of the storytelling boom. Therefore it should not be idealized as a locus of "non-instrumental" narratives but instead critically examined as affected by the storytelling boom yet possessing unique affordances for its contestation. In what follows, we take up both the story logic of social media and the story-critical affordances of fiction as central elements of our theoretical project of reevaluating the storytelling boom. We then move on to suggest narrative hermeneutics as one possible paradigm for the critical examination of our storytelling cultures, and conclude by envisioning future forms of public critical engagement for narrative theorists.

Social Media as the Decisive Inducer of the Storytelling Boom

Social media make the best out of the didactic potential of narratives and foreground the moral of the story, already recognized as a recurring element of everyday oral storytelling by twentieth-century sociolinguistists (e.g., Pratt 1977: 136). New platforms, together with professional story-talk exemplified by storytelling consultants above, affect thus the way we understand "narrative" and what it can do. While social media have made us all storytellers and "consum[ers] of others" (Fernandes 2017: 2), both the rhetoric and the ethics of narrative (e.g., the terms of tellability; see Georgakopoulou, Iversen, and Stage 2020) are being radically transformed by its storytelling affordances such as liking, sharing, and algorithms that support strong and collective, "networked" affect (e.g., Hillis, Paasonen, and Petit 2015; Papacharissi 2015; Page 2018). As the storytellers of our time suggest, the ultimate power of instrumental storytelling does not reside in simple cognitive immersion and embodiment but in the moral positioning and claims to universal truth that such vicarious experientiality permits. This is a conclusion that can be easily drawn by simply looking at the persistent masterplots on our social media feeds: politicians draw moral lessons from their touching encounters with troubled citizens; citizens draw moral lessons from their random encounters with public institutions; marketers use "true" survival stories of illness and burnout to sell products that have nothing to do with recovery; charity organizations look for—or increasingly curate, as Fernandes claims—inspirational stories of deserving individuals. With its increased emphasis on human interest, journalism fishes for the same kind of affective consensus generated by social media shares that "true stories" by individuals arouse.

Maria Mäkelä and her research team have studied the social media storytelling mechanisms that generate such didacticism with the concept of the "viral exemplum."

> We define the viral exemplum as the chain reaction, typically fueled by social media shares, from narrative experientiality to representativeness and normativity. Spurred in the first place by experientiality, this chain works in such a way that even when challenged by subsequent evidence, the initial interpretation and affective reactions may persist and lead to normative conclusions and political action. (Mäkelä et al. 2021: 154)

We argue that this chain reaction from experientiality to representativeness and normativity is the single most significant "danger" of narrative brought about by the twenty-first-century narrative platforms. It transforms the parameters of tellership, narrative audiences, and the "occasion" for telling (see, e.g., Phelan 2017); social media scholars call this transformation "context collapse" (Marwick and boyd 2010) when they attempt to describe how unprecedented, uncontrollable, and undetectable the tellers, audiences, and occasions of viral storytelling can be. The "compellingness" of a social media story is dependent upon an emergent narrative authority (Dawson and Mäkelä 2020), created by the affective networks of the like-minded who validate even anonymous or falsified experiences through sharing. No individual can thus be considered responsible for the ultimate rhetoric and ethics of such "shared stories" (Page 2018). Yet the requirements of authenticity and particularity often mean that the lives and identities of the individuals whose story is being told are instrumentalized, with scarce consideration of "narrative entitlement" (see Shuman 2005). Universal lessons are being drawn from random experiences and storyworld particulars, affective resonance and bodily immersion are taken for representativeness, and the rhetoric of viral storytelling guarantees the status of this doxa as the "truth" (Mäkelä 2021).

Losers in this game of narrative attention economy are tellers who cannot instrumentalize personal stories (such as health care or social service professionals), tellers whose story does not provide easy affective resonance ("undeserving" individuals), or tellers whose concern exceeds the parameters of human experientiality (such as climate scientists trying to warn us of dangers that do not yet manifest themselves in our daily lives). Sharing content that audiences might consider ambivalent is a social risk, and therefore easily recognizable masterplots with stock roles and clear moral positioning thrive. Yet even more crucially, the search for a maximally compelling story for social media platforms can backfire even in the hands of the storyteller who succeeds in creating a viral story—and this is a point that is difficult to communicate to actors such as politicians or activists whose main target is to gain maximum attention (see Mäkelä 2018). If one succeeds in creating a touching and inspiring story for a good cause, what can go wrong? When a prototypical narrative of disruptive personal experience, affording embodied immersion, storyworld construction by inference, and moral positioning on an individual level collides with the social media affordances that turn experientiality into representativeness and moral norms, the results can be unanticipated and even unwanted. Moreover, the interactive effects of these colliding affordances may further collide with the advocated idea. For example, when a leftist politician creates a viral social media story of her transformative encounter with a "deserving" individual, the affective chain reaction of viral storytelling, reinforcing the positioning of the sharers of the story as benefactors, ultimately counteracts the political ideal of non-individuating social welfare the politician attempts to promote.

This is not to say that viral storytelling would not come to any good in, for example, politics. A case in point, and an example of both beneficial and misguided uses of personal storytelling online, would be the #MeToo movement which succeeded in precisely matching the forms of the "story," the platform, and the political structure under attack: patriarchy. The fact that the majority of the stories shared with the hashtag were stripped to the bare minimum, from any storyworld or experiential particulars, made the collective narrative effort the very picture of patriarchy as a *structure*. As far as the campaign succeeded in directing the attention away from particular experiences, by simply prompting the victims to share the hashtag #MeToo, it was able to make the invisible power structure visible. Patriarchy affords individuals with certain patterns of behavior while inhibiting others (from other individuals). The minimal narrative elements were enough to convey the essence of the problem: the "me" signaling the disruptive personal experience and the "too" activating the pervasive structure of oppression. In contrast, some of the more elaborate narratives of sexual harassment by celebrities were much more likely to backfire, or to hand a loaded gun to the agents of the backlash, as they were more easily refuted by appealing to unlikeliness of details or biased representation of intentions and interpretations (see Dawson and Mäkelä 2020: 32). In fact, while contemporary storytelling consultants are currently making considerable profit among political parties and organizations, research rather consistently shows that political stances are rarely altered by stories of personal experience; consumers of emotional investment narratives are more likely to embrace even more fervently opinions they already possess, particularly when it comes to structural political issues (Polletta and Redman 2020).

The Role of Fiction in the Storytelling Boom

In today's storytelling boom, fiction writers do not hold a place of honor as conveyors of meaning but are forced to compete with other "influencers" within a single "attention economy." A totalizing conception of the author as a brand that should secure its consistency across media and genres dominates the literary sphere. In addition to brandization, the current media environment is dominated by discourses on the moral and cognitive benefits of literature. Today, narrative fiction is instrumentalized and even medicalized in the service of the well-being and self-help industry. It is particularly common to claim that literature makes us more empathetic (Kidd and Castano 2013), which, in popularizing media reports, is turned into simplistic advice of how to capitalize on this benefit, for example on the job market: "For Better Social Skills, Scientists Recommend a Little Chekhov" (Belluck 2013). For the purposes of critical engagement with the storytelling boom, however, it is worth looking at how fiction itself critically engages with narrative. Narrative fiction has a long tradition of such engagement, and, in fact, one of its affordances is that, due to its self-reflexivity, it is well equipped to provide critical insights on the problematic aspects of storytelling.

Story-critical views have a long literary history. Classics such as *Don Quixote* and *Madame Bovary* famously ridicule the way in which literary narratives create false expectations of a life that follows a narrative arch full of meaning, adventure, and fulfillment. Modernists, however, were the first ones to explicitly engage in a fully fleshed-out criticism of narrative form, pointing out that life and human experience do not follow the form of narrative. Virginia Woolf (1925: 188–89), for example, argued that fiction aspiring to "likeness to life" has "no plot, no comedy, no tragedy," for "life is not a series of gig-lamps symmetrically arranged." Jean-Paul Sartre ([1938] 1965) raised the issue of the relationship between life and narrative in his novel *Nausea*. Its protagonist, Roquentin, famously suggests that there is something fundamentally dishonest and problematic about our tendency to narrativize our experiences: "This is what fools people: a man is always a teller of tales, he lives surrounded by his stories and the stories of others, he sees everything that happens to him through them; and he tries to live his life as if he were recounting it. But you have to choose: to live or to recount" (61). In the postwar period, the French *nouveaux romanciers* adamantly rejected narrative and developed arguments that anticipate the antinarrativist views that theorists formulated over the following decades. In 1950, Nathalie Sarraute ([1956] 1990: 61) questioned storytelling as a convention that gives characters a false "appearance of cohesiveness" and masks reality, which is in a state of constant transformation; in 1957, Alain Robbe-Grillet ([1963] 1989: 28–29, 33) declared that narrative is an "obsolete notion" because it "represents order" and creates "the image of a stable, coherent, continuous, unequivocal, entirely decipherable universe."[6]

Postmodernist fiction is permeated with a playful and often ironic relationship with the story economy that constitutes late modern society. Even more pertinent from the perspective of critical engagement with the storytelling boom, however, is twenty-first-century fiction, which has been characterized by various labels ranging from post-postmodernism to metamodernism (Vermeulen and Akker 2010). Over the past few decades, much fiction has specifically problematized narrative as a form of representation, questioning various uses of narrative from ontological, epistemological, and ethical perspectives. Hanna Meretoja (2014, 2018, 2022) has suggested conceptualizing such fiction as *metanarrative fiction*, which is not only characterized by reflection on processes of narration, as suggested by previous discussions of metanarration (see Fludernik 1996, 2003; Neumann and Nünning 2012; Macrae 2019) but also by critical reflection on the significance and roles of cultural narratives in our lives. Much of metanarrative fiction has a strong story-critical dimension: it critically explores the risks and limits of problematic narrative practices. By making visible cultural narrative models that limit our narrative imagination without our awareness, story-critical fiction can expand our "sense of the possible" (Mere-

---

6. On the problematization of storytelling in literary fiction and particularly in the *nouveau roman*, and on the relationship between the narrative turn in fiction and theoretical discourse, see Meretoja 2014.

toja 2018)—that is, our capacity to imagine beyond what appears to be self-evident in the present and how things could be otherwise. The cognitive, affective, social, psychological, and ethical relevance of these fictions inheres in how they disturb the experiential recourse to culturally dominant narrative models of sense-making.

Story-critical reflection is particularly prominent in much of contemporary *metanarrative autofiction* (Meretoja 2022), from J. M. Coetzee's brutal exploration of narrative as a form of self-deception in *Summertime* (2009) to Annie Ernaux's turn away, in *The Years* (*Les années*, 2008), from individual-centered autobiography to a collective "impersonal autobiography" that charts the change of times through the itinerary of the author's own life. The latter relates the unfolding of an individual life to historical events and change of fashions and mentalities, showing how even highly subjective bodily experiences, such as those linked to illness or sexuality, are mediated by cultural narrative models of sense-making. To take another example, Karl Ove Knausgaard's autobiographical series *My Struggle* (*Min kamp*, 2009–11) critically engages with conflicting narrative models of masculinity, in the context of contemporary Nordic welfare society, but at the same time Knausgaard creates a brand of his ethos of "brutal honesty." The way he capitalizes on his struggle with dominant cultural narratives exemplifies the way writers are enmeshed in the current story economy even when criticizing it (Meretoja 2022).

Zadie Smith argues that the answer to the question "why write" cannot be "to satisfy a pre-existing demand"; instead, "at the heart of creativity lies a refusal" (Gonzalez 2014). Part of this is the refusal to simply follow preexisting narrative models. Critical engagement with such models is pervasive, for example, in her recent collection of short stories, *The Grand Union* (2019). "Two Men Arrive in a Village" begins with reflection on a certain story type, an archetypal story of two men arriving in a village: "our example is representative; in fact, it has the perfection of parable" (135). While narratives are typically characterized by particulars—something happens to a particular person in a particular situation—this short story focuses on how the recounted story is a variation of a transculturally circulating narrative model with stock roles: "It goes without saying that one of the men is tall, rather handsome—in a vulgar way—a little dim and vicious, while the other man is shorter, weasel-faced, and sly" (136). The two men assault girls who may be "preparing food or grinding meat or texting on their phones" (135–36).

The archetypal story progresses through certain types of scenes: a tense welcome, eating together, the first violence that descends into bloody chaos, "the time of stealing" ("The two men will always steal things, though for some reason they do not like to use this word" [137]), "pointless courage of our women" ("though it could not keep two men from arriving in the village and doing their worst—it never has and never will"), until the moment arrives when "bloody chaos found no more obstruction to its usual plans" (138). The highly self-reflexive narrator draws attention to the rhetorical effects of the narrative devices employed: "And yet the effect was the same: the dread stillness and the anticipation" (137).

After the violent incident, there is a series of retellings: "The next day the story of what happened is retold, in partial, broken versions that change depending very much on who is asking" (138). The chief's wife compares the two men to a mythical whirlwind (*ga haramata*) in which their names and faces are lost, and the narrator ironically remarks: "This is of course a metaphor. But she lives by it" (138). The chief's wife finds a girl who "told her story in full" (138), but when the girl comes to a point that does not fit the archetypal story, a point where the "short, sly man" wanted to reveal his name and present himself as a vulnerable human being, the chief's wife stops the hearing. In a parable, men do not have names; they are not particular individuals, they are archetypes. In this metanarrative short story, Zadie Smith draws our attention to the archetypal narratives that circulate in popular culture and affect how we understand ourselves and others, such as those that repeat scenes of nameless sexual violence, or conflicts between "us" and "them," the latter anonymous intruders who come to the community and degrade "our girls." The point is not to repeat an archetype or reinforce its universality, but rather to critically engage with such archetypes in order to draw our attention to how such narrative models are repeated and through repetition naturalized.

Narrative Hermeneutics

We propose that one solution to the need for narrative scholarship that critically engages with the current storytelling boom is narrative hermeneutics, which approaches narratives as culturally mediated interpretative practices.[7] Against the backdrop of the polarized debate between narrativists and antinarrativists, the narrative hermeneutics developed by Hanna Meretoja provides a theoretical-analytical framework that acknowl-

---

7. Narrative hermeneutics draws on the Ricoeurian tradition of narrative theory and has been formulated in its current form by Hanna Meretoja (2014, 2018), Jens Brockmeier (2015), Mark Freeman (2015), etc. See also Brockmeier and Meretoja 2014; Korthals Altes 2014; Korthals Altes and Meretoja 2018; Brockmeier 2016. Here, we focus on Meretoja's version of narrative hermeneutics, as it is the version that explicitly engages with the current storytelling boom and focuses on the potential and risks of different narrative practices.

edges equally "*both* the ethical potential *and* the risks of storytelling" and addresses "the ethical complexity of the roles that narratives play in our lives" (Meretoja 2018: 2). This approach offers an analytic model which questions universalizing claims according to which narrative form in itself is either beneficial or harmful. It argues that "there is nothing in stories to guarantee that their possible ethical potential will be actualized. Narrative form makes a narrative neither inherently harmful nor beneficial; instead, its ethical value is *contextual,* that is, dependent on how the narrative is interpreted and put to use in a particular social, historical, and cultural world" (Meretoja 2018: 170). Meretoja proposes "a hermeneutic narrative ethics, which acknowledges that narrative practices can be oppressive, empowering, or both, and provides resources for analyzing the different dimensions of the ethical potential and dangers of storytelling" (2).

While traditional narratology approaches narrative as a form of textual discourse (providing a representation of a series of events), cognitive narratology in terms of universal cognitive models, and rhetorical narratology as a mode of communication, narrative hermeneutics conceptualizes narratives as *culturally mediated practices* of *sense-making* that—as explicit narratives—present experiences as part of a meaningful, connected account or—as implicit narratives—provide models of sense-making; they have a dialogical and a performative dimension and are relevant for our understanding of *human possibilities.* "Instead of being mere representations, narratives have a performative character that is intertwined with practices of power. As interpretations of the world, narrative practices have real-world effects. This is precisely what their (per)formative and productive character means: they take part in constructing, shaping, and transforming human reality" (Meretoja 2018: 47). Many sociologically oriented approaches to narrative similarly acknowledge the performative dimension of narrative and pay attention to how narratives take shape in social interaction and at the same time participate in molding the narrative environments in which social actors can take up different subject positions (see, e.g., Riessman 2008; Georgakopoulou 2015). Meretoja's (2018) narrative hermeneutics draws particular attention to how we are constituted in a constant dialogical engagement with cultural narrative models of sense-making and to the existential relevance of narratives practices—that is, to how they shape our sense of what is possible or impossible for us as actors in certain social situations and cultural contexts. Arguably, the social pressure, in the current story economy, to reduce one's experiences, lives, and identities to easily shareable and sellable narratives has a huge impact on how social actors perceive their selves and their possibilities.

Hermeneutic narrative ethics provides a heuristic model for evaluating the ethical potential and dangers of different kinds of narratives. Mereto-ja's (2018, 2021) model provides six evaluative continua on which narratives can be placed in context-sensitive ethical evaluation of social and cultural narrative practices. These continua explore whether narratives: (1) expand or diminish our sense of the possible; (2) cultivate or distort personal and cultural self-understanding; (3) promote or impair our ability to understand the experiences of others in their singularity; (4) participate in building inclusive or exclusive narrative in-betweens; (5) develop or impede our perspective-awareness; and (6) function as a form of ethical inquiry or dogmatism. This model is applicable in the ethical evaluation of any cultural narratives, including "implicit narratives" that function as cultural models of sense-making but are not necessarily anywhere available in explicit, textual form (Meretoja 2021). These continua not only draw attention to aspects of narratives but can also be seen as interpretative strategies that can be helpful in the critical analysis of the narrative practices that dominate the current story economy.

Toward Engaged and Story-Critical Narrative Theory

Above we have contextualized narrative studies within and vis-à-vis the contemporary storytelling boom, trying to provide some critical perspectives that might help us grasp this complex phenomenon and approach it with concepts and theories that move us beyond the general and easy storytalk abounding in public parlance and, to some degree, in academic settings. Narrative scholars should more eagerly pursue the role of a public intellectual, helping one's community to become aware of cultural narratives that surround them and shape the public space and imagination. Moreover, narrative scholars should take up the task of introducing analytical and critical aspects into the general storytalk, in order to provide different audiences with critical tools with which to encounter the torrent of touching, inspiring, and transformative narratives directed at us as citizens, voters, consumers, and constructors of identities. The promotion of storytelling on different fronts uses the language of authenticity, diversity, and interpretative freedom, concealing the fact that instrumentalized and easily shareable narratives often thwart such good intentions and misdirect our attention. The greatest challenges of our time—climate change, fluctuations in the global economy that perpetuate and contribute to global inequality and injustice, changes in the population structure, or pandemics—are supraindividual developments that defy narrativization (see, e.g., Raipola 2019; Björninen and Polvinen 2022). Scholars of narrative are the ones who should make visible the limits of narrative.

In 2018 we launched our consortium project "Instrumental Narratives: The Limits of Storytelling and New Story-Critical Narrative Theory,"[8] with the explicit aim of promoting a critical approach to the storytelling boom, not only within narrative studies but in contemporary societies at large. We have invited our narrative colleagues across disciplines to address exciting or irritating cases of instrumental storytelling in our *Instrumental Narratives* blog aimed at both academic and nonacademic audiences. Currently the blog features entries, for example, on Donald Trump's rhetoric (by Marie-Laure Ryan and James Phelan), the instrumental uses of fiction (Brian McHale, Peter Lamarque), epidemics (by Hanna Meretoja and Avril Tynan), mental health (by Lasse Gammelgaard), fictional Amazon reviews (Lyle Skains), and medieval exempla (Robert Appelbaum). Many of us have noticed that scholarly commentary is made challenging in contemporary media platforms that—following the story logic of social media—favor clear-cut moral and antagonistic positioning (see, e.g., Lasse Gammelgaard's blog entry[9]).

Our "Instrumental Narratives" consortium was anticipated by two research projects that involved public engagement. In "Dangers of Narrative" (led by Maria Mäkelä, 2017–20), narratologists crowd-sourced examples of dubious, unnecessary, or amusing storification in different spheres of life. The project, with its hashtag #mindthenarrative, proved a genuine success among the Finnish social media audience, attracting approximately one thousand reports and ten thousand Facebook followers, and resulting in two national podcasts and collaboration with professional groups ranging from journalists and advertisers to artists and health care professionals. The key to the success were the popularizing critical analyses of the reported stories posted on Facebook by the research team members; these postings allowed the social media audience to partake in the quasi-affective evaluation of the "dangers" of storytelling while at the same time familiarizing the reader with the terminology and approaches of narrative studies in an easily digestible and shareable form. The price to pay for all the social media visibility and popularity was, however, the project's constant exposition to the very same laws of the storytelling boom that the research team was criticizing: the most liked and shared narrative analyses were those that the audience interpreted as conforming to a preferred ideology, while critical analyses of, for example, storytelling by the literary left was considered a biased "narrative" generated by the research project.

8. More on our website instrumentalnarratives.wordpress.com/.
9. instrumentalnarratives.wordpress.com/2020/06/29/lasse-gammelgaard-mental-illness -costumes/.

One of the greatest lessons of "Dangers of Narrative" lay in the ways in which it allowed its readers to recognize the pervasiveness of the drive for moral positioning as a feature of the storytelling boom that not even the dissemination of research can escape. Currently the crowdsourcing activity provides the "Instrumental Narratives" project with a corpus of instrumental storytelling and the accompanying notes by audience reporting the cases, a corpus that reflects the audience's affective yet critical engagement with the stories. What still remains to be done is to find the right balance between descriptive and normative analysis of contemporary narrative practices, as we believe that while it is common to separate normativity and descriptiveness in research, a cultural-critical approach aiming at societal engagement needs to be both.

Such an ethos of socially engaged narrative scholarship characterized another interdisciplinary research project anticipating the consortium, "The Ethics of Storytelling and the Experience of History in Contemporary Arts" (led by Hanna Meretoja, 2013–16, Emil Aaltonen Foundation), which analyzed how contemporary literature and visual arts engage with the ethical potential, risks, and limits of different narrative practices in dealing with such issues as social injustices and histories of violence (see Meretoja and Davis 2018). It contributed to public discussion on how to distinguish between narratives that function as forms of appropriation and ones that enhance our understanding of violence and trauma, alerting us to the need for evaluative tools to differentiate between productive and problematic narrative practices and thereby giving impetus to the development of the aforementioned evaluative continua.[10]

The "Instrumental Narratives" consortium continues to promote public debate on storytelling that, instead of rewarding "good causes" and condemning storytelling by heretics, recognizes the ambiguities brought about by the clashes between forms, genres, uses, platforms, and contexts of narratives. A case in point would be the current coronavirus pandemic that is dominated by certain patterns of narrativization. As Hanna Meretoja (2020) has analyzed, the narrative of war has dominated the public discourse on the pandemic. The narrative of battle is used, in problematic ways, to attribute agency to patients, health care professionals, and "us" collectively so as to turn us from passive victims into courageous sol-

---

10. The project involved, e.g., an exhibition, in the Turku City Library, featuring the documentary photography by the photojournalist and filmmaker Louie Palu, and a public discussion event on the creation, use, control, and censoring of visual narration in the media in the post-9/11 age of terror. The project aimed at addressing the historicity of experience in ways that have been generally lacking in narrative studies and at providing conceptual tools to articulate the ways in which narratives are entangled with practices of power.

diers in a fight against a common enemy. Politicians use it, for example, to convey the gravity of the situation, to justify emergency legislation, and to legitimize sacrificing lives of minimum-wage nurses. Narrativizing the pandemic in terms of war is an example of the workings of *implicit narratives* (Meretoja 2021) that are not necessarily anywhere explicitly fleshed out in textual form but function as models of sense-making that steer us to attach certain meanings to certain phenomena. Articulating such implicit narratives could have a major impact in amplifying cultural self-understanding, providing critical insights on the dangers and limitations of dominant narratives, and opening up alternative ways of making sense of complex social phenomena.

Outline of the Special Issue

This special issue at hand features a selection of articles that we hope provide both methodological groundwork and inspiration for further engagement with the contemporary instrumental uses of narratives. The special issue is divided into three thematic parts. The first section engages with the social and political context of the storytelling boom from the perspective of political campaigning; the second addresses specifically the instrumentalization of storytelling in social media; and the third suggests story-critical alternatives by drawing on the affordances of contemporary literary fiction.

The first section, "Narrative Politics and Campaigning," focuses on politics and campaigning in the age of the storytelling boom. Andrea Macrae provides new insights into the UK storytelling boom by discussing emotive storytelling within UK charity fundraising letters. Drawing and building on research in philanthropy communications, she analyzes the typical linguistic constituents and narrative conventions of these stories, combining cognitive linguistics and classical models of narrative arcs. Kristiana Willsey looks at how veterans' stories are used in political campaigns to make war meaningful. Her article juxtaposes a "vernacular critique of the storytelling boom" with the idea of "management of narrative" linked to the veterans' need to curate the situations in which storytelling could keep its promises.

In the second section, "Social Media Identities," five scholars offer their take on social media as the quintessential platform for the instrumentalization of storytelling. Alexandra Georgakopoulou shows how small stories research functions as a paradigm for critically interrogating the current storytelling boom on social media. She analyzes, in particular, the *directive of authenticity* guiding influencers' self-presentation in Instagram Stories. Directives and other platform affordances shape social media small stories into recognizable formats with particular values attached to them. Against the backdrop of how research on illness narratives has been based on a largely underdeveloped and essentialized notion of voice, Korina Giaxoglou's article discusses a new type of illness stories emerging in digital contexts, *entrepreneurial narratives* characterized by the connective mobilization of illness for producing economic and social value. She focuses particularly on how sharing stories of illness online is associated with the growing commoditization of the "wound." Matias Nurminen analyzes how radical, online masculinity groups and mainstream populist rhetoric use memetic narratives that function as *allusive cognitive metaphors* which are effective in conveying thought patterns and activating masterplots in the viral storytelling environment. Showing how narrative strategies do not discriminate between aims, he contributes to the discussion on the ethical responsibilities of narrative scholars. Hanna-Riikka Roine and Laura Piippo engage with the concepts of affordance and affect to show how computational agents such as platform logics give shape to experiences and prompt narrativization. Their discussion and analyses promote what they call the *semiotics of the imperceptible*; they suggest a critical approach to contemporary storytelling cultures that accounts for the entanglement of individual agents in collectivities and points the way toward recognizing the ethics of shared responsibility.

The third section, "Story-Critical Affordances of Contemporary Literary Fiction," articulates interpretative resources that narrative fiction provides for critical engagement with the current storytelling boom. Anne Rüggemeier considers the role of non-narrative literary practices as an antidote against simplistic understanding and uses of storytelling. She explores the story-critical affordances of literary forms that rely on fragmentation, slowness of action, and intensity instead of plot and embodied experience, thereby problematizing conventional conceptions of what life is and drawing attention to small episodes, sensations, and passing impressions. In the final article, Hanna Meretoja, Päivi Kosonen, and Eevastiina Kinnunen lay out a theoretical-analytic framework of narrative agency and their new model of metanarrative reading groups. They discuss the potential of reading together metanarrative fiction, which critically engages with problematic aspects of narratives, to amplify narrative agency understood in terms of our ability to navigate our narrative environments.

References

Abbott, H. Porter. 2008. *The Cambridge Introduction to Narrative*. 2nd ed. Cambridge: Cambridge University Press.

Alanne, Katja. 2019. "Tarinankerronta tavaksi strategisella otteella." https://hyplus.helsinki.fi/tarinankerronta-tavaksi-strategisella-otteella/ (accessed February 1, 2022).

Attebery, Brian. 2014. *Stories about Stories*. Oxford: Oxford University Press.

Battersby, James. 2006. "Narrativity, Self, and Self-Representation." *Narrative* 14, no. 1: 27–44.

Belluck, Pam. 2013. "For Better Social Skills, Scientists Recommend a Little Chekhov." *New York Times* (blog), October 3. https://well.blogs.nytimes.com/2013/10/03/i-know-how-youre-feeling-i-read-chekhov/.

Björninen, Samuli. 2019. "The Rhetoric of Factuality in Narrative: Appeals to Authority in Claas Relotius's Narrative Journalism." *Narrative Inquiry* 29, no. 2: 352–70.

Björninen, Samuli, and Merja Polvinen. Forthcoming, 2022. "Limits of Narrative." Special issue, *Partial Answers* 20, no. 2.

Boyd, Brian. 2009. *On the Origin of Stories: Evolution, Cognition, and Fiction*. Cambridge, MA: Harvard University Press.

Brockmeier, Jens. 2015. *Beyond the Archive: Memory, Narrative, and the Autobiographical Process*. Oxford: Oxford University Press.

Brockmeier, Jens, ed. 2016. "Narrative Hermeneutics." Special Issue, *Storyworlds* 8, no. 1.

Brockmeier, Jens, and Hanna Meretoja. 2014. "Understanding Narrative Hermeneutics." *Storyworlds* 6, no. 2: 1–27.

Brooks, Peter. 2001. "Stories Abounding." *The Chronicle of Higher Education*, March 3. https://www.chronicle.com/article/stories-abounding/.

Bruner, Jerome. 1991. "The Narrative Construction of Reality." *Critical Inquiry* 18, no. 1: 1–21.

Campbell, Joseph. 1949. *The Hero with a Thousand Faces*. Princeton, NJ: Princeton University Press.

Caracciolo, Marco. 2021. *Narrating the Mesh: Form and Story in the Anthropocene*. Charlottesville: University of Virginia Press.

Coetzee, J. M. 2009. *Summertime*. London: Harvill Secker.

Currie, Gregory. 2010. *Narrative and Narrators: A Philosophy of Stories*. Oxford: Oxford University Press.

Dawson, Paul, and Maria Mäkelä. 2020. "The Story Logic of Social Media: Co-construction and Emergent Narrative Authority." *Style* 54, no. 1: 21–35.

Dicks, Matthew. 2018. *Storyworthy: Engage, Teach, Persuade, and Change Your Life through the Power of Storytelling*. Novato, CA: New World Library.

Eakin, Paul John. 2006. "Narrative Identity and Narrative Imperialism: A Response to Galen Strawson and James Phelan." *Narrative* 14, no. 2: 180–87.

Ernaux, Annie. 2008. *Les années*. Paris: Gallimard.

Fernandes, Sujatha. 2017. *Curated Stories: The Uses and Misuses of Storytelling*. Oxford: Oxford University Press.

Fludernik, Monika. 1996. *Towards a "Natural" Narratology*. London: Routledge.

Fludernik, Monika. 2003. "Metanarrative and Metafictional Commentary: From Metadiscursivity to Metanarration and Metafiction." *Poetica* 35, no. 1/2: 1–39.

Freeman, Mark. 2015. "Narrative Hermeneutics." In *The Wiley Handbook of Theoretical and Philosophical Psychology*, edited by Jack Martin, Jeff Sugarman, and Kathleen L. Slaney, 234–47. Malden, MA: Wiley-Blackwell.

Gallagher, Shaun, and Daniel Hutto. 2008. "Understanding Others through Primary Interaction and Narrative Practice." In *The Shared Mind: Perspectives on Intersubjectivity*, edited by Jordan Zlatev, Timothy P. Racine, Chris Sinha, and Esa Itkonen, 17–38. Amsterdam: John Benjamins.

Gammelgaard, Lasse. 2020. "Mental Illness Costumes: Divisive Discourse and Untold Stories of Stigma." *The Instrumental Narratives Blog*, June 29. instrumentalnarratives.wordpress .com/2020/06/29/lasse-gammelgaard-mental-illness-costumes.

Georgakopoulou, Alexandra. 2015. "Small Stories Research: Methods—Analysis—Outreach." In *The Handbook of Narrative Analysis*, edited by Anna De Fina and Alexandra Georgakopoulou, 255–71. Chichester: Wiley Blackwell.

Georgakopoulou, Alexandra, Stefan Iversen, and Karsten Stage. 2020. *Quantified Storytelling: A Narrative Analysis of Metrics on Social Media*. London: Palgrave Macmillan.

Gonzalez, Susan. 2014. "'Why Write?': To 'Refuse,' Answers Author Zadie Smith in Festival's Keynote." *Yale News*, September 16. news.yale.edu/2014/09/16/why-write -refuse-answers-author-zadie-smith-festival-s-keynote.

Herman, David. 2009. *Basic Elements of Narrative*. Chichester, UK: Wiley-Blackwell.

Herman, David, Manfred Jahn, and Marie-Laure Ryan. 2005. Introduction to *Routledge Encyclopedia of Narrative Theory*, edited by David Herman, Manfred Jahn, and Marie-Laure Ryan, ix–xi. London: Routledge.

Hillis, Ken, Susanna Paasonen, and Michael Petit, eds. 2015. *Networked Affect*. Cambridge, MA: MIT Press.

Keen, Suzanne. 2007. *Empathy and the Novel*. Oxford: Oxford University Press.

Kidd, David Comer, and Emanuele Castano. 2013. "Reading Literary Fiction Improves Theory of Mind." *Science* 342, no. 6156: 377–80.

Knausgaard, Karl Ove. 2009–2011. *Min kamp 1–6*. Oslo: Oktober.

Korthals Altes, Liesbeth. 2014. *Ethos and Narrative Interpretation*. Lincoln: University of Nebraska Press.

Korthals Altes, Liesbeth, and Hanna Meretoja. 2018. "Ethics and Literature." In *The Palgrave Handbook of Philosophy and Literature*, edited by Barry Stocker and Michael Mack. London: Palgrave Macmillan, 601–21.

Kuzmičová, Anežka. 2014. "Literary Narrative and Mental Imagery: A View from Embodied Cognition." *Style* 48, no. 3, 275–93.

MacIntyre, Alasdair. 1984. *After Virtue: A Study in Moral Theory*. 2nd ed. Notre Dame, IN: University of Notre Dame Press.

Macrae, Andrea. 2019. *Discourse Deixis in Metafiction: The Language of Metanarration, Metalepsis, and Disnarration*. London: Routledge.

Mäkelä, Maria. 2018. "Lessons from the *Dangers of Narrative* Project: Toward a Story-Critical Narratology." *Tekstualia*, no. 4: 175–86.

Mäkelä, Maria. 2020. "Through the Cracks in the Safety Net: Narratives of Personal Experience Countering the Welfare System in Social Media and Human Interest Journalism." In *Routledge Handbook of Counter-Narratives*, edited by Klarissa Lueg and Marianne Wolff Lundholt, 389–401. Abingdon: Routledge.

Mäkelä, Maria. 2021. "Viral Storytelling as Contemporary Narrative Didacticism: Deriving Universal Truths from Arbitrary Narratives of Personal Experience." In *The Ethos of Digital Environments*, edited by Susanna Lindberg and Hanna-Riikka Roine, 49–59. Abingdon: Routledge.

Mäkelä, Maria, Samuli Björninen, Laura Karttunen, Matias Nurminen, Juha Raipola, and Tytti Rantanen. 2021. "Dangers of Narrative: A Critical Approach to Narratives of Personal Experience in Contemporary Story Economy." *Narrative* 28, no. 2: 139–59.

Marwick, Alice, and danah boyd. 2010. "I Tweet Honestly, I Tweet Passionately: Twitter Users, Context Collapse, and the Imagined Audience." *New Media and Society* 13, no. 1: 114–33.

Meretoja, Hanna. 2014. *The Narrative Turn in Fiction and Theory: The Crisis and Return of Storytelling from Robbe-Grillet to Tournier*. London: Palgrave Macmillan.

Meretoja, Hanna. 2018. *The Ethics of Storytelling: Narrative Hermeneutics, History, and the Possible*. Oxford: Oxford University Press.

Meretoja, Hanna. 2020. "Stop Narrating the Pandemic as a Story of War." *openDemocracy*,

May 19. www.opendemocracy.net/en/transformation/stop-narrating-pandemic-story -war/.

Meretoja, Hanna. 2021. "A Dialogics of Counter-narratives." In *The Routledge Handbook of Counter-narratives*, edited by Marianne Wolff Lundholt and Klarissa Lueg, 30–42. Abingdon: Routledge.

Meretoja, Hanna. 2022. "Metanarrative Autofiction: Critical Engagement with Cultural Narrative Models." In *The Autofictional: Approaches, Affordances, Forms*, edited by Alexandra Effe and Hannie Lawlor, 121–40. London: Palgrave Macmillan.

Meretoja, Hanna, and Colin Davis, eds. 2018. *Storytelling and Ethics: Literature, Visual Arts, and the Power of Narrative.* New York: Routledge.

Mink, Louis. 1970. "History and Fiction as Modes of Comprehension." *New Literary History* 1, no. 3: 541–58.

Neumann, Birgit, and Ansgar Nünning. 2012. "Metanarration and Metafiction." In *The Living Handbook of Narratology* (online), edited by Peter Hühn, Jan Christoph Meister, John Pier, and Wolf Schmid. Hamburg: Hamburg University Press.

Nussbaum, Martha 2010. *Not for Profit: Why Democracy Needs the Humanities.* Princeton, NJ: Princeton University Press.

Page, Ruth E. 2018. *Narratives Online: Shared Stories in Social Media.* Cambridge: Cambridge University Press.

Papacharissi, Zizi. 2015. *Affective Publics: Sentiment, Technology, and Politics.* Oxford: Oxford University Press.

Peterson, Lani. 2017. "The Science Behind the Art of Storytelling." November 14, https://www .harvardbusiness.org/the-science-behind-the-art-of-storytelling/.

Phelan, James. 2017. *Somebody Telling Somebody Else: A Rhetorical Poetics of Narrative.* Columbus: Ohio State University Press.

Polletta, Francesca. 2006. *It Was Like a Fever: Storytelling in Protest and Politics.* Chicago: University of Chicago Press.

Polletta, Francesca, and Nathan Redman. 2020. "When Do Stories Change Our Minds? Narrative about Social Problems." *Sociology Compass* 14, no. 4: e12788.

Pratt, Mary-Louise. 1977. *Toward a Speech Act Theory of Literary Discourse.* Bloomington: Indiana University Press.

Raipola, Juha. 2019. "Unnarratable Matter: Emergence, Narrative, and Material Ecocriticism." In *Reconfiguring Human, Nonhuman, and Posthuman in Literature and Culture*, edited by Sanna Karkulehto, Aino-Kaisa Koistinen, and Essi Varis, 263–80. New York: Routledge.

Ricoeur, Paul. 1983. *Temps et récit.* Vol. 1. Paris: Seuil.

Riessman, Catherine Kohler. 2008. *Narrative Methods for the Human Sciences.* Los Angeles: SAGE.

Ritivoi, Andreea Deciu. 2009. "Explaining People: Narrative and the Study of Identity." *Storyworlds* 1, no. 1: 25–41.

Robbe-Grillet, Alain. (1963) 1989. *For a New Novel: Essays on Fiction*, translated by Richard Howard. Evanston, IL: Northwestern University Press.

Ryan, Marie-Laure. 2001. *Narrative as Virtual Reality: Immersion and Interactivity in Literature and Electronic Media.* Baltimore, MD: The Johns Hopkins University Press.

Sachs, Jonah. 2012. *Winning the Story Wars: Why Those Who Tell—and Live—the Best Stories Will Rule the Future.* Boston, MA: Harvard Business Review Press.

Salmon, Christian. 2007. *Storytelling: La machine à fabriquer des histoires et à formater les esprits.* Paris: La Découverte.

Salmon, Christian. 2010. *Storytelling: Bewitching the Modern Mind*, translated by David Macey. London: Verso Books.

Sarraute, Nathalie. (1956) 1990. *The Age of Suspicion: Essays on the Novel*, translated by Maria Jolas. New York: George Braziller.

Sartre, Jean-Paul. (1938) 1965. *Nausea*, translated by Robert Baldick. Harmondsworth, UK: Penguin.

Sartwell, Crispin. 2000. *End of Story: Toward an Annihilation of Language and History*. Albany: SUNY Press.

Schechtman, Marya. 2007. "Stories, Lives, and Basic Survival: A Refinement and Defense of the Narrative View." In *Narrative and Understanding Persons*, edited by Daniel D. Hutto, 155–78. Cambridge: Cambridge University Press.

Schiff, Brian, A. Elizabeth McKim, and Sylvie Patron, eds. 2017. *Life and Narrative: The Risks and Responsibilities of Storying Experience*. Oxford: Oxford University Press.

Sellars, Wilfrid. 1963. *Science, Perception, and Reality*. London: Routledge and Kegan Paul.

Shiller, Robert J. 2019. *Narrative Economics*. Princeton, NJ: Princeton University Press.

Shuman, Amy. 2005. *Other People's Stories: Entitlement Claims and the Critique of Empathy*. Urbana: University of Illinois Press.

Smith, Zadie. 2019. *The Grand Union: Stories*. New York: Penguin.

Strawson, Galen. 1999a. "The Self." In *Models of the Self*, edited by Shaun Gallagher and Jonathan Shear, 1–24. Thorverton, UK: Imprint Academic.

Strawson, Galen. 1999b. "The Self and the SESMET." *Journal of Consciousness Studies* 6, no. 4: 99–135.

Strawson, Galen. 2004. "Against Narrativity." *Ratio* 17, no. 4: 428–52.

Vermeulen, Timotheus, and Robin van den Akker. 2010. "Notes on Metamodernism." *Journal of Aesthetics and Culture* 2, no. 1: 5677.

White, Hayden. 1981. "The Value of Narrativity in the Representation of Reality." In *On Narrative*, edited by W. J. T. Mitchell, 1–23. Chicago: University of Chicago Press.

Woolf, Virginia. 1925. *The Common Reader*. London: Hogarth Press.

Zahavi, Dan. 2014. *Self and Other: Exploring Subjectivity, Empathy, and Shame*. Oxford: Oxford University Press.

NARRATIVE POLITICS AND CAMPAIGNING

Small Stories in Charity Fundraising Letters and the Ethics of Interwoven Individualism

Andrea Macrae
Oxford Brookes University

Abstract   The explicit imperative to "tell a story" recently dominating UK and US fundraising discourse refers specifically to the central compelling "story" of the representative victim/beneficiary, and yet there are multiple stories at work in charity fundraising letters, with interdependent narrative trajectories. This article draws on small stories research and on scholarship on storytelling and ethics to explore the relative narrativity of the stories within charity fundraising letters and their marked contingence upon lack of resolution. This article also disentangles and investigates the interactions among the stories of the representative beneficiary, the addressee as potential donor, and the charitable organization. It discusses the affirmation and exploitation of Western neoliberal individualism in the selective spotlighting of an individual beneficiary, and in the individualized appeal to the addressee. It discusses the tensions between the charitable organization and the addressee as competing contenders for the archetypal role of the "hero" in the narrative of the victim/beneficiary, and reflects on the ways in which the complex narratives of supraindividual social processes involved both in the causes of suffering and need and in their alleviation are downplayed in the service of more impactful individualistic narratives.

Keywords   ethics, fundraising letters, small stories research

Poetics Today 43:2 (June 2022)   DOI 10.1215/03335372-9642581
© 2022 by Porter Institute for Poetics and Semiotics

1. The Narrativity of Charity Fundraising Letters: Small Stories and Ethics

The instruction to "tell a story," as a central constituent of an effective direct mail fundraising appeal, has become increasingly prevalent in the UK and US charity sectors. The value of good storytelling is the focus of several popular sector trade books (e.g., Brooks 2014; Burnett 2014; Lockshin 2016), guides for practitioners which are more explicitly informed by academic research (e.g., Sargeant and Shang 2017), formal sector training (e.g., Chartered Institute of Fundraising 2021; Get Grants 2022), and online sector guides (e.g., Boulton 2014; Community Funded 2021; Ibrisevic 2018; Jacobwith 2021; Keating 2019). The "story" referred to in much of this discourse is ostensibly the brief personal story of a representative "victim," or "beneficiary."[1] This story is an illustrative narration of an ongoing crisis, or of a risk of a future crisis, which serves to establish the need for the appeal. However, discussions of storytelling in fundraising guidance and research tend to swiftly shift their focus from the story of the beneficiary to the engagement of the recipient of the letter (usually referred to within the sector as "the donor") with that story, and their potential role in the story of the beneficiary—usually as an agent who "helps" or "saves," through their act of donating. Thus, the story of the beneficiary becomes subsumed within the story of the donor. Charities often use the number and size of donations a campaign receives as an indirect measure of the emotional impact upon the donor of their engagement with the beneficiary's story, while academic researchers sometimes use study participants' self-reported hypothetical "intention to donate" to measure this (e.g., Merchant, Ford, and Sargeant 2010). Beyond these particular measures, though, there has been little attention to the relative narrative nature of, and relationship between, the stories of the donor and of the beneficiary. The narrative of the charitable organization within fundraising letters, usually presented via a more or less individualized representative speaker who may also function as a "witness," in practice often contains a further distinct story involving the organization as an agent. The narrative nature of this third story, and its relationship to the other two, tends to receive even less attention in both academic philanthropic research and in practical sector guidance.[2]

Though the call within fundraising guidance to "tell a story" has been prominent for some time, research within the sector has only recently begun to engage with theories of narrative. This engagement with narratology is usually specifically in relation to donors' emotional responses

1. For many charities, impact upon humans is not the primary concern. This article focuses only on fundraising letters which prioritize impact on humans.
2. See Mitchell and Clark 2020 for analysis of broader nonprofit organizational storytelling.

(and the link to intention to donate), and it is often indirect, via research in marketing and consumer psychology, where in turn some narratological understanding comes from film and television theory (see Merchant, Ford, and Sargeant 2010 for an example of this path of influence). There has been limited direct engagement with the extant body of narratological research across various fields, and in particular literary narrative research, the main exception being reference in some publications to ideas grounded in Joseph Campbell's (1968) work on archetypal hero myths (e.g., Ascough 2018; Community Funded 2021). Though much of the attention to storytelling in the philanthropic sector has centered around its ability to arouse the emotions of the potential donor, the bridge has yet to be built between sector research and practice and leading scholarship on narrative, emotion, and empathy in literary and cognitive studies (e.g., Bortolussi and Dixon 2003; Green and Fitzgerald 2017; Keen 2007; Mar 2011; Nünning 2014). As Sujatha Fernandes (2017: 4) states, the twenty-first-century prevalence of instrumentalized forms of storytelling has tended to involve "constructing a genealogy of an essentialized, universal formula." Within current storytelling formulae in fundraising research and practice, the three forms in which narratological concepts do seem to have been adopted are: (1) an understanding of some version of the basic narrative arc; (2) a conceptualization of the story of the beneficiary as constituting an emotive "inciting action" in the story of the donor; and (3) the depiction of the donor in the prototypical narrative role of either "helper" or "hero."

The aims of this article are to develop a richer account of the complex network of stories and plotlines, and narrative roles and relationships, within the common discourse conventions of UK and US fundraising letters,[3] using ideas and approaches developed within work on storytelling and ethics (in particular Meretoja 2018a and Shuman 2005) and within "small stories research" (Bamberg and Georgakopoulou 2008; Georgakopoulou 2015). Small stories research explicitly encompasses stories which diverge from the norms of singular, linear, totalizing, and lengthy narratives in response to which much of traditional narratology has evolved. It recognizes that "in reality many of our stories are 'messy,' developing

---

3. Due to space and copyright constraints, whole letters or large extracts cannot be replicated within this article. A bank of illustrative examples of fundraising letters exhibiting the narrative features analyzed in this article is openly accessible online at the Showcase of Fundraising Innovation and Inspiration (Burnett 2018). Though the extracts from letters used for illustrative discussion within this article are from the author's own UK-based private collection, many discourse conventions are shared across UK and US fundraising practices (and other Western English-speaking contexts), as are leading sources of philanthropic research and trends in sector guidance.

without easily identifiable endpoints and in different environments and media" (Georgakopoulou 2015: 258). Small stories research aligns with the narratological approach of David Herman (2009) and the sociolinguistic approach of Elinor Ochs and Lisa Capps (2001), both of which retain basic definitional criteria of narrative but view these criteria as each presenting "a continuum of possibilities from more to less prototypical," or as dimensions which may be realized to a greater or lesser extent, in any narrative, and in a variety of different ways (Georgakopoulou 2015: 259). Alexandra Georgakopoulou juxtaposes Herman's (2009) criteria of situatedness, event sequencing, world-making/world-disruption, and conveying an experience with Ochs and Capps's (2001) dimensions of tellability, tellership, embeddedness, linearity, and moral stance. These two lists of narrative criteria overlap in different ways with each other and with Georgakopoulou's (2015: 258) own proposed "levels of analysis": sites, tellers, and "ways of telling"—the last of this list including the "more or less conventionalized semiotic and . . . verbal choices" within a story, and the "iterativity" of "types of stories told as ways of (inter)acting, embedded in recurrent social practices."

An underlying principle stressed in small stories research is that "any definitional criteria should be seen as context-specific" (Georgakopoulou 2015: 259). In this light, small stories research includes stories in which some or most of the sequenced events may be "non- or multilinear," and may be "future or hypothetical events," "unfolding" as a sequence in potential "further narrative-making" (260). This inclusive approach to relative linearity, temporality, and closure is particularly pertinent to charity fundraising letters, the essential pragmatic function of which lies in outlining and using a prior, ongoing or pending potential crisis to influence what happens next, beyond the cessation of the letter's storylines. The effect of the storying in charities' fundraising letters is contingent upon this lack of closure, so much so that readers are likely to accept these unfinished storylines as "a valid component of the text's signifying practice" (Herman, Jahn, and Ryan 2005: 359), in accordance with the conventions of the discourse genre. In a popular fundraising guidance trade book, Jeff Brooks (2014: 40) goes so far as to present it as a form of (non-)ending in its own right, with its own term, arguing that every letter must have "a *fundraising ending*. That is, it's not quite finished." The incomplete narrative structure plays upon the reader's desire for closure. The message of each letter conveys an implicit promise that the decision to act—to donate—will facilitate that resolution. Through this inherent lack of closure, the letters are also often "tellings [which] are fragmented," in which "more storying is added," and different kinds of tellability occur, "as more events unfold" (Georgakopoulou 2015: 263), beyond the textually inscribed narratives, determined by the choice that the reader then makes in response—specifically in their subsequent act of donating or otherwise.

Equally relevant to charity fundraising letters is the attention within small stories research not only to complicating world-disruption, via one or more extraordinary events, but also to world-making, which includes the "telling of mundane, ordinary, everyday events" (Georgakopoulou 2015: 260). The stories of representative beneficiaries tend to involve markedly radical world-disruption (significant change, caused by, for example, war, natural disasters, injury, etc.), and/or forms of unusually highly iterative or constrained world-making (unchanging, repeated, negative, or very limited experiences, such as spending a large portion of every day walking to fetch water, or being routinely abused or neglected, etc.). These forms of extreme world-disruption and iterative and/or constrained world-making, and the relationships between them, are relatively uncommon in nonfictional narrative outside of this discourse genre (excluding world-disruption in news discourse). Equally uncommon is their doubled narrative function: the radical world-disruption or iterative world-making in the story of the representative beneficiary primarily serves to create world-disruption—a narrative complication or crisis—in the story of the potential donor.

Small stories research also acknowledges and addresses the implications of the "detachability and recontextualization" of stories—their scope for extraction and (re)deployment in different tellings and texts (Georgakopoulou 2015: 260). The story of the beneficiary within charity fundraising letters is always re(con)textualized: it is detached from the original instance and environment of telling, and then reframed as an embedded tale within the charity's narrative(s). It is often reformed and rephrased during that process. This recontextualization can be considered appropriation, and even commercialization, of an individual's story, in the service of the stories of others and of the broader cause. Here the events of the beneficiary's story are simultaneously events in larger sociopolitical narratives and also in the narratives of the charity as agent and donor as agent—an example of the "productive co-existence of narrative activities, big and small, in the same event" (Georgakopoulou 2015: 256).

In some charity fundraising letters, though, the representative beneficiary's story is not rephrased: the voice of the beneficiary-as-teller is retained, and their story is shared in their own words, sometimes dispersed throughout various sections of the letter. This is one way in which the narratives within charity fundraising letters can be viewed as co-constructed, with multiple tellers contributing. A different kind of co-construction, however, of the "point, events and characters" of a story (or stories) within a charity fundraising letter, can be identified as occurring "between teller and audience" (Georgakopoulou 2015: 260)—between the charity and the potential donor(s).

The ownership of stories and the ethics of storytelling within charity fundraising letters are highly complex. Small stories research foregrounds the epistemological aspects of stories, in that it explicitly identifies storytelling, and cultural circulation of stories, as ways of knowing, in the Foucauldian sense—as ways of discursively constructing and fixing categories and positions, iterating sociocultural roles and hierarchies, and affirming dynamics of power, agency, and ownership (Foucault 1990). This highlighting of the epistemological aspects of stories is in line with arguments made within Amy Shuman's (2005) and Hanna Meretoja's (2018a, 2018b) ethics of storytelling, and coalesces at points with Phelan's rhetorical approach to the "ethics of the told" and "the ethics of the telling" (Phelan 2007: 203; see also Phelan 2005). In an analysis of stories circulated on social media, Georgakopoulou (2015: 267) discusses the ways in which stories may be "embedded into a variety of . . . environments with different semiotic modes (e.g., verbal, visual), and may be sanctioned and recontextualized in unforeseeable ways and by networked audiences." Relatedly, there is usually no public transparency about the level of informed consent given by a representative beneficiary for the form in which their story is embedded (e.g., with what introduction and further framing comment), presented (e.g., with what images), and circulated (e.g., using what media, in what contexts) by the charity, and subsequently consumed and implicitly sanctioned by potential donors, and recontextualized within donors' own stories as helpers or heroes. In later work, Georgakopoulou (2017: 272) stresses the need to consider "the trajectory of texts," noting that "all discourse shifts across contexts" and arguing that "any act of re-entextualization both produces new meanings and depends on who has access to which contextual space, who selects what to carry forward and how, what the conditions of say-ability are in the first place, and what the potential may be for subsequent circulation." Georgakopoulou draws upon the work of Charles L. Briggs (2005: 275), who calls for the interrogation of the ways in which discourse can "structure means of systematically producing marginalization and subordination," and writes that "we need to ponder not just the content of messages but how the ideological construction of their production, circulation, and reception shapes identities and social 'groups' and orders them hierarchically." Cultural and social narrative studies have increasingly foregrounded the fact that narratives are "entangled with relations of power" and, as such, tend to "marginalize experiences which do not fit white, male, heterosexual and anthropomorphic normativity" (Meretoja and Davis 2018: 5). Though charity sector guides profess the value of "leveraging personal stories in the change-making process, and learning techniques to tell a story that transcends the status quo" (Ibrisevic 2018), Fernandes (2017: 3) draws attention to the potential for "curated personal stories" to "shift the focus away from structurally defined axes of oppression" and to "inhibit social change" at a deeper level.

These points are particularly pertinent with regard to the trajectory of the story of the representative beneficiary, and also with regard to what experiences and narratives are inevitably occluded in the process of the selection, reformulating, and foregrounding of that individual story. Contemporary media and marketing practitioners recognize the emotive value of representing experiences on a "human scale," often reduced to ideologically imbued crisis-resolution narrative arcs (Fernandes 2017: 4). By contrast, complex sociopolitical and environmental issues which have evolved due to many causes over a long period of time are "unnarratable at heart" and "not amenable to emplotment" (Mäkelä 2018: 180). Maria Mäkelä (2018: 182) warns of the risk that the dominance of marketization and consumption of human scale, individualized stories may enable dominant cultural groups to ignore, oversimplify, defer, or efface larger, more complex narratives of structural injustice, and to reaffirm biased norms and values.

If the attention, within Georgakopoulou's (2017, 2015) small stories research, to the context-dependency of narrativity and to context-specific variations is combined with critical view of the motivated construction of "genealogies of storytelling, story prototypes and voice" (Fernandes 2017: 5), and applied to storytelling practices within charity fundraising letters, several questions arise: What prototypes of stories are being created and curated within charity fundraising letters? Whose voices are bestowed telling rights? What kinds of experiences are considered tellable? What kinds of narrative arcs are privileged? What kinds of roles and actions are inscribed? And what cultural webs of narratives, and social structures of power distribution, are transformed or perpetuated, shaped or questioned, in that storytelling (Meretoja 2018a)? The rest of this article brings together these lines of narratological and ethical questioning to examine the workings, interweavings, interdependencies, and contradictions of the stories of the beneficiary (section 2), the donor (section 3), and the charity (section 4) within charity fundraising letters. Section 5 of the article presents conclusions and reflections on implications for theory and practice.

2. The Representative Experiencer's Story

Drawing on evidence-based studies, philanthropic researchers Adrian Sargeant and Jen Shang (2017: 81) argue that "real victims generate the strongest emotional response, the most positive attitude toward the communication, and the highest proclivity to donate," and they add that "in many cases, a single identifiable victim generates more support than thousands of unidentified victims in aggregate." This corroborates the "identifiable victim effect" originally put forward by Thomas C. Schelling (1968; see also Small, Loewenstein, and Slovic 2007). To offer just one example of how this is transferred into sector trade books, Brooks (2012: 38) writes that "so many fundraisers think the size or intractability of a problem is what makes it compelling. What they're missing is that donors don't want to solve a problem because it's big. They want to solve it because it's solvable." Brooks continues, "the fundraising that works is always about a sick baby. Or a father who couldn't grow enough food for his family" (38). These are examples of individual stories of problems which have solutions, each "an account of *one person*" (39). Shuman (2005: 130–32) proposes that the use of a personal narrative testifies to the reality of the need, creates the impression of a singular, authoritative, firsthand, and thereby reliable *interpretation* of the need, and lends legitimacy to charity's appeal, while backgrounding the paternalistic context.

The individuals whose stories are leveraged within fundraising letters as a central emotive device are commonly referred to within the sector as "victims" (e.g., Sargeant and Shang 2017; Small, Loewenstein, and Slovic 2007) or "beneficiaries" (e.g., Breeze and Dean 2012; Hibbert 2016; Merchant, Ford, and Sargeant 2010). Jess Crombie (2020: 8) critically reflects on the passive, one-way interaction and disempowered receivership inscribed by the term *beneficiary*, and advocates for the use of the alternative term *contributor* (i.e., a partner in the work of the charity). The story of this individual, meanwhile, is sometimes referred to within the sector as a "case story" (e.g., Chang and Lee 2010) or "case study" (e.g., NCVO 2020), which foregrounds the representative or allegorical function of these stories and elides the original teller, their individual identity and personal experience. This article instead uses the terms *representative experiencer* and *representative experiencer's story*.[4] These terms reflect the spotlighting, within this article, of the individual's firsthand experience, and of their discursive role in letters as an experiencer (i.e., as someone who has experienced, or is experiencing, something which has given rise to a need), and also draw attention to the function of the story as representative of others'/collective experiences. They also avoid the (occasionally assumed) implication that the individual whose story is told is necessarily a direct "beneficiary" of any donation made in response to reading that story, do not position the individual as

---

4. These terms are not unproblematic, in that, for example, they background the individual's identity and agency.

a "victim," and create space for querying how routinely such individuals have informed and empowered agency over how their stories are selectively narrativized, presented, and circulated.

As Mäkelä (2018) points out, an embodied individual experience, and the mediation of this experience, seem to be at the crux of most definitions of narrative. The mediation of an individual representative experiencer's story can be located on three continua. The first continuum is a scale from positive (e.g., happy, healthy, strong) to negative (e.g., intensely pitiable) framing of the representative experiencer.[5] The second continuum is a scale from first-person presentation to third-person presentation. The third continuum relates to the overall proportion of letter that is dedicated to presentation of this single representative experiencer's story—that is, the extent to which the individual experiencer story is foregrounded (and other stories backgrounded). In addition to the three continua, there are arguably three different narrative trajectories. The first narrative trajectory presents a crisis which has been resolved, but there is subsequent risk of a new crisis (e.g., a flood has been survived, but there is risk of future flooding, of starvation due to crop damage, etc.). The second narrative trajectory presents a crisis which has been resolved for some people but not for others (e.g., a health condition for which some have received medical care, but others are still in need). The third narrative trajectory simply presents an ongoing crisis (e.g., long-term famine or civil war). The choices made with respect to these continua and trajectories, combined with the choice of using one individual's story as representative of others, entail ethical implications.

The second continuum, relating to the narrative voice used to present the representative experiencer's story, has a bearing on claims to authenticity, ownership, immediacy, and empathy. Shuman (2005: 3) raises the problem of entitlement in storytelling, asking, "Who has the right to tell a story, who is entitled to it?" Representative experiencer stories which are presented in the first-person voice arguably carry a greater sense of embodied immediacy, evoking the reader's empathy with the individual concerned (Keen 2007). Use of stories in the first person also implies that the original speaker has bestowed the charity telling rights, with permission to recontextualize and convey their words, rendering charities less open to allegations of misappropriation or misrepresentation.

A first-person story will nonetheless be edited and textually framed. Shuman (2005: 125) suggests that in the context of charity fundraising letters

---

5. The first continuum is less directly relevant to this article, but for valuable critical discussions see Breeze and Dean 2012; Bünzli 2021; Chang and Lee 2010; Crombie 2020; New Venture Fund 2016.

there is the possibility that "quotation erases rather than makes present the quoted person." Selective quotation can be read as representing the quoted person—as standing in for, summarizing, and epitomizing—thereby presenting a reductive portrayal of the individual's experiences, roles, and identities in ways which risk reaffirming stereotypes. Moreover, Georgakopoulou describes some of the editorial practices and "entextualization choices" that quoted and inscribed small stories can be subjected to, such as "erasing hesitations, uncertain looks toward the interviewer, false starts [and] long pauses." Georgakopoulou (2017: 273) argues that "entextualization encompasses a host of choices of form from layout to . . . transcription . . . with a host of implications for what may be foregrounded or overlooked." Further to the potential problems of quotation and entextualization, any editing, translation, or reformulation of the original first-person storytelling involves a subtle form of erasure of that individual's voice. A rendering of the representative experiencer's story in the third person assumes the authority to interpret, paraphrase, summarize, and "speak for," entailing a greater erasure of the original voice.

The portrayal of an experiencer's story as representative also carries ethical implications. Shuman (2005: 4) highlights how, despite their basis in individual experience, these stories "stray beyond the personal," by being presented as allegorical—functioning "to represent not just individual, but collective, experience." Representative experiencer stories, positioned as bearing a metonymic relation to the voices and experiences of others, are vulnerable to ethical queries regarding the entitlement of that story to represent (and thereby arguably silence) those others (121).

The British Red Cross's (2015) Nepal earthquake appeal letter offers one example of the privileging of an individual's experience. A report of the radical, world-disrupting event of the earthquake is followed by iterative world-building, in the descriptions of the daily lived experiences of consequent poverty, homelessness, and fear of recurrence. The letter presents the story of a named individual, Bijay, whose experiences are partly conveyed through direct quotation—for example, "'As I was running down the stairs with my boys, my elderly parents were clinging to each other in the bedroom,' Bijay said. 'My dad is 79 and paralysed—my mum would not leave his side.'" The last segment of Bijay's story, though, is narrated in the third person: the charity selectively describes his and his family's feelings of relief over their survival and despair over the devastation. The next sentence portrays the story of Bijay and his family as metonymically representative of the experiences of many: "They now face weeks of uncertainty ahead of them, as so many other families do." Bijay's story lacks closure: the story is presented as ongoing, awaiting an intervention.

Discussing the advantages and disadvantages of recontextualization and circulation of others' stories, Shuman (2005: 5) notes that "storytelling provides some hope for understanding across differences," but also argues that in some contexts "the appropriation of stories can create voyeurs rather than witnesses and can foreclose meaning rather than open lines of inquiry and understanding." What is being occluded by this privileging of the individual are the larger and more complex narratives of how the representative experience came about. Fernandes (2017: 13) argues that "disconnecting . . . personal experiences" from the "broader geopolitical contexts" in which they occur can reinforce stereotypical narratives about the causes of the situations which have led to those experiences. Mäkelä (2018: 175) probes the sociopolitical consequences of twenty-first-century transmedial "radical storification—the focusing on individual experience instead of macro-level or complex phenomena." Mäkelä finds "tear-jerking fundraising stories" to be a more "harmful or misleading" form of "instrumentalised story[ing] of personalised experiences" (178), partly because, as Fernandes (2017: 29) writes, they foreground the individual and the immediate, and background the bigger picture: they prioritize the satisfaction provided by "practical problem solving over confronting power and class conflict."[6]

A further example illustrates this issue.[7] Roughly 25 percent of a letter by Action Aid (n.d.-a) is dedicated to telling the story of Nikita. The letter begins, "Born and raised in the slums of Mumbai, Nikita lives in a tiny hut made of metal sheets and plastic with her parents and her younger sister." Notably, she is introduced via a locative prepositional phrase that situates her using the word *slum*, which tends to be used by more powerful and privileged people to marginalize and misrepresent more impoverished communities (Mayne 2017). The charity's presentation of Nikita's story deploys iterative world-making—the portrayal of unchanging lim-

6. See Moore et al. 2021 for one example of an empirical study which found that including information about systemic issues which have created the situation of need increased the likelihood of inspiring belief in the need for broader systemic social change, without deleterious effects on reader engagement, empathy, and willingness to act. The study warrants replication in varied charity contexts, but suggests that the complex social and structural narratives which representative experiencer stories tend to occlude could potentially be incorporated into fundraising letters without reducing revenue generation.

7. This article's re-entextualization and recirculation of the individuals' stories in the illustrative letters is arguably more ethically problematic than the charities' use of these stories, in that the individuals have no awareness of, and thus have not permitted, the author's use of their stories in this context. Additionally, it should be noted that the two examples have been selected based on their illustrative potential, with no intended critique of the practices of the two charities involved, both of which are widely respected within the sector.

ited or negative experiences: "There's no electricity and oil is so expensive her parents have to ration the use of their only lantern. Nikita's father earns a few rupees selling garlic, but it's never enough and Nikita often goes hungry." Nikita's story is presented in the third person, with no indication that Nikita's own words have been used or even paraphrased. Her voice is thereby elided from the story (as are the voices, and names, of her parents and siblings). Nikita's experience becomes metonymic: the next sentences of the letter are: "Thousands of children in Mumbai and other deprived communities around the world are growing up in poverty. . . . Children like Nikita can't depend on hope or luck." The storytelling thereby moves on to portray Nikita's story as illustrative of the experiences of "thousands of children in Mumbai," children "like Nikita" who are represented only through her. The letter invites the reader to become a child sponsor, or make a donation, with the promise of this act "making a difference." The causes of this poverty—the wider, longer-term, more complex, and less directly remedied issues—are elided by the selective, micronarrative focus of the storytelling.

Meretoja (2018a; see also Meretoja 2018b) distinguishes between subsumptive and non-subsumptive narrative practices. Subsumptive narrative practices "function appropriatively and reinforce cultural stereotypes by subsuming singular experiences under culturally dominant narrative scripts." They also "reinforce problematic stereotypical sense-making practices," those which "tend to hinder our ability to encounter other people in their uniqueness and perpetuate the tendency to see individuals as representatives of . . . groups" (Meretoja 2018b: 107). They present an authoritative, naturalizing interpretation of the events and experiences they depict. Subsumptive narratives reduce and appropriate the individual, and, as per the view of Emmanuel Levinas (1991: 42; cited in Meretoja 2018b: 105), subsume "singular experiences, events or persons . . . into a coherent system of representation: narrative represents them as 'fixed, assembled in a tale,'" within a sequence of events presented as inevitable. While subsumptive narrative practices present storyworld events as "self-evident and inevitable," non-subsumptive narrative practices instead present counternarratives, challenge oversimplifying stereotypes and categorizations, and have the potential to expand our "sense of the possible," to change perspectives and modes of thinking and perspective-taking (Meretoja 2018a: 90). Some presentations of the representative experiencer's story in charity fundraising letters risk reaffirming stereotypes, such as positioning the less privileged as "other" (Hall 1997) and as "the oppressed" (Shuman 2005: 148), and reducing complex narratives to naturalized crisis-resolution dynamics on a human scale. In Meretoja's terms, the nature of the appropriation and mediation of experiencers' narratives within charity fundraising letters, and the use of them as representative, arguably tends toward subsumptive narrative practices. The same could be said of the presentation of the potential donor's story.

This section has explored the way in which the crisis within charity fundraising letters is located within a story of an individual representative experience. One of the contradictions inherent within the use of a representative experiencer's story is the way in which the letter conventionally moves away, toward the end, from any implication that the potential donor can directly aid that individual with whom a personal empathic connection has been facilitated, and draws the potential donor toward the idea that "you could help someone *like* [the named individual]"—for example, "Please make a difference to a child like Nikita today" (Action Aid, n.d.-a). The representative experiencer is no longer the sole occupant of the role of the Object, within Algirdas Julien Greimas's (1983) actantial model: that position becomes, usually latterly and briefly, occupied by multiple, anonymous people "like" that named individual.

This shift in attention from the one to the many arguably addresses one particular critique of individualized representations of need in charity fundraising letters and elsewhere: that evoking empathy toward an individual creates only a very limited form of empathy, and obstructs the formation of a more "universal compassion" which is likely to be a more powerful force for positive social change (Bloom 2016). However, the marked extent to which most fundraising letters foreground the individual representative experiencer's story prior to this shift in attention limits the potential compassion-enabling gains.

Shuman (2005: 5) calls for a different but connected critique of empathy in the context of charity fundraising letters, arguing that a letter's primary provision of an opportunity for the potential donor to feel a prosocial emotional response to the named individual reaffirms "the privileged position of empathizer." Relatedly, Meretoja (2018a) asks whose agency is enabled through the representative experiencers' stories. The story of the potential donor, as the key agent in the letter's multiple narratives, is the focus of section 3.

3. The Potential Donor's Story

The term *supporter* is often used within the fundraising sector, rather than *donor*: *supporter* encompasses other kinds of giving to the cause (e.g., volunteering), and backgrounds the monetary exchange. Interestingly Merchant, Ford, and Sargeant (2010) use the term *consumer*, which is arguably more fitting in some ways, not least in view of the "consumption" of an other's story. In this article, the term *potential donor* has been adopted, because the focus of this section is upon the narrative path that hinges precisely upon that potentiality; the reader's agency, opportunity, and privilege, to choose to donate financially (i.e., to become a "donor"), or choose not to.

The three different narrative trajectories through which the representative experiencer's story can be presented (i.e., a crisis survived but with risk of recurrence or subsequent crisis; a crisis resolved for some but not others; and an ongoing crisis—see section 2) offer the potential donor different points of intervention in the story, and different kinds of agency and levels of impact. Multiple roles also exist for the potential donor: from "hero" to "helper"—or, in Greimas's (1983) terms, from Subject (as hero-protagonist, providing aid to the experiencer as Object), to Helper (as an agent who supports the charitable organization as Subject).

The representative experiencer's story often begins on the front of the envelope of the charity fundraising letter, as does the positioning of the potential donor, with text such as "Will you save *x* from a harsh winter on the streets?" or "Please help us save *x*," for example. On the envelope, and within the letter, the verb choices, and the inclusion (or otherwise) of the charitable organization as an agent with a more or less direct relationship to the representative experiencer, can position the potential donor in a direct relationship with the representative experiencer and/or the group they are representing, as the principally empowered agent and protagonist (e.g., "Will you *be there to help* families on the edge of survival?" [Oxfam, n.d.]; "Will you *protect* children like Omar from the bitter cold?" [UN Refugee Agency 2016]). Alternatively, they can position the potential donor primarily in relation to the charitable organization and in a secondary agentive role (e.g., "Please *help us save* women like Maria from this evil in our midst" [Salvation Army 2019; emphasis mine]). This latter position also notably presents the remedial action as collaborative (see section 4).

The more individualistic narrativizations which position the potential donor as a hero and savior are expressed through invitations to "perform a miracle" (Sightsavers 2014), to "save a child the world forgot" (Action Aid, n.d.-b), and to "giv[e] the gift of childhood" (Action Aid 2016), and assertions that "you can transform a life," "your gift . . . could save lives" (Action Aid 2021), "your generosity will change lives" (Christian Aid 2016), and so on. In these examples, the second-person pronoun (or a noun phrase using the second-person possessive pronoun) is the grammatical subject—the sole agent. This is combined with verb-phrase and object pairings implying high impact (e.g., "could save lives," "will change lives"). The potential donor, and/or their actions (i.e., their "gift" or "generosity"), are presented as significantly, and solely, empowered. Brooks (2014: 41, 42) advocates this approach in their sector guidebook: "The best story of all is the story where the donor is the hero. . . . You never go too many sentences without shining the spotlight back on the donor. You make it clear she has the power, the will, and the compassion to make the world a better place by giving. . . . Make it clear the donor is the hero." Positioning the donor as a hero, "as an agent capable of changing the world" (Shuman 2005: 148), however, diametrically positions the representative experiencer, and the group(s) they represent, as needing to be saved—as lacking the agency to change their own circumstances without dependency upon others. This reiterates and reinforces disempowering narrative patterns, and undermines attempts to present the representative experiencer, and the group(s) they represent, with dignity.

The charitable organization instrumentalizes the story of the representative experiencer for financial gain to alleviate the central need. Concurrently, storytelling within charity fundraising letters serves a self-oriented need in the potential donor (e.g., of empowered altruism), while simultaneously and relatedly backgrounding more complex narrative situations and the potential donor's relationship to those narrative situations (e.g., of complicity). Shuman (2005: 5) discusses the ways in which "appropriation can use one person's tragedy to serve as another person's inspiration and preserve, rather than subvert, oppressive situations." The relationship between the representative experiencer's story and the potential donor's narrative trajectory provides an illustrative example of uses of storytelling to marshal reactive "moral energy," and appeal to emotions, values, and self-identity, rather than to issues-based analysis (Fernandes 2017: 33). Lois Presser (2018: 21) proposes that, among different readers, "different stories provoke emotional reactions of varying force and engagement . . . depending on how much preferred experiences and identities are under threat." Though such short narratives have limited potential to achieve reader immersion, the dramatic intensity of the story of the representative experiencer, and the positioning of the reader as someone who either is or is not the kind of person who would choose to help, are impactful through the arousal of the reader's emotion and their desire to perform an act, completing a narrative which reaffirms their preferred self-identity. As Presser (2018: 20) states, the attraction of the "resolution" of the story is the illusion of agency and control, and of "a recognizably stable self."

As mentioned in the previous section, a tension arises toward the end of many charity fundraising letters in the shift away from the individualized empathetic (albeit unidirectional) relationship that has been implicitly established between the potential donor and the representative experiencer. While much of the letter may offer the opportunity to "save x," the last lines are more likely to imply the potential donor could "save people like x" (as per the close of the Action Aid letter discussed in section 2). The prior implicit avenue for achieving narrative closure, by resolving the problems faced by x, is latterly negated and frustrated. Despite this, many recipients take the next step in the narrative journey, and donate. This suggests that while the one-to-one individualized relationship may be important in evoking engagement, the potential donor does not need, or can readily see beyond, that individualized depiction of need, once they are engaged.

Unusually, this juncture of the potential donor's completion of their narrative lies beyond the remit of the textually inscribed discourse. Many charities send thank-you letters, or make thank-you phone calls, and so on, which carefully convey some kind of impact alongside gratitude, thereby providing some textual or verbal narrative resolution.[8] The deferral (at best) of that final step, however, beyond the cessation of the narratives within original letter, as well as the possibility that the charity may not be able to report precisely the impact originally implied in the letter, risks achieving only weak narrative satisfaction in that closure.

The penultimate section of this article devotes some attention to the most backgrounded of the three narrative strands within charity fundraising letters: the story of the charitable organization.

4. The Charitable Organization's Story

The charitable organization conventionally functions as the primary narrator—the dominant voice in the letter through which all entextualized storylines are framed and mediated. As the main and framing teller, the charitable organization is in control of the presentation of other two stories. Unlike the other stories, however, the story of the charitable organization is not usually presented as the story of an individual, though, but rather of a depersonalized collective. A caveat is required in that, as will be discussed, this story is often attributed to an individual, at least at the point of the letter's close.

Again, a continuum may be useful in appreciating the affordances of the story of the charitable organization: a continuum of different degrees of presence or absence of reference to the work of the charity. As mentioned

---

8. As with fundraising letters, there are many templates and guides for thank-you letters online (e.g., Bishop 2021; Sargent 2011). The discourse conventions of impact updates and thank-you letters, and their relation to storytelling continuation or closure, warrant further research.

in section 3, in narrative configurations in which the potential donor is presented as the hero, the story of the charitable organization tends to be backgrounded: here their role is that of the Sender, in Greimas's terms, and reference to the work of the charitable organization will be minimal. In narratives which present the charitable organization as Subject, reference to the work of the charitable organization is likely to occupy a larger proportion of the text. Relatedly, the charitable organization is more likely to be depicted in the syntactic role of active agent in verbal processes. Consider, for example, the ask "Will you be there to help families on the edge of survival?" (Oxfam, n.d.) which positions the potential donor as the directly impactful agent and elides the charity. Compare the ask, "Could you give £5 to ensure we can respond when we are needed?" (British Red Cross 2010). Here the potential donor ("you") is the actor in the main clause, but the charity ("we," implicitly excluding the potential donor) is the agent which responds and which is needed.

A further continuum may be relevant, one in which the voice of this teller narrates as an individual predominantly using first-person singular reference (e.g., "I have seen . . .") or first-person plural reference (e.g., "We have built . . ."), or referring to the charity by name (e.g., "[name of the charity] has developed . . ."). There is different rhetorical value in presenting the charity as a legitimate organization comprised of a collective body of people, and presenting the charity via a single, seemingly authentic, relatable individual. Charities tend to, at minimum, present the letter as signed by a named individual, creating a personal touch, signaling the legitimacy of the letter, and suggesting its author has a position of responsibility or is a reliable source. For example, within a Christmas appeal letter from Crisis (2020), while the letter makes occasional first-person plural reference to "us" and "our" work, the first-person singular pronoun "I" is used only in the final line, latterly developing the impression of a personal message from an individual, identifiable, authoritative author: "From all of us at Crisis, I wish you a very happy Christmas" is followed by a signature and the signatory's name and role—"Head of Crisis Christmas Team."

When first-person reference is more prominent, is it usually to voice a form of witness testimony, for example with phrases such as "I've seen a great deal of cruelty and suffering" (Salvation Army 2019), "I'll never forget my first winter in Jordan" (UN Refugee Agency 2016), and "I saw for myself the unprecedented scale of the flooding" (British Red Cross 2010), testifying to both the reality of the need and the authority of the teller. Such individual testimony, as per the representative experiencer story, provides a first-person perspective with which the potential donor can empathetically connect. This voice has different empathy-inducing affordances, however, in that the teller may be more likely to be (perceived as) a member of the "in-group" of the potential donor, and they model an emotive response to the experience of witnessing—a response thereby presented as appropriate—which can guide the potential donor toward feeling and acting in the desired way.

Notably, the donor's act of donation will not complete the narrative trajectory of the charitable organization or the witness/teller/author: their work and story is generally implied to be unending, each appeal part of a continuous series. The need-generating situation that functions as radical world-disruption or repetitive world-building in the story of the representative experiencer, and the donor's purportedly crisis-resolving, climactic act of donating, both constitute a different kind of mere world-building in charity's ongoing story.

There are inevitable tensions between positioning the potential donor as the protagonist and key agent of change, and positioning the charity as the protagonist—as the primary agent whose role the donor merely facilitates.[9] As has been illustrated throughout this article, this is but one example of the ways in which the positioning, and narrative trajectories, of the potential donor, charitable organization, and representative experiencer are interdependent, and but one manifestation of the challenges of mapping complex processes, involving multiple agents and stakeholder groups, onto individualistic cultural codes.

5. Conclusions and Implications for Theory and Practice

While the immediate need presented in a charity fundraising letter is often intended to create a degree of world-disruption for the recipient, that world-disruption is framed in such a way as to suggest the act of donating as the recognizable and ready means by which that disruption can be resolved. The broader "untellable" sociopolitical narratives which have led to the circumstances of need, and which have not only created the necessity for the charity fundraising appeal, but have also contributed to the normalization of the dynamics of power, privilege, and agency inscribed in the web of relations within philanthropy, are not disrupted, and nor are the discourse conventions or the wider systems of communication through which philanthropic appeals make meaning (Meretoja 2018a). In one view, the individualistic, emotion-arousing, self-identity-affirming nature of con-

---

9. Some charities are increasingly presenting experiencers as agents, e.g., explicitly portraying local communities as initiating and driving change, with charities' collaborative support. This shift is sometimes as part of programs to decolonize Western philanthropy.

ventional storytelling practices within charity fundraising letters tend to reduce or distort sequences of events into a crisis-resolution narrative arc and an individualistic, rather than collective or collaborative, model of experience, empowerment, and agency, and to problematically perpetuate patriarchal and paracolonial relationships between those who have historically been among the privileged and empowered peoples of the world, and those who have not. In another view, the charity sector is both mindful of, and cannot escape, its difficult position with regard to the ethics of its storytelling practices.[10] Instrumentalizing stories of representative experiencers is highly effective in generating funding needed to facilitate charities' work. Just as those who design systems using artificial intelligence cannot control the inherent misogyny within the data on which those systems are based, the charity sector cannot control the broader culturally dominant patterns of consumerist engagement with individual, problem-resolution/trial-triumph narratives. While many charities also work hard to effect significant structural and social change in complex contexts, most are responding to urgent need with limited resources. Charities make choices about which stories to tell, and how, but they do so within a cultural context in which views on what kinds of stories are "tellable," relatable, and powerful are deeply entrenched. Fernandes (2017) and Presser (2018), as leading critics of instrumental storytelling and the ethics of narrative, foreground the role and responsibilities of charities, as agents given telling rights and/or asserting telling privileges, to examine the ethics of their storytelling practices and to engage critically with the discourse conventions and encoded power structures involved, but both critics extend this responsibility to readers too, as consumers of and actors within these stories and the cultural norms within which they operate.

It is important to note that the outline of narratives within charity fundraising letters in this article deliberately focuses on the prototypical. There is wide variation (not least spurred by the need for novelty to attract readerly attention). Some charities prefer to provide lengthy first-person letters from representative beneficiaries as separate enclosed (rather than embedded) texts, for example. Different causes have slightly different conventions, codes of practice, and affordances. Some organizations and campaigns are less individualistic (particularly religious charities), and appeal more to in-group identities. Different nations, and more so cultures, operate via slightly different discourse conventions, within different embed-

10. For an exploration of the deeper ethical contradictions underlying conventional Western philanthropy, see Slavoj Žižek's compelling animated lecture (RSA 2010), and Glennie 2011 as an example of an opposing position.

ded, foregrounded, and backgrounded power structures, and with different conceptualizations of tellability and the unnarratable. The ethics of representation of animal beneficiaries differs, within current culturally dominant views, from that of humans. It is hoped that the discussion of the more prototypical charity fundraising letters presented here may inform and support analyses of the narratives and ethics of wider varieties.

Finally, the three core strands of a charity letter, and the hypothetical future events they project, can be usefully recognized as stories in their own right, and, while a charity fundraising letter as a discrete textual unit is difficult to conceptualize as a coherent narrative, its strands do nonetheless closely fit aspects of the conventional definition of a multiplot narrative: they "frequently . . . include embedded narratives," and "new plot lines are initiated when intersecting destinies create new personal relationships, new goals, and new plans of action, which interact in various ways with the previously establish[ed] plot lines" (Herman, Jahn, and Ryan 2005: 368, 324). The application of ideas from small stories research to charity fundraising letters shows how taking an inclusive and context-sensitive approach to narrativity facilitates a deeper narratological appreciation of the multiple plotlines, protagonists, tellers, and tales in this discourse genre, and enables a means by which to constructively accommodate and explore their often nonlinear, fragmented, and ongoing/unfinished form.

References

Action Aid. 2016. Myanmar appeal letter. Chard, Somerset: Action Aid. Author's private collection.
Action Aid. 2021. Afghanistan appeal letter. Chard, Somerset: Action Aid. Author's private collection.
Action Aid. n.d.-a. Child sponsorship appeal letter. Chard, Somerset: Action Aid. Author's private collection.
Action Aid. n.d.-b. Burma appeal letter. Chard, Somerset: Action Aid. Author's private collection.
Ascough, Hannah. 2018. "Once upon a Time: Using the Hero's Journey in Development Stories." *Canadian Journal of Development Studies (Revue Canadienne d'études du développement)* 39, no. 4: 533–49. doi.org/10.1080/02255189.2018.1479634.
Bamberg, Michael, and Alexandra Georgakopoulou. 2008. "Small Stories as a New Perspective on Narrative and Identity Analysis." *Text and Talk* 28, no. 3: 377–96.
Bishop, Jordan. 2021. "How to Write a Thank-You Letter for Donations: A Nonprofit Guide." *Donorbox Nonprofit Blog,* July 15. donorbox.org/nonprofit-blog/thank-you-letter -for-donations/.
Bloom, Paul. 2016. *Against Empathy: The Case for Rational Compassion.* London: Penguin.
Bortolussi, Maria, and Peter Dixon. 2003. *Psychonarratology: Foundations for the Empirical Study of Literary Response.* Cambridge: Cambridge University Press.
Boulton, Laura. 2014. "The Storytelling Secrets Charities Can Learn from Gandalf." *Voluntary Sector Network* (blog), *Guardian,* July 30. www.theguardian.com/voluntary-sector -network/2014/jul/30/successful-charity-storytelling-a-little-bit-of-give-and-take.

Breeze, Beth, and John Dean. 2012. "Pictures of Me: User Views on Their Representation in Homelessness Fundraising Appeals." *International Journal of Nonprofit and Voluntary Sector Marketing* 17, no. 2: 132–43. doi.org/10.1002/nvsm.1417.

Briggs, Charles L. 2005. "Communicability, Racial Discourse, and Disease." *Annual Review of Anthropology*, no. 34: 269–91. doi.org/10.1146/annurev.anthro.34.081804.120618.

British Red Cross. 2010. Urgent autumn appeal letter. London: British Red Cross. Author's private collection.

British Red Cross. 2015. Nepal earthquake appeal letter. London: British Red Cross. Author's private collection.

Brooks, Jeff. 2014. "Persuade with Story, Not Statistics." In *The Fundraisers' Guide to Irresistible Communications: Real-World Field-Tested Strategies for Raising More Money*, 35–44. Medfield, MA: Merson and Church.

Bünzli, Fabienne. 2021. "Improving the Effectiveness of Prosocial Advertising Campaigns: Message Strategies to Increase Support from Less Empathetic Individuals." *Journal of Philanthropy and Marketing* 26, no. 2: e1711. doi.org/10.1002/nvsm.1711.

Burnett, Joe. 2018. "Welcome to SOFII's Direct Mail Showcase: Contents and Index." SOFII, December 11. sofii.org/article/welcome-to-sofiis-direct-mail-showcase-contents-and-index.

Burnett, Ken. 2014. *Storytelling Can Change the World*. London: White Lion.

Campbell, Joseph. 1968. *The Hero with a Thousand Faces*. 2nd ed. Princeton, NJ: Princeton University Press.

Chang, Chun-Tuan, and Yu-Kang Lee. 2010. "Effects of Message Framing, Vividness Congruency, and Statistical Framing on Responses to Charity Advertising." *International Journal of Advertising* 29, no. 2: 195–220. doi.org/10.2501/S0265048710201129.

Chartered Institute of Fundraising. 2021. "The Power of Storytelling for Fundraisers." *Chartered Institute of Fundraising*. ciof.org.uk/events-and-training/training/2022/the-power-of-storytelling-for-fundraisers-(7-mar-2 (accessed February 28, 2022).

Christian Aid. 2016. DCR Light the Way appeal letter. London: Christian Aid. Author's private collection.

Community Funded. 2021. "Storytelling: The Four Core Fundraising Narratives." www.communityfunded.com/blog/storytelling-4-core-fundraising-narratives/ (accessed February 28, 2022).

Crisis. 2020. Christmas appeal letter. Slough, Berkshire: Crisis. Author's private collection.

Crombie, Jess. 2020. *Putting the Contributor Centre Frame: What the People in Our Pictures Think about the Way We Tell Their Stories*. You've Been Reframed, paper 3. London: Rogare.

Fernandes, Sujatha. 2017. *Curated Stories: The Uses and Misuses of Storytelling*. Oxford: Oxford University Press.

Foucault, Michel. 1990. *The Archaeology of Knowledge*. London: Routledge.

Georgakopoulou, Alexandra. 2015. "Small Stories Research: Methods—Analysis—Outreach." In *The Handbook of Narrative Analysis*, edited by Anna De Fina and Alexandra Georgakopoulou, 255–71. Oxford: Wiley.

Georgakopoulou, Alexandra. 2017. "Who Tells Whose Story? Beyond Everyday and Literary Stories, Fact and Fiction." In *Life and Narrative: The Risks and Responsibilities of Storying Experience*, edited by Brian Schiff, A. Elizabeth McKim, and Sylvie Patron, 271–75. Oxford: Oxford University Press.

Get Grants. 2022. "Online Storytelling for Fundraising Training Course." www.getgrants.org.uk/online-storytelling-for-fundraising/ (accessed February 28, 2022).

Glennie, Jonathan. 2011. "Slavoj Žižek's Animated Ideas about Charity Are Simplistic and Soulless." *Guardian*, April 22. www.theguardian.com/global-development/poverty-matters/2011/apr/22/slavoj-zizek-animated-ideas-about-charity.

Green, Melanie C., and Kaitlin Fitzgerald. 2017. "Fiction as a Bridge to Action." *Behavioral and Brain Sciences* 40: e363. https://doi.org/10.1017/S0140525X17001716.

Greimas, Algirdas Julien. 1983. *Structural Semantics: An Attempt at a Method*, translated by

Daniele McDowell, Ronald Chliefer, and Alan Velie. Lincoln: University of Nebraska Press.

Hall, Stuart. 1997. "The Spectacle of the 'Other.'" In *Representation: Cultural Representations and Signifying Practices*, edited by Stuart Hall, Jessica Evans, and Sean Nixon, 215–87. London: SAGE.

Herman, David. 2009. *Basics Elements of Narrative*. Oxford: Wiley-Blackwell.

Herman, David, Manfred Jahn, and Marie-Laure Ryan, eds. 2005. *Routledge Encyclopedia of Narrative Theory*. New York: Routledge.

Hibbert, Sally. 2016. "Charity Communications: Shaping Donor Perceptions and Giving." In *The Routledge Companion to Philanthropy*, edited by Tobias Jung, Susan D. Phillips, and Jenny Harrow, 102–15. New York: Routledge.

Ibrisevic, Ilma. 2018. "The Ultimate Guide to Nonprofit Storytelling (30+ Tips)." *Donorbox Nonprofit Blog*, May 17. donorbox.org/nonprofit-blog/nonprofit-storytelling-guide/.

Jacobwith, Lori L. 2021. "Engagement: The Secrets of Storytelling." Association of Fundraising Professionals, January 1. afpglobal.org/news/engagement-secrets-storytelling.

Keating, Chris. 2019. "Secrets of Direct Mail 4: Storytelling, Fundraising and the Dialogue Method." SOFII, September 12. sofii.org/article/secrets-of-direct-mail-4-storytelling -fundraising-and-the-dialogue-method.

Keen, Suzanne. 2007. *Empathy and the Novel*. Oxford: Oxford University Press.

Levinas, Emmanuel. 1991. *Otherwise than Being; or, Beyond Essence*, translated by Alphonso Lingis. Dordrecht: Kluwer.

Lockshin, Vanessa Chase. 2014. *The Storytelling Non-profit: A Practical Guide to Telling Stories That Raise Money and Awareness*. Victoria, BC: Lockshin Consulting. Kindle.

Mäkelä, Maria. 2018. "Lessons from the *Dangers of Narrative* Project: Toward a Story-Critical Narratology." *Tekstualia* 1, no. 4: 175–86.

Mar, Raymond A. 2011. "Deconstructing Empathy." *Emotion Review* 3, no. 1: 113–14. doi.org /10.1177/1754073910384158.

Mayne, Alan. 2017. *Slums: The History of a Global Injustice*. Chicago: University of Chicago Press.

Merchant, Altaf, John B. Ford, and Adrian Sargeant. 2010. "Charitable Organizations' Storytelling Influence on Donors' Emotions and Intentions." *Journal of Business Research* 63, no. 7: 754–62. https://doi.org/10.1016/j.jbusres.2009.05.013.

Meretoja, Hanna. 2018a. *The Ethics of Storytelling: Narrative Hermeneutics, History, and the Possible*. Oxford: Oxford University Press.

Meretoja, Hanna. 2018b. "From Appropriation to Dialogic Exploration." In Meretoja and Davis 2018: 101–21.

Meretoja, Hanna, and Colin Davis, eds. 2018. *Storytelling and Ethics: Literature, Visual Arts, and the Power of Narrative*. London: Routledge.

Miall, David S. 2011. "Emotions and The Structuring of Narrative Responses." *Poetics Today* 32, no. 2: 323–48.

Mitchell, Sarah-Louise, and Moira Clark. 2020. "Telling a Different Story: How Nonprofit Organizations Reveal Strategic Purpose through Storytelling." *Psychology and Marketing* 38, no. 3: 1–17. https://doi.org/10.1002/mar.21429.

Moore, Melissa M., Melanie C. Green, Kaitlin Fitzgerald, and Elaine Parvati. 2021. "Framing Inspirational Content: Narrative Effects on Attributions and Helping." *Media and Communication* 9, no. 2: 226–35. https://doi.org/10.17645/mac.v9i2.3788.

NCVO. 2020. "How to Write More Effective Fundraising Letters." *NCVO Knowhow.* know how.ncvo.org.uk/how-to/how-to-write-more-effective-fundraising-letters (accessed February 28, 2022).

New Venture Fund. 2016. *Road-Testing the Narrative Project*. May. static1.squarespace.com/static /56b4f3fb62cd948c6b994bd2/t/577d22b9d1758e79c8b1712f/1467818683314/New +Venture+Fund+-+Full+Evaluation+Report.pdf.

Nünning, Vera. 2014. *Reading Fictions, Changing Minds: The Cognitive Value of Fiction*. Heidelberg: Universitätsverlag Heidelberg.

Ochs, Elinor, and Lisa Capps. 2001. *Living Narrative*. Cambridge, MA: Harvard University Press.

Oxfam. n.d. Be Humankind appeal letter. Annesley, Nottinghamshire: Oxfam. Author's private collection.

Phelan, James. 2005. *Living to Tell about It: A Rhetoric and Ethics of Character Narration*. Ithaca, NY: Cornell University Press.

Phelan, James. 2007. "Rhetoric/Ethics." In *The Cambridge Companion to Narrative*, edited by David Herman, 203–16. Cambridge: Cambridge University Press.

Presser, Lois. 2018. *Inside Story: How Narratives Drive Mass Harm*. Oakland: University of California Press.

RSA. 2010. "RSA Animate: First as Tragedy, Then as Farce." YouTube video, 10:56. July 28. www.youtube.com/watch?v=hpAMbpQ8J7g.

Salvation Army. 2019. Kidnapped into Slavery appeal letter. London: Salvation Army. Author's private collection.

Sargeant, Adrian, and Jen Shang. 2017. *Fundraising Principles and Practice*. 2nd ed. San Francisco: Jossey Bass.

Sargent, Lisa. 2011. "How to Write a Better Thank-You Letter (and Why It Matters)." SOFII, May 21. sofii.org/article/how-to-write-a-better-thank-you-letter-and-why-it-matters.

Schelling, Thomas C. 1968. "The Life You Save May Be Your Own." In *Problems in Public Expenditure Analysis*, edited by Samuel B. Chase, 127–62. Washington, DC: Brookings Institute.

Shuman, Amy. 2005. *Other People's Stories: Entitlement Claims and the Critique of Empathy*. Urbana: University of Illinois Press.

Sightsavers. 2014. Christmas appeal letter. Melksham, Wiltshire: Sightsavers. Author's private collection.

Small, Deborah A., George Loewenstein, and Paul Slovic. 2007. "Sympathy and Callousness: The Impact of Deliberative Thought on Donations to Identifiable and Statistical Victims." *Organizational Behaviour and Human Decision Processes* 102, no. 2: 143–54. https://doi.org/10.1016/j.obhdp.2006.01.005.

UN Refugee Agency. 2016. Winter Survival Fund appeal letter. London: UNHCR. Author's private collection.

At War with Stories: A Vernacular Critique of the Storytelling Boom from American Military Veterans

Kristiana Willsey
University of Southern California

Abstract   In a post-draft era in which American civilians have grown increasingly apart from their military, veterans are urged to share their stories, to personalize distant and poorly understood conflicts—to make war meaningful. But individual veterans can't control the larger conversation in which their stories are interpreted or used. Veterans' stories are ventriloquized by candidates in campaign rallies, recapped in late-night news monologues, retweeted by celebrities, optioned for film, and consistently cited as evidence of why we should, or shouldn't, be at war. This politically charged landscape for the telling of personal narrative (and the speed and ease with which stories circulate via mass media) creates unique challenges for veterans, who need to find meaning in their experiences for their own sakes, but resist the ready-made plots and morals imposed on them by politicians and popular culture. Caught between what Amy Shuman calls "competing promises of narrative," veterans learn how to *not* tell war stories, relying on the denial or deferral of storytelling to assert small-scale meanings that resist recirculation and politicization. But to reject narrative outright is antisocial at best, and at worst pathological. Instead, the *management* of narrative—learning to select and edit stories for a given audience— is critical to avoiding the stigmatized identity of the traumatized veteran, who is either stubbornly silent or disturbingly voluble. Framing the withholding of narra-

This article draws on material from my doctoral dissertation, "Narrative Battlegrounds: Entitlement and Tellability in Veterans' Narratives," based on research with veterans of Iraq and Afghanistan in the greater Los Angeles area between 2011 and 2012. Unless otherwise indicated, quotes from veterans are from my fieldwork, and pseudonyms are used throughout.

Poetics Today 43:2 (June 2022)   DOI 10.1215/03335372-9642595

tive in positive rather than negative terms, my interlocutors stressed their need to curate the situations in which storytelling could keep its promises.

Keywords   personal experience narrative, folk narrative, military, veterans

In 2017, at the height of debates over National Football League (NFL) players "taking a knee" to protest police brutality and racial injustice, an image of a Marine veteran and double amputee went viral on Twitter. The caption read: "I wonder what this BRAVE American would give to stand on his OWN two legs just ONCE MORE for our #Anthem?" The image was liked and retweeted thousands of times, including by then-president Donald Trump. The subject of the photograph, Staff Sergeant John Jones, did not appreciate his image being used to promote a political agenda, nor being framed as what disability advocates call "inspiration porn." As he told Buzzfeed News, "The thing is, I do stand. Hello, I have technology" (quoted in Bergengreun 2017). Jones went on the record to clarify that he personally did not have an issue with athletes peacefully protesting, despite the political narrative his image was spun to support: "So many people have taken that photo and never even contacted me, never found out who I was or anything to say, 'Hey can I utilize your photo for this?'" (quoted in Kirkland 2017). In interviews, Jones focused on his postwar career providing jobs training for veterans through the nonprofit Workshop for Warriors, seeking to retake control of the narrative as an active author rather than a passive prop in other people's stories.

The image of a disabled veteran gave the political message of the tweet a persuasive charge that it would not have otherwise: who better to address the meaning of American democracy than someone who (the story goes) sacrificed their body in service of it? At a time when American culture is increasingly concerned with the question of who has the right to tell a story or speak on an issue, military veterans are often upheld in popular media and political discourse as the "true" or "real" Americans, whose emotional and physical investment in their nation gives them an indisputable moral authority over it. Particularly since the end of the draft, voluntary military service is framed (in recruitment ads, in political rhetoric, in many veterans' personal narratives) as a rarefied and moral act, the choice to stake one's life (or at least a few years of one's lifespan) on America's system of government. A history of military service bolsters the speaker's political claims: when cell phone footage of a confrontation on the steps of the Lincoln Memorial between a Native American protestor and a group of high school boys in red "Make America Great Again" hats went viral, news outlets quickly identified the protestor at the center of the video, Nathan

Phillips, as a Vietnam veteran. The irony made for social media magic: a Native American elder who had fought in the service of the government that dispossessed his culture, versus a group of smirking, privileged children? Phillips's indictment of Trump's border wall could not have a more credible, retweetable source. But when Phillips's service record was called into question (he never deployed to Vietnam), newspapers issued embarrassed corrections, and the story became too messy for easy virality (Lamothe 2019).

Feeding into the symbolic utility of veterans and their stories is the widening gap between the military and the general public: less than 1 percent of American adults are active-duty military, and only 7 percent are veterans, down from 18 percent in 1980 and steadily declining (Schaeffer 2021). Detailing the political history that has led to the creeping alienation of the American military from the American public, Rachel Maddow (2012: 199) notes in *Drift*: "The American public has been delicately insulated from the actuality of our ongoing wars. While a tiny fraction of men and women fighting our wars are deploying again and again, civilian life remains pretty much isolated in cost-free complacency." These statistics set up a strange terrain for storytelling: veterans are urged to tell their stories to provide a human face for war, to offer evidence of the global stakes of stateside politics. But the compartmentalization of America's military actions from everyday civilian life has simultaneously created an eager market for (the right kind of) soldiers' stories, and audiences ill informed to understand them. Storytelling is dialogic co-performance—stories are not handed off like static, bounded objects, but are scaffolded by audience feedback and participation (Duranti 1986; Ochs and Capps 2001; Reissman 2008). The post-draft distance of the public from American foreign policy sets up veterans' storytelling for failure.

After the 2011 troop withdrawal from Iraq, Americans looked to veterans to provide what Frank Kermode called a "sense of an ending," and a wave of military fiction and memoir found a receptive mainstream audience. As a *New York Times* article from 2012 puts it (prematurely, it would turn out), "Now that the American involvement in Iraq and Afghanistan is winding down, the warriors are telling their stories" (Bosman 2012). Autobiographical works like Chris Kyle's *American Sniper*, Matt Bissonnette's *No Easy Day*, and Howard E. Wasdin and Stephen Templin's *Seal Team Six* were runaway bestsellers: the public was ready for military memoirs, so long as they weren't too grim or morally conflicted. A buyer for a bookshop interviewed in the article explains "they're doing heroic things, and you don't have to wade into the politics of anything. . . . People feel like they're reading about the war, but it's not as hard to swallow. How many books can you read about how we shouldn't be there?" (quoted in Bosman 2012). "Heroic" books are, of course, hardly exempt from politics—their popularity relies on the narrative that war is a necessary evil, hard choices to entrust to hard men. Conversely, an article in the *Guardian* on the publishing trend for war stories focuses on the moral imperative to narrate, suggesting that a "flood" of books by veterans (in this case, critically acclaimed fiction like Kevin Powers's *The Yellow Birds* or David Abrams's *Fobbit*) had the potential to "stop the next conflict," with "veterans themselves leading the charge" (Harris 2013). People might *want* books that aren't "hard to swallow," but they *need* books that depict the brutality of war, because only a vicarious firsthand experience could sufficiently convince the reading public that war is bad.

The "warriors [were] telling their stories" all along, but now the public was buying them, perhaps hoping to read and then close the book on war in Iraq and Afghanistan. This desire for closure without conversation was a source of frustration to veterans like Phil Klay, who won the National Book Award for his short story collection *Redeployment*. In a 2014 interview with NPR, Klay states, "What I really want—and I think what a lot of veterans want—is a sense of serious engagement with the wars . . . without resorting to the sort of comforting stories that allow us to tie a bow on the experience and move on." But if (given the growing divide between civilians and an all-volunteer military) only veterans have the lived experience and moral authority to speak about war, then the ongoing dialogues about war that Klay and other writers hoped to spark through their work often stayed between veterans: in literary journals like *Consequence* and *Wrath-Bearing Tree*, communities like the Military Writer's Guild, and news sites like *Task and Purpose* and the *Duffel Blog* (the military's answer to the *Onion*). Venues for military storytelling in print, similar to oral storytelling, found their most engaged and receptive audience among military readers; the *New York Times*'s site for veteran-reporters, *At War*, was shuttered in 2021 for lack of interest.

Personal narratives of war always have more-than-personal stakes: public programs like the Library of Congress's Veterans History Project and StoryCorps's Military Voices Initiative record and preserve the oral narratives of military veterans, upholding shared storytelling as socially unifying and individually cathartic. Civilians seek out soldiers' stories to determine what meaning to take from war. After President Biden's 2021 announcement of a troop withdrawal from Afghanistan, a *New York Times* article asks the question, "Was it worth it?" (Philipps and Ismay 2021).[1] The

---

1. That the *Times* published two stories on the function of storytelling for closure at the end of war, nearly a decade apart, is a testament to the challenges of personal narrative on the constantly shifting ground of an endless war.

question isn't posed to American civilians, who would have no real way to answer—worth what? What changed in everyday life? What was lost or given up? Instead, this article and others like it ask a handful of veterans for their stories, to personalize and contextualize the impact of war on the small sliver of the population who lived it. Air Force veteran and author Brian Castner points out that the withdrawal timing is not for any military reason, but rather a politically savvy narrative move: "'In terms of story, it's genius,' he said. 'The Biden administration figured out a way to give the withdrawal meaning: Do it on the anniversary of 9/11, remind people why we were there—say we stayed for 20 years, then chose to leave. Tell them we did our part, put your chin up. It's a myth,' he said, 'but at least it's something'" (quoted in Philipps and Ismay 2021). Veterans who thought of themselves as active agents in a physical war come home and find themselves passive characters in a war being fought through political rhetoric: as heroes of a just war, or victims of an unnecessary one.

This is the cultural landscape in which individual veterans must tell their stories—media saturated with always-already politicized military narratives, for audiences uniquely, historically disassociated from American foreign policy. As a folklorist, my interest is in the stories a culture holds in common, particularly the role those stories play in forging national identity.[2] Just as traditional plot structures are constantly renewed and revoiced by individual tellers, personal narratives can travel far from their author and become the collective knowledge of a culture, at the expense of the individual at the center of them. Stories survive by becoming other people's stories; the emotional and corporeal particularities of embodied knowledge must be translated into shared representational codes and shaped by prior discourse. What Hannah Arendt describes as the private "passions of the heart, the thoughts of the mind, the delights of the senses [are] transformed, deprivatized and deindividualized, as it were, into a shape to fit them for public appearance" ([1958] 1998: 50). How has the storytelling boom shaped the conditions and possibilities for individual veterans' stories? How do personal narratives become—or resist becoming—political resources? The tension between the necessity and the impossibility of narrative parallels what Amy Shuman (2005: 150) calls the failed promise of narrative, that "narrative promises mutual understanding (empathy) and entitlement, and these are competing promises." Because the experience

---

2. Folklore is a discipline historically rooted in Romantic nationalism—early folklorists like the Grimm brothers' collected folktales in service of the political philosophies of Herder, who argued that political legitimacy came not from the ruling elites but from the common people—*das Volk* (see Abrahams 1993; Zipes [1988] 2002).

of war is seen as something of profound, universal human significance, the stakes for veterans—who want to own their stories, whose stories only exist because they are shared—are critically high and deeply felt. Caught between Shuman's "competing promises of narrative," veterans learn how to *not* tell war stories, relying on the denial or deferral of storytelling to assert small-scale meanings that resist recirculation and politicization.

How to Not Tell a True War Story

Narratives provide scripts for living that can be both defining and confining; as Hanna Meretoja (2018: 98) notes, "Our self-narratives include elements linked to cultural narrative scripts such as those of a 'devoted mother,' a 'loyal friend,' a 'social phobic,' and so on. Our narrative self-understanding has direct ethical consequences: it shapes how we act in the world." Narrators can engage with these cultural models reflexively: my interlocutors were highly conscious of and resistant to the script of the "stoic, broken vet" who refused to tell his stories, who insisted that his experiences were too singular and terrible to be understood by anyone. The reluctant narrator was a tragic cliché, a character satirized in veteran blogs and viral videos. As I was doing fieldwork at a private barbeque in someone's backyard, a vet I had not met before that night told me I shouldn't be there, could not understand their experiences. Angrily, he interrupted other people's stories to tell them not to talk to me. His friends apologized for him, embarrassed. "Don't be *that guy*," they kept saying to him. "I can't believe you're being *that guy*." Former Army Sergeant Brad Fox told me he had started out with every intention of bucking this trope: "I wanted to be like, open . . . *Some*body that would, like, t-*talk* about it, as opposed to somebody that *wouldn't* talk about it?"[3] But he quickly found his stories were only isolating him further; a story that can be told with other vets doesn't necessarily translate to an audience that doesn't have the specialized knowledge or the lived experience to make sense of it. Brad revised his approach, learned to "edit [him]self more." Differing backgrounds between speaker and audience can be minimized by spending more time setting up and framing the story, but this can also lead the story to collapse

---

3. Quotes from fieldwork and interviews have been transcribed with attention to the performance (volume, emphasis, hesitation, etc.). See the transcription key at the end of this article for reading notes. Though speakers do not divide utterances into paragraphs, I have included paragraph breaks in the transcribed personal narratives for ease of reading and clarity on the page. Paragraph breaks are not determined by topic shifts, but by parallel language such as "so" and "and then," the repetition of which structured the emergent performance.

under the weight of exposition. Sometimes there is no way to contextualize a story in a way that the audience will accept. Former Marine Corporal David Sharp noted that he tried to "veer away from it [the subject of his combat experience]" when non-veterans brought it up, because "there's certain things that I've noticed that I said that *bothered* people." Rather than needing social encouragement to open up about their experiences, veterans learn how *not* to tell a war story.

Veterans cannot outright refuse to narrate without risking being read as the stigmatized, traumatized veteran (see Willsey 2015). So instead, they learn (with difficulty, through trial and error) which stories are "safe" for which audiences, how to diplomatically substitute tellable stories for untellable ones, and how to render the management of narrative seamless and invisible. In order to not tell certain stories, soldiers will offer more socially viable alternatives; "the narrative which is untellable is often replaced by a narrative which is less risky and which is imminently tellable" (Goldstein 2009: 252). This kind of strategizing was made explicit in some of my interviews: when I asked former Army Sergeant Mike Graves to tell me about a memorable experience in either of his tours in Iraq, there was a lengthy pause before he initiated a redirection of the conversation.

M: (5 seconds) Hmm. Aahm. (3 seconds) There's like, a few (.) Aahm, I don't wanna talk about any of the bad stuff. Like, okay there's this one, on the *first* deployment we had, we had a dude named [Mitchell]? He's reeeally skinny, like really—not *short*, he was taller than I was, but super skinny? Like, just one of those weirdly skinny flexible dudes? (chuckle) And I remember we were just kinda like—this was at night, we're all just kinda chillin' in our ahm (.) Like, our (1 sec) called 'em like pods—like our rooms?

K: Mm-hmm.

M: Just like, imagine like a trailer with rooms in it. So we're all just chillin', like watchin' movies or whatever (brief interruption from the waitress)
So we're all just doing our own little thing like uh (.) Oh, so there's like a knock on our door like (lowers voice) bam bam bam bam! Ok, so we answer the door—[Mitchell's] *in*, like a *duffel* bag. He's like folded himself into a duffel bag (laughter) and he's being like carried around by this other dude named [Dupont] who's a Specialist. [. . .] It was just *hilarious*. Like, I don't think I stopped laughing for like, four hours.

We had met for our interview at a diner near his campus, and sat opposite each other in a red vinyl booth, a plate of french fries neglected between us and Johnny Cash filtering from the speakers overhead. In the long pause following my question—eight seconds altogether, which would have been more than enough time to lose the floor if this had been an ordinary social interaction as opposed to an interview—Mike is sorting through his "most memorable" experiences, looking for one that he can safely tell without alienating his audience. This is, as Diane Goldstein (2009: 252) calls it, an "audible silence"—a lack of story that speaks for itself. The story he does tell—a silly and accessible account of a skinny soldier who folded himself up small enough to fit into a duffel bag and entertain his friends during their monotonous downtime—could just as easily have taken place in a college dorm.

Over time, these stories become part of veterans' repertoire of personal narratives: polished artifacts that function not as risky self-exposure, but rehearsed performance of a preferred self. Bruce Jackson (2007: 35–36) has a name for this kind of exchange, calling these "preemptive strikes of personal narrative,"

> "Barabas stories," after the protagonist in Christopher Marlowe's *The Jew of Malta*, who is stopped on the road by Friar Barnardine immediately after Barabas has set fire to a convent [. . .]. Friar Barnardine points a finger at him and says, "Barabas, thou hast committed—." The homicidal arsonist Barabas famously picks up and continues the sentence with another narrative entirely: "Fornication? But that was in another country, and besides, the wench is dead."

This is a fitting parallel to the kinds of stories I got when I asked for war stories—issues of life and death parried with a dirty joke. I asked about memorable experiences, strange or dangerous things that had happened to them, and I was deferred with a succession of funny, outrageous, occasionally mildly obscene stories that I began thinking of as "cover stories" or "not-war stories."

Though they may be strategic, it would be a mistake to think of these colorful, tellable stories, rife with sensory detail but low on moody introspection, purely as deceptions or a special smoke screen to keep nonveterans out. These stories help vets create coherent pasts that incorporate their military histories into their post-military lives in meaningful ways, because "sense-making is also emergent. Individuals are constantly updating, reinterpreting, reforming, or abandoning their 'understandings' as needed and as required by subsequent experience" (Braid 1996: 16). Narrative is a means for reshaping identity—through the reiteration of stories, good memories are revisited and reinforced, encouraged to overwrite the grimmer or less interpretable experiences. It isn't that veterans are only telling this lighter fare to sheltered folklorists and other non-military friends—they tell them the most overall. This, according to one of anthropologist Erin Finley's informants, "is pretty much the way veterans talk to each other about it. You don't ever get in-depth enough about it that it bothers you [. . .]. And they're usually funny. Not sad" (quoted in Finley 2012: 28). The military is an institution that deals with life-and-death decision-making and relies on uniformity and hierarchy. So naturally, the stories that get told the most emphasize idiotic invincibility in the face of mortality, the humiliation or outsmarting of superior officers, and the individuality of the tellers. We are clever, deathless, and irreplaceable, these stories say.

Personal Narrative, Public Meaning-Making

Veterans' storytelling is popularly held to be therapeutic for the teller and cathartic for the audience: if untold stories are evidence of repressed trauma, narrative is purgative, like lancing a wound. Veterans must tell their stories so that they, and by proxy the nation, can heal. Veterans are tasked with recovering a usable past from the experience of war, to model meaning-making for the American public. But vets often feel that what civilians think they know about the military makes it harder, not easier, for their stories to be heard. Dutiful civilians say "Thank you for your service," a phatic phrase that performs connection it doesn't accomplish (Samet 2011). Oblivious acquaintances ask them nervously, "Did you ever kill anyone?" invoking the well-worn character of the "broken" vet that haunted soldiers' storytelling. Alienated by the simplified frameworks and ready-made morals of political discourse and popular culture, veterans defensively assert idiosyncratic personal meanings that would lose much of their resonance if separated from their teller. Shared public narratives of war and the personal stories told by individuals do different work, as veteran Thomas Burke clarifies to the *New York Times*: "Was it worth it? I could answer both ways. [. . .] There has been so much suffering by the Afghan people. In that sense, it's not worth it. But for individuals, there are experiences and realizations from Afghanistan that will always shape their lives. [. . .] I can't say that doesn't have real value. There are experiences I treasure, people I love who I met there" (quoted in Phillips and Ismay 2021).

Burke essentially splits his answer along the lines of what Michael Bamberg (2006: 2–3) labeled "big" and "small" narrative: "a *social* or *plot orientation*" and a "*'person'* or *'subjectivity-centered'* approach." The former centers on how "dominant" or "master" narratives—or what Jean-François Lyotard ([1979] 1984) called "grand narratives"—shape identity at a community-wide level; the latter focuses on the ways in which individuals use narrative to construct a stable and coherent sense of self. Recognizing that he is speaking to a national news outlet in service of the construction of the "grand narrative" of the war, Burke answers "both ways": was the war in

Afghanistan "worth it" in a global, political sense? No. But for veterans themselves, it has to be.

Individuals veterans can't rely on the constantly shifting political justifications for going to war, or wait for closure on a "grand narrative" decades in the making—they need small stories they can live with, narratives they can safely incorporate into a coherent sense of self. A representative example comes from David Sharp, who described his most memorable experience as a freak hailstorm that awed American troops and Iraqi civilians alike:

> D: During my deployment—as a civilian, ahm, I went over as a private contractor after I got out of the military—Ahhm (.) Iraq is typically hot desert. (.) When the sun goes down, it can get cold, it can get *damn* cold. It can drop below freezing, rarely. Ahm, and it rains, eeevery so often. But, typically, like when the sun's up, midday, during the winter months it's actually gorgeous weather, kinda like right now, it's actually really comfortable.

> K: Mm-hmm.

> D: Um, excuse me, *any*ways. (.) Ahah. It was just, I don't know *what* the deal was and a-a-a *We're*. Anyways, OK, to boil it down for ya,[4] we're, uh, we're protecting a company, the, the company we're working for were protecting *another* company of *demotechs*—what they do is they gather up a bunch of ordnance and at the end of the day they *blow* it all up.

> K: Mm-hmm.

> D: Um. (.) There was—it, so we saw like a fog, a wall of fog in the distance?
> . . . We see this *wall* of *fog*, it's comin' at us *really fast!* It's like, somethin' out of a movie or somethin', it was kinda wiggin' us out a little bit? We're—initially you see something like that and you think, sandstorm. But it *wasn't*. You could tell it wasn't a sandstorm. And they don't *come* at you like that either, like this wall.
> And suddenly this fog? Uh, hits us, and uh, this *blast* of wind starts comin', right? We're like, did a frickin' bomb go off in the distance or somethin'? It's *weird*, it's, the weather's weird. It's just, it's goin' nuts. Even the *loc*als are wiggin' out. They're like, (softly) What the fffuck is this, Y'know? (.) Ahm.
> And then, uh, it starts *hailin'* like crazy, I'm talkin' like, like, golfbaaall, y'know, close to a fist. sized. hail, comin' down, like, like Armageddon. Y'know? We getting, we're gettin' in our *vehicles*, and everyone's getting *shelt*er, and we're all just kinda *lookin'* at each other like, what the fuck is goin' on? Where we at again? What part of the world's this?

> K: Mm-hmm.

---

4. Note that this is the only point in the story at which David struggles, as he attempts to create a visual of the work he is doing for someone who has never seen it. The rest of the story is comfortable and coherent.

D: Ahand, (soft chuckle) a lot of the *loc*als, y'know, they're super*stit*ious, they're very re*ligiou*s, and they're like, ready to *pray*. Like, *what* is goin' on. And they said, ah, it only lasted (1 sec) seven to ten minutes, and then it just went away and you could see, like, it was like a gigantic (.) *cloud* of whatever this weather was and then it was moving on, you could see it *pass* us, and then it was like movin' on to the next area.

And I remember askin' the, ah, locals, and some of the workers and stuff, like, "Has that *ever* happened before, in your *lifetime* of livin' here," and they're like, Nope. Never. *Strangest* thing that's ever happened. So to *me*, that was like, (.) Yeah. Really, ah, really weird. You'd think that it'd be something, y'know, *combat* related? But it wasn't. It was weather. (laughs) That was the strangest memory I have.

David acknowledges the unlikeliness of this story as his "most memorable experience," laughing as he says, "You'd think that it'd be something, y'know, combat related." Relative to the surrounding conversation, the narrative is notably light on hesitation markers, self-correction, and frame-breaks, and confidently incorporates sensory descriptions and figurative language. This is not just an experience reported or described, but *performed*, part of David's repertoire of personal narratives. This is the experience he keeps returning to in order to draw a coherent relationship between his deployments and how he has come to understand them. On a day, as David says, "kinda like right now," a typical, breezy blue spring day in Los Angeles, American soldiers and Iraqi citizens alike were reduced to vulnerable human beings caught up in forces larger than themselves. At multiple points throughout his narrative, David draws clear linguistic parallels between his company of soldiers and "the locals"—"It was kinda wiggin' us out a little bit," he says. "Even the *locals* are wiggin' out." It's important to the story that this is like nothing either side has ever experienced, a freak hailstorm quite literally out of the blue, coming down "like Armageddon." David's story underscores the shared humanity of American soldiers and Iraqi civilians, just passing the time together, waiting out a storm that feels like the end of the world.

This sense of identification with Iraqi and Afghan civilians was a persistent theme in the stories of the vets I spoke with, who were highly conscious of and resistant to an existing narrative of the US military as brutal, aggressive invaders with little regard for local custom or human life. Narratives tend to occur in conversational cycles: "second stories" can either validate or complicate the moral position advanced by the first story (Allen [1987] 1989; Linde 1993; Ochs and Capps 2001). I often encountered narratives like David's, operating like counternarratives to stories that were not told—what Meretoja (2021: 37) calls "implicit narratives," or "*models of sensemaking* that underlie specific narratives but may not be anywhere available in a material form. They need to be constructed by interpreters of explicit narratives, which carry implicit narratives within them—as that which they resist or reinforce." I didn't discuss politics with David, nor did I ask any of my interlocutors whether they thought the work they had done in the military was necessary or moral. I never asked them, "Should the United States have invaded Iraq?" or "Did the military's involvement in Afghanistan make the United States safer from terrorism?" Yet they could not help but respond to these unasked questions; such questions occupied a kind of negative space in our conversations that my participants structured their responses around. David does not so much contradict the expectations created by political discourse as he does carve out a neutral zone within it, via a surreal, experience-centered story without heroes or villains.

Even a more plot-driven, action-packed narrative works best when the moral is tethered to the individual teller rather than the larger geopolitical context. After all, who would rely on the remote and ambiguous outcome of a forever war to derive a stable sense of self? A story by Special Forces vet Stan Reznik is a compelling example of keeping the stakes personal:

> S: You're always afraid, ah, that you won't be the person you wanna be, y'know, at the right time. And I think if anything terrified any of us, it was l-letting each other down? Or not being, exactly what we wanted to be when that moment came. And, ah, I was really de*light*ed, ah, when ah (.) W-w-well this is a story that you might find, ah, um, interesting. [. . .]
>
> My buddy [Bill] was out on a patrol, and I was on se*cur*ity that day. This is the fourth day we'd been there. Now, this guy said these guys will hit us within four days. (.)
>
> So, for four days, I slept, uh, in my *pants*, and my long underwear, and sometimes, even with my *boots* on. And, when you're in a *sleeping* bag, because it's *freezing* outside, you get out, and your pants are wet with sweat (singsong) aand that kinda stuff and so it b-began to *piss* me *off*, because I kept getting out of this sleeping bag with my, my pants like, drenched in sweat y'know
>
> K: Mm-hmm.
>
> S: Besides it's not like laundry was the order of the day, y'know? [. . .]
>
> So, everybody tells you about, y'know a-ah (.) M4s, or M16s, or pistols and that kinda stuff, but the real thing in war is if you have a machine gun, you're right where you wanna be, and if you don't, you're not. M-machine guns are everything. [. . .]
>
> Y'know one of the things about a Range battalion is, our motto of the Ranger regiment is "Of Our Own Accord."
>
> So people are supposed to be highly motivated.
>
> So people who were brand new would immediately, uh, clean anything that needed cleaning.

So you never take anything down and clean it like you would in normal life, you always have to have things ready.

SO the way it goes is someone takes the one that's not on, puts that on the tower, takes the other one down and *cleans* it.

So [Bill] had gone on patrol, I'd given him my M9 which is a 9-millimeter pistol. (1 sec) I *just* got off of, uh, guard duty, and our machine gunner, [Jack], who normally carries a *machine* gun and a pistol wanted to have my M4 for guard duty.

K: Mm-hmm.

S: So I gave him my M4. The last thing I saw before I went to sleep—the floor of our tent had haji prayer mats, as the carpet. And there was a prayer mat with my machine gun on it. [. . .]

So that's the last thing I saw before I went to sleep, is this is the machine gun, and this is the ammunition. So, I-I was comfortably armed. (.)

So I thought, y'know, I'm going to take off my pants because I'm tired of waking up with my pants, wet. And uh, y'know, got naked from the waist down, got into bed, and, y'know, you sit there for about forty-five minutes and *finally* I drift off to sleep. About the minute I fall into REM sleep: zhhhhhooo BKOW! Zhhhooooo BEW! DA-DA-DA-DA-DA-DA. So somebody says, "incoming," like, yeah, no shit!

So, I'm outta bed, and into my pants in twenty seconds, and I have my body armor on, and while I'm doing this I'm focusing my eyes and looking over and the machine gun is not there. Somebody's taken our machine gun and put it in another tower and taken down the gun from another tower so they can clean it. (I gasp)

So now I'm thinking, this is great, someone's attacking the safehouse and I can't find anything to kill anybody with, y'know? (.) And so I grabbed the ammunition, cause I knew I had to get that to the gun, I was running out the door, there was a small breeching shotgun. [. . .]

SO as I was running out, I turn the gun over in my hand, and I release the slide, and I looked in there, and all I had was a single (.) *hatton* round—which is one of these breaching slugs. They always joke to me about this afterwards and call me "Shotgun [Stan]" y'know? (.)

But anyway, that was the first time ah, anyone ever uh, *shot* at me. (.) It was good because everyone around me, ah, y'know was just the way I would want 'em to be, and I like to think that I-I was that way *too,* y'know? [. . .]

We didn't end up fighting anyone, it was a small outbuilding in an apple orchard that we got into Humvees and the squad I was attached to went to and flushed out just to make sure we weren't taking fire from there, but (briefly summarizes the actual engagement that happened the next night)

All you want to be is where you're supposed to be, and all you want to do i-is, do what you're supposed to do at the right time.

Vietnam memoirist Tim O'Brien ([1990] 2009: 65) famously wrote that "a true war story is never moral. [. . .] It doesn't instruct or encourage virtue." On the other hand, according to the psychologist Jerome Bruner (1990: 51), "to tell a story is inescapably to take a moral stance, even if it is a moral stance against moral stances." Caught between the impossibility of making war meaningful and the necessity of finding meaning in one's own experience of war, Stan's story stakes out a moral that is understated and intimate rather than overtly political. At one level, it's an ironic commentary on how the can-do, be-prepared ethos of his Ranger unit left him unprepared (his gun taken away to be cleaned while he slept), but how his own willingness to work with what he had (even if that were a breaching pistol with a single shot) earned him the respect of his peers. Yet the more significant takeaway is contemplative rather than humorous. Stan opens and closes his narrative with an opaque yet resonant sense of quiet satisfaction, of an orderly universe, in which the objective is not to kill anyone, nor even to neutralize a violent ideology, but simply to "be what you're supposed to be, and . . . do what you're supposed to do." Stan does no actual fighting in the story, and the outcome of the engagement is irrelevant, tossed off as an aside. What matters to Stan is how his war gave him a new name and social identity, showed him who he was under pressure—a highly personal meaning that would be difficult to package and repurpose.

Real and Ideal Narrative

When I asked veterans, "Who is allowed to tell a war story, and who is allowed to hear one?" I was given two answers: the diplomatic response was "anyone," while the more nuanced follow-up was some variation on "anyone who will (really) listen," or even "anyone who was there," sketching out the subjective, contingent nature of narrative as it *does* happen, rather than as it *should*. The inability of shared narrative to transcend dramatic differences in experience was a starting point, but not a socially viable end point. If veterans were to dwell on the precariousness of narrative, they would be denying trust in their community and undermining, simultaneously, the power of shared story and the bonds of brotherhood. My interlocutors instead emphasized the need to control the contexts of storytelling, not as a rejection of narrative, but insurance against its failure, framing the management of narrative in positive rather than negative terms.

Though I have titled this a vernacular critique of the storytelling boom, my interlocutors consistently confronted and resisted the notion that narrative was a false savior. To reject narrative outright was seen as antisocial at best, and at worst, pathological. Elinor Ochs and Lisa Capps (2001: 278) describe humans as being "caught between the desire for coherence and the desire for authenticity of life experience," between the social and the individual. The rhetorical construction of narratives in suspension imagines authenticity and coherence, self and other, as discrete possibilities—but this is an oversimplification. Michael Jackson (1998: 6), summarizing the wave of scholarship known as the "intersubjective term," calls selfhood a "bipolar notion" that emerges in the act of measuring reality: "What we commonly call 'subjectivity' or 'selfhood' are simply arrested moments artificially isolated from the flux of 'interindividual' life." The trouble with the notion of "private stories" and "master narratives" is that being-for-another is interpolated into being-for-oneself: individuals anticipate and internalize the responses of their audiences, and this internalized other is incorporated into the individual's idea of self (Ricoeur 1992; Schütz 1945; Duranti 2010).

Scholarly fixation on the theoretical impossibilities of breaching the divide between ways of seeing and knowing—that sensitivity to the impossibility of objective knowledge that characterizes the "reflexive turn" in anthropology—can blind us to the strategies at work within the communities we study (see Ruby 1982). My interlocutors were wary of these kinds of essentializations, of what Jackson (1998: 6) calls "a notion of the subject or of selfhood as some skin-encapsulated, seamless monad possessed of conceptual unity and continuity." There was little patience among veterans for reluctant storytellers, because there were no individual, privately owned narratives—only stories with smaller communities/audiences, and the extent to which these stories could help their tellers survive depended upon the purpose and commitment of that circle of tellers.

What many of my interlocutors identified as *ideal* conditions for storytelling defined narrative in the narrowest possible sense: it involved no artful translation of experience for new audiences, but rather what Edna Lomsky-Feder (2004: 84) calls the "field of memory," wherein shared experiences are jointly remembered and narrativized. As former Army Airborne infantryman Sam McDuggan explains, "It works better if it's a group of people that were there together." When storytelling expands beyond the confines of shared experience, the scope of potential narratives adjusts accordingly: "It's like a ((nested)) hierarchy, the more (.) up on the level you are the more stories *will* be shared back and forth? And so, if like me and one of my friends are sittin' down and talking (.) we *prob*ably wouldn't share *quite* as much. Of. Um. Our more combat-related stories? If it was someone we knew who had a desk job."

Stories seek common ground, Sam emphasized—if a group of vets includes one young soldier who has just completed boot camp, then boot camp stories will be told, even though, "no one really tells boot camp type stories . . . stuff that I guess just sorta gets pushed down as the deployment stories get added on top, I guess they just don't seem quite as interesting (chuckling)." Though Sam clearly understands combat experience as a higher order of access than support work, even dangerous work, it's significant that he stresses not narrative entitlement or exclusivity, but rather the importance of collaboration and community. As Courtney Cazden and Dell Hymes (1978: 28) point out, a narrative is a legitimate source of authority only "when it is used *among co-members of a group*." If a round of storytelling threatens to make one individual the "odd man out," the stories told are selectively edited to ensure that the conversation is appropriately inclusive and dialogic.[5]

Once narratives travel beyond their immediate contexts, beyond the circle of one's unit or even one's branch, the line between using narrative to lay claim to an identity and using narrative to create an entirely new identity for oneself was difficult to draw. As Roger Abrahams (1986: 233) notes, "Storytelling involves one of the most complicated of all playful complicitous activities, for it allows speakers to use language in a way that immediately denies all claims for veracity." The slippery, relativistic continuum between truth and fiction, real identity and fabrication, makes calling out another story as a lie or its speaker as a fraud a risky proposition. Army infantry vet Jun Zhu tried to avoid any kind of storytelling that glamorized or celebrated combat, something he felt often happened when veterans with different backgrounds and service records told stories together: "It seems like everybody just wants to like, one-up each other or something ah-ah I don't know exactly (.) Cause they just go there [the veteran's center student lounge] and it's just this massive, crazy, 'Oh yeah you did this? Well I was there for the in*va*sion, I did this, this and this.'" Like many of my interlocutors, he insisted that this kind of competitive one-upmanship was not how storytelling was *meant* to function; rather, it was an example of the failures of narrative. When I asked vets what a failed narrative looked like, I received a description of competitive storytelling (verging on fraud) more often than descriptions of a breakdown. Sometimes the two were clearly linked; saying too much and saying too little were both seen as forms of insecurity, a lack of ownership over one's stories which my interlocutor had pity or contempt for.

---

5. This is, perhaps, the essential distinction between oral storytelling and literary narratives authored by veterans: print cannot control where, and by whom, it is read. Anxiety about the circulation and misinterpretation of personal narratives beyond the initial performance has become newly urgent, given the ways in which social media straddles the line between speech and print—digital orality.

In order for storytelling to take place, it must be recognized at some level as shared experience, which means that the implicit awareness that no experience is entirely shared must be tactfully deferred or otherwise managed. Storytelling must be constantly *described* as collaborative, dialogic, and open, precisely because it is so frequently *enacted* as conflicted, competitive, and rife with critiques of entitlement. When attention shifts to the inconvenient impossibility of shared language to reflect the variety of experiences of war, whatever social work narrative could accomplish collapses into anxiety over its failures. It must be "anyone" who can tell a war story, because otherwise, it might very well be "no one."

Fighting Stories with Stories

When open critiques of another narrator's entitlement can slip too easily into an outright rejection of narrative and community cohesion, the best way to accomplish such a critique can be through another story. Earlier in our interview, Jun had mentioned dismissively how other veterans would brag about working with the SEALs or Special Forces, in order to borrow a little of those elite soldiers' glamour and boost their own stories' relative importance. Here, he describes how his friend Jeff would puncture the inflated stories of his peers: he performed an exaggerated parody of them that commented ironically on the ego-driven posturing of competitive storytelling.

> This uh, this other guy that [Brad] and I usually hang out with? He-he's very vocal, so he'll be like, y'know he'll tell his own war stories and he'll usually s-start something *ridiculous*, y'know he'll be like, (deepened, "tough" voice) "Y'know what, one time, I did *gate* guard, and this Navy SEAL came up to me, and he *touched* me, and he says (.) 'Now you have my Navy SEAL powers.' And I had his Navy SEAL powers!" (drops the exaggerated voice at the end, both of us laughing) like stuff like that!
>
> And everyone'll just be like, (deflated, soft voice) "Um, I guess we're all assholes for" (.) I dunno. Like, trying to have like a, pissing contest with each other cause it's just *stupid*, y'know? And everybody'll usually just *shut up* afterwards cause it's like so *riDICulous* and *stupid*.

Jeff performs a typical tough-guy story with an absurd twist—the Navy SEAL passes on his skills through an extended index finger reminiscent of E.T., which Jun imitated in his abbreviated restaging. The parody of storytelling acts as a comic corrective (Burke 1989) to overly ego-driven narratives—it occupies and explodes the narrative genre established by previous tellers. As Jun retells the story, he deepens his voice and speaks in a more clipped, direct tone, a mocking exaggeration of performative masculine speech patterns. His stylized (see Abrahams 1986) performance of masculinity, as Jun re-voices it, is indistinguishable from the surrounding, "real" stories until the final twist, which draws the audience's attention (and embarrassment) to the performativeness of their own narratives.

Jeff's critique of narrative rights—of tellers whose stories exceed their real military roles—is also an implicit critique of narrative itself. The parody comments not just on absurdity of that teller's exaggerated story, but on the flawed premise of narrative: experiences (or Navy SEAL powers) can't be handed off or transmitted via a supernatural touch. Neither our identities nor our experiences are so easily transferred: contact with a Navy SEAL does not confer SEAL-ness upon one, and hearing another person's stories does not give us privileged access to their past experiences. Entitlement critiques are a species of what Katharine Young ([1986] 2006) calls "edgework," the negotiation of the boundaries between the *narrated* event, and the *narrative* event (see also Bauman 1985). Calling out a story as a lie reframes it, redirects attention from the content of the story to the context of storytelling, to the constructedness, not just of that specific story, but of storytelling altogether. Puncturing the narrative would overturn the smaller world of the story and replace it with the larger, more complex world that the narrative is needed to contain. But safely within the frame of a story, the speaker can play with the dangerous rejection of sociality and narrative coherence. In this way, he avoids an open critique of the entitlement claims of others that could overset the vital, fragile faith that words map neatly and wholly onto images and ideologies, that the past we create for ourselves is the only past, and that we are the people we pretend to be.

Veterans' narratives carry moral authority and act as political currency, not in spite of the gap in understanding between the public and the military, but because of it: the same conditions that make storytelling vital make successful storytelling impossible. The assumption that stories are inherently transformative, redemptive, or unifying obscures the dialogic demands of narrative and the responsibility of the audience in co-constructing meaning. Narratives can create mutual understanding, but they can also be exploitive, voyeuristic, or oblivious, solidifying reductive and prejudicial versions of events. They can bridge gaps, or they can be a hollow performance, staging empathetic connection without accomplishing it. Lacking the context or stakes to understand the stories they want to hear, Americans fall back on the stock characters of political rhetoric and popular culture: veterans as victims to be pitied or feared, or as heroes to be vaguely and ritualistically thanked for their service. Conscious of the contradictory expectations and constraints for their personal narratives, veterans offer an emic antidote to an impossible, wholesale rejection of narrative. They redefine narrative in order to salvage it, discreetly curating the conditions for storytelling in order for narrative to function on the terms that it promises. The storytelling boom creates a market that commodifies and politicizes veterans' experiences, but "real" storytelling is a gift economy.

Transcription Key

[. . .] short section omitted
[ ] text altered (usually a name or place name anonymized)
italics word or syllable stressed
? rising intonation
. falling intonation, closing an utterance
, breath pause
(.) beat, pause of less than one second
(sec) longer pause, indicated with number of seconds
(( )) uncertain hearing, indecipherable (possible word in double parentheses)
CAPITALS volume
. . . searching, anticipatory pause
(xx) description of scene, gestures, transcriber's notes

References

Abrahams, Roger. 1986. "Complicity and Imitation in Storytelling: A Pragmatic Folklorist's Perspective." *Cultural Anthropology* 1, no. 2: 222–37.

Abrahams, Roger. 1993. "Phantoms of Romantic Nationalism in Folkloristics." *Journal of American Folklore*, no. 419: 3–37.

Allen, Barbara. (1987) 1989. "Personal Experience Narratives: Use and Meaning in Interaction." In *Folk Groups and Folklore Genres: A Reader*, edited by Elliott Oring, 236–45. Logan: Utah State University Press.

Arendt, Hannah. (1958) 1998. *The Human Condition*. Chicago: University of Chicago Press.

Bamberg, Michael. 2006. "Introductory Remarks." *Narrative Inquiry* 16, no. 1: 1–5.

Bauman, Richard. 1985. *Story, Performance, and Event: Contextual Studies of Oral Narrative*. Cambridge: Cambridge University Press.

Bergengreun, Vera. 2017. "Veteran Who Lost Both Legs in Iraq Says NFL Controversy Is beside the Point." *Buzzfeed News*, September 27. www.buzzfeednews.com/article/verabergengruen/veterans-are-sick-of-being-used-as-patriotic-memes-in-the.

Bosman, Julie. 2012. "A Wave of Military Memoirs with You-Are-There Appeal." *New York Times*, March 18. www.nytimes.com/2012/03/19/books/new-military-memoirs-find-an-audience.html.

Braid, Donald. 1996. "Personal Narrative and Experiential Meaning." *Journal of American Folklore*, no. 431: 5–30.

Bruner, Jerome. 1990. *Acts of Meaning*. Cambridge, MA: Harvard University Press.

Burke, Kenneth. 1989. *On Symbols and Society*, edited by Joseph R. Gusfield. Chicago: University of Chicago Press.

Cazden, Courtney, and Dell Hymes. 1978. "Narrative Thinking and Storytelling Rights: A Folklorist's Clue to a Critique of Education." *Keystone Folklore* 22, nos. 1–2: 21–35.

Duranti, Alessandro. 1986. "The Audience as Co-author: An Introduction." *Text* 6, no. 3: 239–47.

Duranti, Alessandro. 2010. "Husserl, Intersubjectivity, and Anthropology." *Anthropological Theory* 10, no. 1: 1–20.

Finley, Erin P. 2012. *Fields of Combat: Understanding PTSD Among Veterans of Iraq and Afghanistan.* Ithaca, NY: Cornell University Press.

Goldstein, Diane. 2009. "The Sounds of Silence: Foreknowledge, Miracles, Suppressed Narratives, and Terrorism—What Not Telling Might Tell Us." *Western Folklore* 68, no. 2/3: 235–55.

Harris, Paul. 2013. "Emerging Wave of Iraq Fiction Examines America's Role in 'Bullshit War.'" *Guardian,* January 3. www.theguardian.com/world/2013/jan/03/iraq-fiction-us-military-war.

Jackson, Bruce. 2007. *The Story is True: The Art and Meaning of Telling Stories.* Philadelphia: Temple University Press.

Jackson, Michael. 1998. *Minima Ethnographica: Intersubjectivity and the Anthropological Project.* Chicago: University of Chicago Press.

Kirkland, Allegra. 2017. "Veteran Whose Photo Trump Retweeted Wants No Part in Politics of NFL Protest." *Talking Points Memo,* September 26. talkingpointsmemo.com/news/sergeant-john-jones-nfl-protests-trump-retwee.

Klay, Phil. 2014. "Reminder from a Marine: Civilians and Veterans Share Ownership of War." Interview, *Morning Edition,* NPR, March 6. www.npr.org/2014/03/06/286378088/reminder-from-a-marine-civilians-and-veterans-share-ownership-of-war.

Lamothe, Dan. 2019. "Nathan Phillips, Man at Center of Standoff with Covington Teens, Misrepresented His Military Service." *Washington Post,* January 24. www.washingtonpost.com/national-security/2019/01/23/nathan-phillips-man-standoff-with-covington-teens-faces-scrutiny-his-military-past/.

Linde, Charlotte. 1993. *Life Stories: The Creation of Coherence.* Oxford: Oxford University Press.

Lomsky-Feder, Edna. 2004. "Life Stories, War, and Veterans: On the Social Distribution of Memories." *Ethos* 32, no. 1: 82–109.

Lyotard, Jean-François. (1979) 1984. *The Postmodern Condition,* translated by Geoffrey Bennington and Brian Massumi. Minneapolis: University of Minnesota Press.

Maddow, Rachel. 2012. *Drift: The Unmooring of American Military Power.* New York: Broadway Books.

Meretoja, Hanna. 2018. *The Ethics of Storytelling.* Oxford: Oxford University Press.

Meretoja, Hanna. 2021. "A Dialogics of Counter-narratives." In *The Routledge Handbook of Counter-narratives,* edited by Klarissa Lueg and Marianne Wolff Lundholt. New York: Routledge.

O'Brien, Tim. (1990) 2009. *The Things They Carried.* New York: First Mariner Books.

Ochs, Elinor, and Lisa Capps. 2001. *Living Narrative: Creating Lives in Everyday Storytelling.* Cambridge, MA: Harvard University Press.

Phillips, Dave, and John Ismay. 2021. "'No Victory Dance': Veterans of Afghan War Feel Torn over Pullout." *New York Times,* April 14. www.nytimes.com/2021/04/14/us/afghanistan-veterans-biden.html.

Reissman, Catherine Kohler. 2008. *Narrative Methods for the Human Sciences.* Thousand Oaks, CA: SAGE.

Ricoeur, Paul. 1992. *Oneself as Another,* translated by Kathleen Blamey. Chicago: University of Chicago Press.

Ruby, Jay, ed. 1982. *A Crack in the Mirror: Reflexive Perspectives in Anthropology.* Philadelphia: University of Pennsylvania Press.

Samet, Elizabeth D. 2011. "On War, Guilt, and 'Thank You for Your Service.'" *Bloomberg View,* August 1. www.bloomberg.com/news/2011-08-02/war-guilt-and-thank-you-for-your-service-commentary-by-elizabeth-samet.html.

Schaeffer, Katherine. 2021. "The Changing Face of America's Veteran Population." *Pew Research Center*, April 5. www.pewresearch.org/fact-tank/2021/04/05/the-changing-face -of-americas-veteran-population/.

Shuman, Amy. 2005. *Other People's Stories: Entitlement Claims and the Critique of Empathy*. Chicago: University of Illinois Press.

Schütz, Alfred. 1945. "On Multiple Realities." *Philosophy and Phenomenological Research* 5, no. 4: 533–76.

Willsey, Kristiana. 2015. "Falling out of Performance: Pragmatic Breakdown in Veterans' Storytelling." In *Diagnosing Folklore*, edited by Trevor Blank and Andrea Kitta, 277–300. Jackson: University of Mississippi Press.

Young, Katharine. (1986) 2006. *Taleworlds and Storyrealms*. Dordrecht: Springer.

Zipes, Jack. (1988) 2002. *The Brothers Grimm: From Enchanted Forests to the Modern World*. London: Palgrave Macmillan.

II. SOCIAL MEDIA IDENTITIES

Co-opting Small Stories on Social Media: A Narrative Analysis of the Directive of Authenticity

Alexandra Georgakopoulou
King's College London

Abstract   Small stories research has recently been extended as a paradigm for interrogating the current storytelling boom on social media, which includes the design of stories as specific features on a range of platforms. This algorithmic engineering of stories has led to the hugely popular feature of Stories on Snapchat and Instagram (also Facebook and Weibo). This article offers a methodology for studying such designed stories, underpinned by a technographic, corpus-assisted narrative analysis that tracks media affordances, including platforms' directives to users for how to tell stories and what stories to tell, discourses about stories as platformed features, and communicative practices. The article specifically focuses on the directive of authenticity in the storytellers' self-presentation with data from influencers' Instagram Stories. Authenticity is attestable in the values underlying the design of stories, the affordances offered, and the storytelling practices that these commonly lead to. The article singles out three constituents of authenticity vis-à-vis each of the above: the design of stories as vehicles for "imperfect sharing" and an amateur aesthetic; visual and textual affordances for sharing life-in-the moment; and the deployment of specific genres of small stories that anchor the tellings onto the here and now. These enregister a type of teller who offers a believable account of themselves and their life through affording an eyewitnessing quality to their audiences and access to their everyday.

Keywords   stories as features, social media, formatting, directives, values in design, authenticity, sharing life-in-the-moment, showing the moment.

Poetics Today 43:2 (June 2022)   DOI 10.1215/03335372-9642609
© 2022 by Porter Institute for Poetics and Semiotics

1. Introduction: Stories on Social Media as Designed Features

Since their inception, social media companies have been keen to evolve their features in ways that offer users facilities for telling stories. Facebook notably introduced the important feature of check-ins as a way for users to locate their stories. The widely recognized power of storytelling for presenting ourselves, making sense of our experience, and connecting with others has been duly harnessed by social media. Early features and prompts, such as "What are you doing right now?" (on Facebook) or status updates as the main function of Twitter, began, however, to direct users to a type of storytelling that is associated with sharing their experiences in the here and now and in short bursts, as opposed to producing lengthy accounts about the past. This early coupling of storytelling with sharing the moment has been crucial for how storytelling facilities have evolved on social media (Georgakopoulou 2017). In a longitudinal study of stories on social media, I have identified a close link between specific media affordances—mainly portability, replicability, and scalability (amplification) of content—and what I have described as *small stories* (Georgakopoulou 2007). Seen through the lens of conventional narrative studies, small stories are atypical: they tend to be brief or signaled elliptically; they are about very recent, ongoing (breaking news) or future events, and they are open-ended and transportable. They are also multiply authored and contested, often across contexts, thus destabilizing the close link between a given teller and their experience. Finally, there is a tendency for reporting mundane, ordinary, and even trivial events from the teller's everyday life, rather than big complications or disruptions.

Given these features, which have by now been well documented as characteristic of much of online storytelling (see, e.g., Giaxoglou 2020; Page 2012), I have argued that small stories research is well positioned to be extended to the study of social media, so as to offer alternative tools and concepts for the inquiry into stories (Georgakopoulou 2016b). I have also identified certain key phases in the development of facilities for posting small stories, in particular in so-called ego-centered platforms such as Facebook and Instagram (Georgakopoulou 2017).

The latest phase I have identified is characterized by big platforms' turn to designing stories as distinct features, integrated into their architecture, and named as such. The introduction of this hugely popular feature of stories began on Snapchat (2014), followed by Instagram Stories (2016), Facebook (2017), Weibo (2018) and lately, Twitter Fleets (2020), which are highly similar to "stories." This phase in the evolution of storytelling facilities online can be characterized as *sharing the moment(s) as stories*: it involves rolling out visual and video facilities that purport to allow users to post beyond single feeds and beyond sharing "a single moment." It is also part and parcel of platforms' ongoing shift toward live streaming formats of sharing (cf. Abidin 2018). In this phase, platforms use and, in many ways, appropriate the term *story* or *stories* as an attractive label that evokes positive associations to do with the "power of stories." As I have shown, the design of stories as a feature, in fact, presents certain mismatches between such associations that are explicitly evoked by the rhetoric of platforms about stories and the actual affordances offered for them (Georgakopoulou 2019). Stories as features are notably brief, visual—that is, photographic (e.g., seven seconds on Instagram) and/or (live) video (fifteen seconds) posts—despite the fact that they are launched as facilities for *telling* stories in a more sustained and continuous way than feeds allow. The stories are also heavily designed, templatized features with bundles of menus and pre-selections, despite the fact that they are hailed by platforms as opportunities for unbridled storyteller creativity (Georgakopoulou 2019).

I have set out to interrogate this story-curation phase on social media as an integral part of the current mobilization of the term *stories* and of storytelling in a variety of domains (see sec. 2, below). To do so, I employ the method of technography of stories which tracks media affordances, discourses about stories as features, and users' communicative practices (see sec. 3, below). I thus document the *formatting* of stories—that is, the processes through which certain types of stories and ways of telling them become recognizable, normative, and sought after on platformed environments. I have shown how the stories' formatting is supported by specific *directives* (cf. preferential conditions, prompts) by platforms to users for how and what kind of stories to share. Our analysis has specifically brought to the fore three directives (cf. preferential conditions, prompts) to users (Georgakopoulou, Iversen, and Stage 2020): these directives affect the types of stories told (i.e., sharing life-in-the-moment), the audience's mode of engagement in them (i.e., quantified viewing) and the tellers' self-presentation (i.e., authenticity).

In this article, I focus on the directive of authenticity in the storytellers' self-presentation. I show how authenticity is understood to be legible in the values in the design of stories, the affordances offered, and the storytelling practices that these commonly lead to, with a focus on female influencers' stories on Instagram. Specifically, stories are designed as vehicles for sharing life-in-the-moment, with tools that support the construction of an amateur aesthetic. Drawing on these tools and affordances, influencers deploy specific genres of small stories so as to anchor the tellings onto the here and now—for example, breaking news, updates, and behind the scenes. These features enregister a specific type of teller as one who offers a "real" (i.e., non-edited, genuine, believable) self-presentation through affording an eyewitnessing quality to their audiences and access to their everyday. The construction of an authentic self thus hinges on the construction of ordinariness and in turn flattens differences among different types of users. I conclude by proposing the sociotechnicity of stories and the role of media-afforded directives in their production and engagement with them as a point of entry into the study of the current instrumentalization of stories, especially as vehicles for truth-telling, in a number of public domains.

2. Context: Stories and Authenticity as Buzzwords in the Digital Era

The mobilization of stories by social media platforms and their integration into the economy of sharing is linked to *the age of life-stories*, also referred to as *the age of the witness* and *testimony* (Jensen 2019). This mobilization is part and parcel of a post-truth, "story-positive culture" (Gjerlevsen and Nielsen 2020), specific to the Western world, where stories are celebrated as liberating, therapeutic activities, central to an individual's personal growth. The term *story* has become somewhat of a buzzword, a powerful evocation of stories' ability to engage on an emotional rather than on a rational level and to persuade on the basis of personal experience (Georgakopoulou, Giaxoglou, and Seargeant 2021; Mäkelä 2018; Mäkelä et al. 2021). As Sujatha Fernandes (2017) shows, from legislation, production, and circulation of stories in legal hearings, to electoral processes and voter canvassing, stories have been commodified and refashioned since the turn of the millennium within a business model so as to bring capital to organizations. Fernandes's critique of this commodification of stories points to a reduction of the vastness of narrative practices and the fullness and complexity of individual experience, in favor of scripted performances.

The current social media curation of stories can be seen as a continuation of such contexts of story-commodification. That said, it also needs to be recognized as a technologically afforded stepping up, an extension that is bound to reduce the variation of storytelling even further, on account of the platformed affordances of portability and distribution that facilitate the wide availability of ready-made, pre-selection templates for storytelling. In a similar vein, such affordances are conducive to the standardization of specific types of stories as normative. The potential for standardization is also facilitated by the abundance of sophisticated metrics and analytics, more or less visible to users, that accompany the platformed design of stories. The proliferation of how-to guides to ordinary users and brands alike for posting "great" stories, and the wide adoption of stories by influencers, suggest that there is already recognizability of what constitutes a typical story on different platforms, alongside a well-developed machinery for the creation of normativity. Finally, the unprecedented popularity and replication of stories as a feature across platforms and types of users, from ordinary users to businesses and influencers, in the Global North and South, also attests to a process of consolidation of specific ways of telling as typical and valued, at the expense of others.[1] All of the above make apparent the need for studying stories as deliberately designed and platformed features within the current storytelling boom.

Stories online are increasingly being promoted by social media and advertising companies as the ideal vehicle for presenting an authentic self. While authenticity is routinely associated with "realness," its specific definitions and conceptualizations at specific points in time and in specific environments have a traceable, historicized heritage, and they are shaped by sociocultural values (Coupland 2003). Within the current association between stories and authenticity online, the prevalent definition of authenticity is that of "genuine," "not fake or manufactured" self and life (Marwick 2013), which presents no gaps or discontinunities in relation to the off-line life. In turn, this definition of authenticity online, often referred to as "mediated authenticity" (see, e.g., Enli 2015), as the genuine presentation of one's off-line reality, is historically linked with the erosion of the audiences' "organizational trust" in traditional broadcast media and its gradual replacement by a "personal trust" in individuals worth following (Enli 2015). At the level of language, mediated authenticity has been found to be expressed with amateurishness and a conversational, immediate style of communication, in distinction from the formal style of traditional broadcasting (see, e.g., Tolson 2010, in relation to YouTube vloggers). At the level of self-presentation, in particular in the case of influencers, mediated authenticity is linked with sincerity and believability of postings which in turn render influencers familiar and relatable to their followers (Abidin 2017).

The association of mediated authenticity with storytelling as its primary vehicle is particularly evident in the case of brand storytelling, where it is promoted as a way for brands to connect with their customers (see, e.g., Patel, n.d.). Market research similarly shows that the majority of customers value authenticity when they are deciding what brands they like. Similarly, users are more inclined to evaluate positively the brand endorsements of influencers who come across as authentic, in the sense of sincere and believable (Lee and Eastin 2020).

1. In the short history of rivalry over story-facilities between Snapchat and Instagram, the latter has emerged as a winner with more than 500 million accounts using Instagram Stories every day (https://www.businessofapps.com/data/instagram-statistic).

As we will see below (sec. 3), the intimate links between stories as a plat-formed feature and authenticity build on the above associations of medi-ated authenticity, but they also extend and add new dimensions to it, as authenticity becomes an integral part of the technological story-design.

3. Methods

3.1. Technography

An interrogation of the design of stories on social media necessitates what can be called, adapting Taina Bucher's (2018: 60) terms, a *technographic* approach to stories: a type of ethnography that attempts to trace the work-ings of technology and the affordances offered for the design of stories, establishing the (dis)continuity of any choices and updates. This requires an element of historicity—that is, tracking and identifying choices and val-ues in the design of stories in the context of antecedents.[2] A technographic approach allows the analyst to document the processes of the stories' *for-matting*: this refers to the recognizability of jointly achieved social actions in specific settings—in this case, digital communication, where large num-bers of users, geographically dispersed and unknown to one another, enter communication "stages" without any prior shared history (see Blommaert et al. 2020: 55–57). The key to formatting is, according to Jan Blommaert, Laura Smits, and Noura Yacoubi, users' repeated exposure to specific social actions. As will be shown below, such actions include the platforms' repeated *directives* (prompts, preferential conditions) to users, in their pro-motional material and in the actual design of stories, for what types of sto-ries to post and how.

Technography allows us to identify the design facilities, tools, and func-tionality of stories. There is increasing recognition within social media stud-ies, in particular in the fields of science and technology studies and of plat-form studies, that the design of features is imbued with values (for a "values in design" perspective, see Flanagan and Nissenbaum 2014; see also Bucher 2018). Social media develop their architecture on the basis of ideas about who their intended users are and what they would like those media to accom-plish (see, e.g., Langlois 2012; van Dijck 2013). The technographic approach thus entails uncovering the views and ideologies underlying a given design. These are encoded in promotional material, companies' briefs and blog posts, documents that outline technical specifications of new features, media reports and interviews with CEOs, and occasional disclosures of how part of

---

2. For details on the methods I have employed for tracking, including the technique of iden-tifying critical moments, see Georgakopoulou 2016a.

their algorithms work. Such material cumulatively produces a widely circulated discourse about a feature, while also including clues of hidden agendas, regarding its marketing and monetization.

To uncover platforms' discourses about stories and the values in their design, I have employed corpus-assisted discourse analytic methods, as one facet of the technographic approach to stories. Corpus methods allow us to retrieve meanings and associations that are salient yet not obvious to the naked eye and which can be established only by seeking out patterns of occurrence in a body of texts (Taylor and Marchi 2018: 61).

We specifically employed advanced Google search facilities on the words *stories, Instagram, Snapchat,* and *Facebook,* and the search engines Google, Bing, and DuckDuckGo, so as to compile a corpus of material (around 1,213 articles, excluding duplicates, amounting to around one hundred thousand words) related to Snapchat Stories (2014) and Instagram Stories (2016).[3] The main types of sources in the corpus (henceforth, the EgoMedia Stories corpus) include: (1) Instagram and Snapchat blogs; and (2) reviews of stories as a feature on a variety of online media such as tech, business, and marketing magazines and blogs (e.g., *BuzzFeed,* the *Verge, TechCrunch, Wired,* Sprout Social, etc.). Using corpus compilation and analysis procedures, we identified keywords and key semantic domains, collocates so as to explore the textual behavior of keywords, and concordances so as to explore patterns of lexical associations. The insights from the corpus-assisted analysis in turn led us to the next phase of data collection and analysis, namely influencers' stories.

Overall, the use of technography has enabled me to uncover the *directives* employed by platforms in the stories' design and in their promotion and marketing. Directives can be seen as prompts to users for engaging in specific posting practices and relational actions. They are supported by an app's tools, features, and functionality: these elements facilitate and activate certain actions at the expense of others, and give more weight to and prioritize certain types of content, so they render specific types of posting, interaction, and behavior by users as more valued and better suited to ensuring popularity for said users.

3.2. Stories as Communicative Practices

It is by now a familiar claim that apps evolve in a mutually feeding relationship with users' practices: far from being passive adopters, users strat-

---

3. The corpus was compiled in collaboration with Dr. Anda Drasovean in February 2018 and includes material published by January 2018.

egize, circumvent constraints, and even game any perceived algorithmic manipulations (Bucher 2018). That said, due to affordances of amplification and scalability and the algorithmic pressures for users to be popular (Bucher 2018), the potential for directives to lead to compliance on users' part and, in turn, to specific communication practices becoming normative and widely available, should not be underestimated. Influencers[4] as hyper-popular power-users were the first point of entry of this study into storytelling practices for two reasons: the style and content of their communication, including their stories, are emulated by ordinary users; features of the apps tend to evolve in response to both the practices of such users and their resistances (cf. Abidin 2018). On Instagram, influencers are clearly positioned as MVPs (Most Valuable Players), as their privileged access to story-analytics and other exclusive features shows (see Georgakopoulou, Iversen, and Stage 2020: chap. 4). Influencers therefore play a key role in the authorization (cf. naturalization, legitimation; see Jaffe 2011) of story-directives, serving as model-setters and cultural mediators between the apps' promoted template stories and the users.

The ongoing study of influencers' Instagram Stories has involved distinct phases of automatic collection period during which Stories, as multimodal data with their metadata, have been mined (with Python command lines and Instaloader) from two largely representative cases of female influencers.[5] This collection has generated a corpus of around 5000 stories. Here, I draw on findings from the 406 stories collected in phase 1 (January 2019) and the 1854 stories collected in phase 2 (April–June 2020) from Lele Pons, American-Venezuelan Instagram and YouTube celebrity, former top female Viner, a top-ten storyteller (with the most watched Stories in 2016 and 2017), according to Instagram's released figures. The coding of stories on NVivo12 has included metadata (e.g., time of posting), types of captions, language of choice in captions, interactive elements (e.g., swipe up features, stickers), format of Stories (e.g., live, photos, videos), mentions of others and mentions in stories of others, and so on. We have also coded the type of experience or happening that the stories report: for example, good morning / good night, travel, outings with friends.

---

4. According to Freberg et al. (2011), social media influencers constitute independent third-party endorsers or opinion leaders with access and reach to a large audience and the ability to shape their attitudes by using blogs, tweets, and other social media.
5. Although the female bias in the gender ratio of Instagram users has recently narrowed, six of the top ten most followed accounts on Instagram are currently owned by women, hence our focus on two female influencers. Kim Kardashian is routinely on the top ten list.

4. The Directive of Authenticity in Self-Presentation

As discussed above, the links between online stories and authentic self-presentation pick up on the prevalent definition of mediated authenticity as being genuine, real, not fake. The expression of a "true self" in stories as a sign of authentic self-presentation has a long-standing tradition in narrative studies as well as corresponding with lay conceptualizations of authenticity.[6] In turn, the definition of authenticity as the teller's presentation of a true self tends to be sought in the accuracy, believability and credibility of a story's events (see, e.g., Labov 2006). For the narrative analyst as well as for the storyteller, authenticity as truth and realness poses from the outset a tension between the inevitably subjective (re)constructions of experience and their tailoring to the here and now, in ways that ensure their reportability in a given context. From this point of view, authenticity has been recognized, especially within constructionist views of narrative, as inevitably "staged" and "strategic," part of a teller's intricate identity work and sensitive to the context of a story's telling (see, e.g., Ochs and Capps 1997; Coupland 2003).

An authentic self-presentation in stories thus needs to be seen through the prism not of the naive presentation of an essentialist self but of the facilities that allow the staging of a self that will be perceived as authentic in a given environment. Indeed, as it has been shown, constructions of authenticity require orientations toward certain semiotic resources that are recognized as emblematic of an authentic self (Blommaert and Varis 2011). As we will see below, the deployment of semiotic means that anchor the stories onto the present and achieve immediacy of tellings are such emblematic features. Jan Blommaert and Piia Varis (2011) argue that, for an authentic identity to be recognizable, any emblematic resources of authenticity need to be supported by regulatory discourses on how to be authentic in specific environments. The internet, they aptly claim, is rife with such discourses.

4.1. Values in Design: Imperfect Sharing

In the case of stories as a platformed feature, a key discourse, directive to authenticity, is that of *imperfect sharing*. Promoted by Kevin Systrom, Instagram CEO at the time of the launch of Stories (2016), as a key communica-

---

6. A case in point is Wilt, Thomas, and McAdams's (2019) study in which undergraduate students were tested on their conceptualization of authenticity in narrative. The analysis of the narrative content in their essays revealed "expression of true self," and the contentment and independence that come with it, as predictors of authenticity.

tive function of theirs, imperfect sharing was equated with the presentation of "real" (unpolished, unfiltered), "silly," and "goofy" selves.

With its "Stories" feature, Instagram incorporated Snapchat's successful introduction of stories as a tool for ephemeral sharing of silly and playful aspects of everyday life into its own platform design (see Kofoed and Larsen 2016). I have shown how imperfect sharing on both platforms grew out of the backlash against posting "glossy, perfect lives" (Constine 2016) and the public moral panic about the "narcissism" involved in young women's posts of edited selfies (Georgakopoulou 2016a). The Stories feature was thus designed as a vehicle for authenticity from the outset, and its tools and functionality were meant to support this aim.

Template stories offered by the platforms as part of their launching documents and how-to guides encourage sharing off-the-cuff, everyday moments (e.g., outings with friends; for examples, see Read, n.d.). Similarly, many of the stories' tools (e.g., animal filters, the boomerang looping effect, Superzoom, a "party hard" visual effect) and editing features are designed to help posters add funny elements to their stories. Such fun elements are promoted in how-to guides as ways of producing creative, original, and authentic stories. It is indicative of this conceptualization of authenticity that the words *creativity*, *authenticity*, and *originality* were strongly associated in the EgoMedia Stories corpus. Research on how Instagram Stories are perceived by users is scarce: a notable exception is Rebekka Kreling, Adrian Meier, and Leonard Reinecke's (2021) study, which has shown that users perceive stories as more authentic than posts, in that they afford a more spontaneous self-presentation. This finding provides evidence for the alignment between the branding of stories as vehicles for authentic self-presentation and users' perceptions of them.

In addition, the built-in ephemerality enables a sense of authenticity in self-presentation. By lasting for twenty-four hours and then disappearing,[7] and by being brief, stories promise users the ability to share in the moment, without worrying about overposting or about spending too much time on editing. As has been argued, the ephemerality of stories has incorporated a new dimension in the concept of ephemerality, a temporal time-bound logic, whereby the ephemeral both refers to the in-the-moment consumption of content in seconds and to the fact that a story can be viewed for a specific amount of time (Vázquez Herrero, Direito-Rebollal, and López-García 2019). This enhances the immediacy of the feature and, in turn, its potential for an authentic self-presentation, as we will see below.

---

7. Currently, users can archive or use highlights to store their favorite stories for longer, if they wish.

4.2. Amateur Aesthetic

Authenticity through imperfect sharing is closely associated with an "amateur aesthetic" (cf. Abidin 2018), which is promoted by minimal simple static graphics, and the facility of brief captions that can be overlaid upon the images. According to Crystal Abidin (2018: 91), an amateur aesthetic "feels less staged and more authentic," given that "the live, moving image affordances of streaming apps tend to enable for little modification and the basic editing affordances restrict modification to preset filters and stickers." The tools provided for this amateur aesthetic build on and are reminiscent of vernacular style photographic visual tropes (cf. Morton 2017): for example, image grain (favored by Kim Kardashian), skewed composition, and unflattering poses. Such tropes have been described as "endemic to a diaristic image-making that has become associated with inherently authentic and real, in-between, moments" (Morton 2017: 16). In the data at hand, the association of the authentic with ordinariness and an accessible aesthetic mode has the added effect of creating a level playing field for all users, be they ordinary users, influencers, or businesses.

In photographic terms, Instagram Stories present a vertical format, departing from the earlier square format of pictures on Instagram that evoke Polaroid pictures, and moving more to the direction of video. (Their size and ratio are the same as those of full high-definition [HD] video). This is yet another design choice with authenticity in mind. Stories are more immersive than anything else on the app, as users can view them full-screen on their smart phones. This format enhances the qualities of immediacy of viewing and the illusion of eyewitnessing, which are important constituents of constructing authenticity, as I will show below.

The constant rolling out of features and tools that allow users to link their stories with other stories, mention other users in their stories, and add location stickers and hashtags, as well as to engage with stories enhance the sense of interactivity around stories, adding to the creation of authenticity. It is notable that adding a CTA (call to action) in a story is promoted in how-to guides as one of the ingredients of authenticity in storytelling alongside "honesty (not faking it)." Elsewhere, we have argued that such features are part of a hybrid style of design in stories that allows users' connections on the one hand while, on the other hand, paying lip service to the platforms' agenda of quantification of every single aspect of a story (Georgakopoulou, Iversen, and Stage 2020). This suggests that the ways in which authenticity has been fashioned into the stories' design serve the twofold purpose of supporting stories as both creations and consumables, often linked with advertising. Influencers' management of the tension between presenting themselves as authentic and self-promoting, as will be discussed below, capitalizes on this hybrid functionality of stories.

4.3. Storytelling in the Moment

The presentation of storytellers and their lives as "authentic" was found in the data to go hand in hand with sharing life-in-the moment. In the Ego-Media Stories corpus, the lexeme *moment(s)* is one of the top fifty keywords. The most frequent modifiers for *moment(s)*, especially the terms *everyday*, *little*, *casual*, and *daily*, suggest a strong association with spontaneity and the mundane, and, in turn, with authenticity. The association of the word *moment* with sharing everyday life is missing from our reference corpora: in the British National Corpus, for instance, *moment* is associated with "an opportune and specific occasion" (e.g., at the last/crucial/right moment).

In a similar vein, the analysis of the key semantic domains suggests that immediacy is a salient, top-twenty domain in the corpus, associated most frequently with words that locate a story's events in the present, such as (*right*) *now*, *update*, *daily*, *current*, and *today*. Immediacy notably collocated with spontaneity and authenticity: the concordance lines suggest that their connection is located in the behind-the-scenes[8] feel that sharing in the moment affords (see Table 1 and Figure 1 at the end of this article for further details on the collocates for *authentic*).

Immediacy and spontaneity are also closely associated with authenticity in how-to guides for brand storytelling. A salient distinction there is between "of the moment" and "scheduled" content: the first is deemed as authentic, while the latter is deemed as "too perfect" and thus alienating for the audiences (Osman 2020).

Sharing-in-the-moment in influencers' stories is closely associated with specific types of small stories well suited to reporting on the here and now: these include breaking news, countdowns, behind-the-scenes views, good-morning/good-night stories, and updates. All these formats of stories have lay names, recognizable to and often employed by the posters themselves. One-third of Lele Pons's stories in the first phase of collection (406) are explicitly labeled (cf. captioned) as countdowns, behind-the-scenes views, and good-morning/good-night stories. There is a strong element of storytelling on the go in all of these formats: the teller moves about with their phone and captures snapshots of travels and everyday outings with friends, but also of their domestic environment, thus diarizing the everyday. Brief captions are recruited to provide an assessment of what is going on as a narrator's voice-over, leaving the visual or video modality routinely in the role of the depiction of the here and now. (Out of 406 stories, 264 comprise photos and 366 contain captions.) This on-the-go posting that invites view-

---

8. *Behind the scenes* is a recurrent phrase in the corpus (it occurs 179 times in total), which is indicative of the promoted spontaneity and authenticity.

ers to follow the storytellers around privileges the depiction of the mundane rather than of complications: for example, only 5 of Lele Pons's 406 stories report a complication (e.g., "broke my whole nail!!!!!"; "I'm still a little sick:/").

Another common thread in small stories of the everyday is the prevalence of temporal marking, linguistically expressed (e.g., with time stamps, temporal adverbs such as *just* and *now,* durative aspects of present tense verbs, etc.). Of Lele Pons's 406 stories, 59 are linguistically marked as being of "the moment;" in addition, there is no use of the past tense in any of the stories' captions, except for cases when a temporal marker of immediacy precedes the verb: for example, "just posted a video." This signposting ensures the stories' anchoring in the here and now, on the one hand, and generates the algorithmically preferred live streaming and timeliness quality, on the other hand. Given that stories last for twenty-four hours, one day is seen as an organizational unit for sharing moments as stories in its duration. This explains the frequency of good-morning/good-night stories, which punctuate the beginning and end of postings for a given day. In addition, such stories as the first and/or last post for the day, are a perfect opportunity for depicting the poster in intimate surroundings—for example, in her bedroom, half-awake and face semi-covered by a duvet or blanket, with no makeup or filters: another depiction of a "genuine self." (Only two out of seventeen such stories show landscape to indicate the time of the day, as opposed to Lele Pons being in bed.)

The immediacy in the temporality of Lele Pons's stories qualifies them for the genre of "breaking news," which I have shown to be a salient storytelling genre since the inception of social media (Georgakopoulou 2017). Breaking news stories set expectations for updates and create conditions for a trajectory of tellings in the near future, based on the ongoingness of events and/or or audience engagement that seeks further elaboration (Georgakopoulou 2017). In the data, this is a common strategy for Lele Pons to segment her day into a series of small stories, linked with one another in a temporally sequential way. For instance, she announces her visit to her middle school in Miami with a story of greeting her "favorite teacher," and a story that includes a picture with current students and is captioned with a durative present ("visiting my middle school!!!!!"). These serve as the first two of several postings for the day, that update on the visit (e.g., "catching up with my History teacher!!"). The final story from the visit is a picture of several pupils and a caption wishing them "good luck" and saying that "2019" is "your year." The event of the visit to her school is therefore told by Lele Pons in an episodic fashion, through a series of small stories of sequentially ordered subevents. This type of episodic, modular telling with breaking news and updates as main formats licenses frequency of postings with the aim of retaining followers' attention. Lele Pons, in tune with what market research has shown especially for influencers, posts stories several times a day (every two to three hours).

4.4. Authenticity and Showing the Moment

By segmenting her day with stories, as discussed above, Lele Pons affords her followers a sense of eyewitnessing. She partly achieves this with manipulations of visual and video elements, including the placement of her phone's camera, which affords her followers different perspectives and degrees of proximity to the unfolding events. These range from letting her followers "see" the events *with her* to them seeing her *as a character* in the unfolding story (Zappavigna and Zhao 2017). In all these cases, the predominance of the visual element, the *showing mode* of storytelling, allows the narrator to take a step back and let the events speak for themselves (Fludernik 2006). This combination of visuality and immediacy adds to the sense of vraisemblance of the stories.

The (re)designation of stories as visual rather than textual or verbal communication places a premium on specific narratorial modes—in particular, the narrator-experiencer, as opposed to the narrator who steps back and reflects on the goings-on. The effect of showing rather than telling is the production of a readerly experience of an "unmediated" story. The privileging of sensory roles for the narrator-recorder of their life (e.g., I see, I hear, I am experiencing now) and for the "audiences" as "live spectators" is evidenced in the corpus in the fact that visuality is a key semantic domain and that the lemma story/stories strongly collocates with a visual language (e.g., watch, view, see, hide, appear, disappear; for details on this association, see Georgakopoulou 2019).

At the level of communicative practices of stories as visual/viewable features, Lele Pons draws on the amateur aesthetic, as discussed above, with certain choices being recurrent in her stories. She specifically uses ugly selfies as a resource for imperfect sharing. She also uses Spark AR Studio filters to achieve fun visual effects. For instance, she places floating particles strategically and humorously in a story of eyebrow waxing. Bigger or differently colored fonts are employed for some words, or capitalization and exclamation points are used in the captions for emphasis and excitement. Among emoji, Lele Pons has a distinct preference for heart emoji. All such choices are available to and widely employed by ordinary users too: a key aspect of the authenticity that the amateur aesthetic brings to a story is that it purports to flatten any differences among users, creating a semblance of equal status, when in reality business accounts and influencers enjoy privileged access to story-analytics and priority in rolling out of new features, among other perks.

5. The Enregisterment of an Authentic Storyteller

Authenticity on social media has been mainly associated with (perceived) personality attributes such as believability and relatability. For example, Abidin (2018) has shown that influencers online place a premium on relatability in how they present themselves to their followers. Authenticity, in the sense of how genuine the influencer is, is a big part of this relatability, conducive to creating intimacy and closeness with their followers.

In the data at hand, the close association of authenticity with specific types of stories, as discussed above, grounds the characterization of an authentic teller both in the communicative practice of storytelling and in a specific mode of presentation of everyday life. Locating stereotypical valuations of a person (or a social group) in communicative practices has been shown in sociolinguistic research to be a process of creating stable, recognizable meanings. Enregisterment, the term for this process, therefore refers to "practices whereby performable signs become recognized (and regrouped) as belonging to distinct, differentially valorized semiotic registers by a population" (Agha 2007: 81). In Asif Agha's description of enregisterment, reflexive and metalinguistic processes are an integral part of such valorizations: our corpus analysis suggests that the proliferating how-to guides online, often produced by users themselves (e.g., Lele Pons has produced guides on how to create the perfect Instagram Story), that bring together stories with authenticity, are evidence of such reflexivity.

From this point of view, we can claim that stories as designed platform features have become a performable practice for enregistering and essentially valorizing the authentic teller as a truth-teller, whereby truth is conceived of primarily in terms of the teller's experientiality rather than referentiality. The authentic teller is one who tells the truth by depicting the minutiae of everyday life, the banal, using equally banal ways of telling and inviting their followers to be witnesses of their "non-edited" daily reality. As the discussion above showed, this mode of storytelling capitalizes on a specific set of semiotic resources supported by the design of stories as vehicles for imperfect sharing and an amateur aesthetic. This finding concurs with Blommaert and Varis's (2011) claim that, in particular in digital environments, constructing an identity of authenticity tends to be a matter of "enoughness." Enoughness is based on the use of a normally limited set of resources that are recognized as emblematic and as doing enough to produce an identity of authenticity in a given environment (Blommaert and Varis 2011). The perspective of "enoughness" on authenticity in Instagram Stories would suggest that authenticity should not be equated with "truth" in a literal sense but in producing accounts of daily life that are believable, trustworthy *and recognizable as "genuine" and "true"* (see Gubrium, Krause, and Jernigan 2014 for a similar point on the identification of authenticity online).

The idea of "enoughness" in authentic self-presentation also explains the potential of specific resources or genres of stories for being used as a vehicle of authenticity by different users, from ordinary users to influencers. We can expect "different degrees of fluency in enregistering discursive orientations" to authenticity by different users, as Blommaert and Varis (2011) show, but at the same time the design of stories facilitates a "normalization of aesthetics" (cf. Abidin 2018). This is a facilitating factor in the enregisterment of specific choices with the potential of flattening differences among different types of users. At the same time, we can also expect that different users put the directive of authenticity into practice in ways that suit local projects and the larger identities they want to project through stories—that is, they strategize the directive of authenticity.

6. The Influencers' Tension between Authenticity and Self-Promotion

In light of the above, although influencers have been instrumental in authorizing the directive of constructing authenticity through stories, it is also notable that putting the directive into practice places them in a double bind: constructing ordinary selves through sharing ordinary life-in-the-moment creates an obvious tension with promoting themselves and their products as well as with creating power-user identities as influencers.[9] Two discursive strategies for self-presentation in my data show how influencers manage this tension. In brief, the first strategy is that of repurposing: this refers to the adaptation of sharing life-in-the moment genres—for example, countdowns, breaking news, and behind-the-scenes stories, to the communicative purpose of (self)-promotion. One-third of Lele Pons's stories are promotions (140 out of 406). For instance, breaking-news stories are often deployed to direct users to postings of pictures or musical videos of Lele Pons. "Just posted a pic. Comment if you can relate." Or, "My next YouTube is my favourite ever!! This Friday!!!!" Similarly, countdowns are often repurposed by LelePons as previews, suspense-creation vehicles for the release and promotion of a video. For example, a sequence of three stories posted within one hour serve as a countdown for the release of her video *Amigos* (a short video parody of the TV show *Friends'* opening credits, featuring Lele Pons and five other friends and replacing the well-known

9. In the case of Kim Kardashian in particular, a large number of her stories (e.g., 347 out of 632 in the first phase of collection) are, thematically speaking, (self)-promotions: e.g., product tutorials and endorsements.

Friends theme with a Latino song). The first story announced that the video would be "coming out in 1 hour," the second that it would be out in thirty minutes, and the third that it was "out now." Similarly, behind-the-scenes stories offer glimpses of shooting music videos.

The second strategy of managing the tension between presenting ordinary selves and self-promotion is that of "commensuration," a term I adapt from Deborah Lupton's (2016) creative reworking of the mathematical notion. Commensuration refers to the systematic coming together of different qualities and properties in certain environments. This unlikely alliance tends to result in a gradual coming together of their diverse meanings. Drawing on this definition, commensuration in my data refers to the coming together of stories as a relational and affective mode with stories in their function as a vehicle for (self)-branding, marketing, and quantification of audience engagement. For instance, stories that depict fun outings and hanging out with friends get blended with the genre of peer-to-peer recommendation and endorsements which influencers use a lot. It is no accident that Lele Pons's friends who feature heavily in her stories (e.g., Hannah Stocking, Montana Tucker, Twan Kuyper) are all influencers, well-known YouTubers or Instagrammers, and every tag and every swipe that is added to her stories about them takes her followers to their products, videos, and so on. They, of course, reciprocate the favors. This relationality is akin to Instagram pods, the influencers' groups who agree to comment on, share, and engage with one another's posts, as part of gaming Instagram's algorithm into prioritizing their content and showing it to a broader audience (Abidin 2018). But what is notable for our purposes is that peer-to-peer recommendation is commensurate with the format of sharing life-in-the-moment and the blurring of daily life and endorsements that stories afford.

This commensuration is facilitated by the Instagram design of stories and algorithms. First, the main interactive elements in stories, such as location stickers, tags, swipes, and any calls to action buttons, are hybrid from the outset: they support the authentic presentation of daily life and the story's interactivity, but at the same time they are resources both for quantifying every behavior and activity that users do with stories (e.g., clicking on a sticker is metricizable) and for being used by influencers and businesses for advertising purposes. In addition, algorithms consistently flatten different types of users on Instagram, for instance by reprogramming "friendship" as "those people you interact most with." The relationship of fandom that followers thus have with influencers can easily be algorithmically computed as friendship. This metric conflates intimate relations with friends a follower may know in their everyday life and with influencers. The viewing engagements are conducive to this conflation, as stories from friends and influencers may appear next to one another and can be viewed one after another. Commensuration therefore works at different levels: not only do influencers commensurate their own relationships with other influencer-friends as endorsements and self-promotions, but they also commensurate their fandom-based relationships with followers as relationships of friendship.

7. Conclusion

This article has focused on the growing and resonant phenomenon in the social media landscape of stories as a designed feature on platforms. With a focus on Snapchat and Instagram, and drawing on real-time tracking, corpus-assisted methods, and a narrative analysis of influencers' Instagram Stories, I put forward a technographic approach that traces the workings of technology in relation to the design of stories, the values underlying their design, the types of affordances offered, and the actual types of stories that they prompt. This approach has allowed me to document how what I have described in previous work as small stories become formatted, that is, recognizable as a specific type of communicative practice and social action. The process of formatting is facilitated by specific platform directives to users for how and what kind of stories to share. I singled out above the directive of authenticity in the tellers' self-presentation. Building on the current close association of authenticity with storytelling and the widely circulating discourse of "being real," in the sense of unfiltered, on social media, I argued that the design of stories has integrated authenticity as a core value into its affordances. In this way, I showed, authenticity has been associated with imperfect sharing, and is supported by tools for ephemerality and an amateur aesthetic in self-presentation. I also showed how this type of authenticity has become closely associated with specific genres of small stories, well suited to providing snapshots of daily life in the moment and on the go. In particular, the format of breaking news lends itself to postings of sequences of stories, intertextually linked, that provide updates on unfolding events. An experience-centered, showing mode of narration affords the viewers a proximity and eyewitness quality. The storytelling is situated in the here and now, with temporal marking of immediacy and ongoingness. Immediacy, therefore, and mining the mundane, are key to this type of telling and to creating authenticity for the teller. In this way, a specific way of telling becomes conventionally associated (*enregistered*) with a specific mode of self-presentation that comes with values and valuations typical of an authentic storyteller.

Finally, I put forward two strategies with which influencers navigate the tension between authorizing the platformed directive of authenticity and promoting themselves and their products, which introduces a marketing and monetization element at odds with the construction of an ordinary self on a par with their followers. The two strategies of repurposing and commensuration capitalize on the fact that the design of stories supports authenticity at the same time as advertising and quantification of audience engagement with stories. We see, then, a parallel instrumentalization of authenticity in the broader context of the instrumentalization of stories as hybrid features, both as content-creation facilities for sharing everyday life and as (microtargeted) marketing.

The present study is aimed at joining and contributing to parallel initiatives that recognize the need to critically interrogate this instrumentalization of stories, especially of personal experience, across various spheres of everyday life. This impulse is variously referred to as a *storytelling boom*, a period of *story-curation*, or a *story-positive culture* (see, e.g., Fernandes 2017; Mäkelä et al. 2021). In light of the present findings, studies of the curation of stories on social media could benefit from combined attention to the communicative how and the sociotechnicity of stories. This requires technographic methods that allow us to uncover the *values* that underlie the design of stories, the tools that accompany stories and become instruments for their *valuation*, and the (in)*visibilitie*s for specific tellers and tales that these, in turn, create. It is within this nexus that agency, creativity, and any empowering potentials of stories for storytellers and audiences online need to be examined.

With attention to the historicity of the platforms' definitions of a "story"[10] and the mobilization of specific types of stories in connection with media affordances, we can uncover the processes through which norms and recognizability of specific stories in association with specific semiotic resources and modes of self-presentation develop. The present study showed this in relation to the directive of authenticity. Going forward, the intimate link between authenticity with specific ways of telling, as uncovered above, can be further investigated for any (shifting) connections of storytelling with notions of truth and credibility, in an era recognized by many as post-truth.

---

10. My corpus analysis has shown that the meaning of the term *story* itself is changing, through developing strong associations with *sharing* and *moment*, on the one hand, and with a language of marketization and quantification, on the other hand (see Georgakopoulou 2019). Even in morphological terms, plural *Stories* with a capital S, referring to the platformed feature, outnumbers in our corpus the word *story*: this, coupled with the fact that the term *Stories* has entered the vocabulary of many languages without it being translated, is indicative of a process of rapid standardization for the term in its meaning as a platformed feature (Georgakopoulou 2019).

Table 1.   Top ten collocates for *authentic* (ranked by logDice score)

Rank	Collocate	Freq.	logDice Score
1	Being	3	9.299
2	spontaneous	3	9.254
3	raw	3	9.133
4	tell	8	9.011
5	feel	7	8.784
6	rather	4	8.687
7	nature	3	8.654
8	storytelling	3	8.613
9	brand	12	8.362
10	visual	3	8.346

1	to build a relationship with their customers through	**authentic**	and personal content. Indeed, Brian Robbins of
2	Footage The key is to make your fans feel like insiders.	**Authentic**	, behind-the-scenes content does just that. This is the
3	to post content that is real-time, spontaneous and more	**authentic**	. For brands there are a number ways Instagram Stories can be
4	and viewing Stories, you were sharing and viewing more	**authentic**	moments in someone's life. It's messier. It's maybe
5	for a company is to tell original stories that reflect	**authentic**	moments, instead of the traditional publicity that can be
6	contests and campaigns, and drive more engagement.	**Authentic**	and visual brand storytelling is the future of marketing,
7	pictures of food and drink, an actual story that conveys an	**authentic**	narrative has a strong chance of standing out. Adding
8	on popular user behavior, 2. It's a great way to share more	**authentic**	moments with followers, and 3. This means one less social
9	stories," says "Today's marketers need todeeper more	**authentic**	stories," says Craig Elimeliah , Director of Creative
10	re asking that because everything in my mind is about real,	**authentic**	engagement. So you need to ask some questions and you need

Figure 1   Examples of concordance lines of *authentic*.

References

Abidin, Crystal 2018. *Internet Celebrity: Understanding Fame Online*. Bingley, UK: Emerald.

Agha, Asif. 2007. *Language and Social Relations*. Cambridge: Cambridge University Press.

Blommaert, Jan, with Laura Smits and Noura Yacoubi. 2020. "Context and Its Complications." In *The Cambridge Handbook of Discourse Studies*, edited by Anna De Fina and Alexandra Georgakopoulou, 52–69. Cambridge: Cambridge University Press.

Blommaert, Jan, and Piia Varis. 2011. "Enough Is Enough: The Heuristics of Authenticity in Superdiversity." Tilburg Papers in Culture Studies 2. www.tilburguniversity.edu ›tpcs paper2_2.

Bucher, Taina. 2018. *If . . . Then: Algorithmic Power and Politics*. Oxford: Oxford University Press.

Constine, John. 2016. "Instagram Launches 'Stories,' A Snapchatty Feature for Imperfect Sharing." *TechCrunch*, August 2, https://techcrunch.com.

Coupland, Nick. 2003. "Sociolinguistic Authenticities." *Journal of Sociolinguistics* 7, no. 3: 417–31.

Enli, Gunn. 2015. *Mediated Authenticity: How the Media Constructs Reality*. Berlin: Peter Lang.

Fernandes, Sujatha. 2017. *Curated Stories: The Uses and Misuses of Storytelling*. Oxford: Oxford University Press.

Flanagan, Mary, and Helen Nissenbaum. 2014. *Values at Play in Digital Games*. Cambridge, MA: MIT Press.

Fludernik, Monika. 2006. *Introduction to Narratology*. Abingdon, UK: Routledge.

Freberg, Karen, Kristin Graham, Karen Mcgaughey, and Laura A. Freberg. 2011. "Who Are the Social Media Influencers? A Study of Public Perceptions of Personality." *Public Relations Review* 37: 90–92. https://doi.org.10.1016/j.pubrev.2010.11.001.

Georgakopoulou, Alexandra. 2007. *Small Stories, Interaction, and Identities*. Philadelphia: John Benjamins.

Georgakopoulou, Alexandra. 2016a. "From Writing the Self to Posting Self(ies): A Small Stories Approach to Selfies." *Open Linguistics*, no. 2: 300–17.

Georgakopoulou, Alexandra. 2016b. "Small Stories Research: A Narrative Paradigm for the Analysis of Social Media." In *The SAGE Handbook of Social Media Research Methods*, edited by L. Sloan and A. Quan-Haage, 266–82. London: SAGE.

Georgakopoulou, Alexandra. 2017. "Sharing the Moment as Small Stories: The Interplay between Practices and Affordances in the Social Media-Curation of Lives." In "Storytelling in the Digital Age," edited by Anna De Fina and Sabina Perrino. Special issue, *Narrative Inquiry* 27, no. 2: 311–33.

Georgakopoulou, Alexandra. 2019. "Designing Stories on Social Media: A Corpus-Assisted Critical Perspective on the Mismatches of Story-Curation." *Linguistics and Education*, no. 62: 100737. https://doi.org/10.1016/j.linged.2019.05.003.

Georgakopoulou, Alexandra, Korina Giaxoglou, and Philip Seargeant. 2021. "Stories in Everyday Life: From Electoral Politics to Instagram." Paper presented to the Contemporary Cultures of Writing research group, the Open University, March 2021.

Georgakopoulou, Alexandra, Stefan Iversen, and Carsten Stage. 2020. *Quantified Storytelling: A Narrative Analysis of Metrics on Social Media*. London: Palgrave.

Giaxoglou, Korina 2020. *A Narrative Approach to Social Media Mourning: Small Stories and Affective Positioning*. London: Routledge.

Gjerlevsen, Simona Zetterberg, and Henrik Skov Nielsen, eds. 2020. "Distinguishing Fictionality." In *Exploring Fictionality: Conceptions, Test Cases, Discussions*, edited by Cindie Maagaard, Daniel Schäbler and Marianne Wolff Lundholt, 19–40. Odense: Syddansk Universitetsforlag.

Gubrium, Aline C., Elizabeth Krause, and Kasey Jernigan. 2014. "Strategic Authenticity and Voice: New Ways of Seeing and Being Seen as Young Mothers through Digital Storytelling." *Sexuality Research and Social Policy* 11, no. 4: 337–47.

Iqbal, Mansoor. 2021. "Instagram Revenue and Usage Statistics (2021)." *Business of Apps*, November 12. www.businessofapps.com/data/instagram-statistic.

Jaffe, Alexandra. 2011. "Sociolinguistic Diversity on Mainstream Media: Authenticity, Authority, and Processes of Mediation and Mediatization." *Journal of Language and Politics* 10, no. 4: 562–86. https://doi.org/10.1075/jlp.10.4.05jaf.

Jensen, Meg. 2019. *The Art and Science of Trauma and the Autobiographical Negotiated Truths*. London: Palgrave.

Kofoed, Jette, and Malene C. Larsen. 2016. "A Snap of Intimacy: Photo-Sharing Practices among Young People on Social Media." *First Monday* 21, no. 11. firstmonday.org/article/view/6905/5648.

Kreling, Rebekka, Adrian Meier, and Leonard Reinecke. 2021. "Feeling Authentic on Social Media: Subjective Authenticity across Instagram Stories and Posts." Preprint, submitted June 17, 2021. PsyArXiv. https://doi.org/10.31234/osf.io/jz3wm.

Labor, William. 2006. "Narrative Pre-construction." *Narrative Inquiry* 16: 37–45. https://doi.org.10.1075/Ni.16.1.07Lab.

Langlois, Gana. 2013. "Participatory Culture and the New Governance of Communication: The Paradox of Participatory Media." *Television and New Media* 14, no. 2: 91–105. https://doi.org/10.1177/1527476411433519.

Lee, Jung Ah, and Matthew S. Eastin. 2020. "I Like What She's #Endorsing: The Impact of Female Social Media Influencers' Perceived Sincerity, Consumer Envy, and Product Type." *Journal of Interactive Advertising* 20, no. 1: 76–91. doi.org/10.1080/15252019.2020.1737849.

Lupton, Deborah. 2016. *The Quantified Self.* Malden, MA: Polity.

Mäkelä, Maria. 2018. "Lessons from the *Dangers of Narrative* Project: Toward a Story-Critical Narratology." *Tekstualia* 1, no. 4: 175–86.

Mäkelä, Maria, Samuli Björninen, Laura Karttunen, Matias Nurminen, Juha Raipola, and Tytti Rantanen. 2021. "Dangers of Narrative: A Critical Approach to Narratives of Personal Experience in Contemporary Story Economy." *Narrative* 29, no. 2: 139–59.

Marwick, Alice 2013. *Status Update: Celebrity, Publicity, and Branding in the Social Media Age.* New Haven, CT: Yale University Press.

Morton, Heather 2017. "The New Visual Testimonial: Narrative, Authenticity, and Subjectivity in Emerging Commercial Photographic Practice." *Media and Communication* 5, no. 2: 11–20.

Ochs, Elinor, and Lisa Capps. 1997. "Narrative Authenticity." *Journal of Narrative and Life History* 7: 83–89.

Osman, Maddy. 2020. "What Is Authenticity on Social Media? We Asked the Experts." *Fanbooster,* June 29, 2020. fanbooster.com/blog/social-media-authenticity/.

Page, Ruth 2012. *Stories and Social Media.* New York: Routledge.

Patel, Neil. n.d. "How to Create and Authentic Brand Story That Actually Improves Trust." *Neil Patel* (blog). neilpatel.com/blog/create-authentic-brand-story/.

Read, Ash. n.d. "What Are Instagram Stories and How You Can Use Them to Boost Engagement for Your Brand." *Buffer Marketing Library.* buffer.com/library/instagram-stories.

Taylor, Charlotte, and Anna Marchi, eds. 2018. *Corpus Approaches to Discourse: A Critical Review.* New York: Routledge.

Tolson, Andrew. 2010. "A New Authenticity? Communicative Practices on YouTube." *Critical Discourse Studies* 7, no. 4: 277–89.

van Dijck, Jose. 2013. *The Culture of Connectivity.* Oxford: Oxford University Press.

Vázquez Herrero, Jorge, Sabela Direito-Rebollal, and Xosé López-García. 2019. "Ephemeral Journalism: News Distribution through Instagram Stories." *Social Media + Society* 5, no. 4. https://doi.org/10.1177/2056305119888657.

Wilt, Joshua A., Sarah Thomas, and Dan McAdams. 2019. "Authenticity and Inauthencitiy in Narrative Identity." *Heyilon* 5, no. 7: e02178. https://doi.org/10.1016/j.heliyon.2019.e02178.

Zappavigna, Michele, and Sumin Zhao. 2017. "Selfies in 'Mommyblogging': An Emerging Visual Genre." *Discourse, Context, and Media*, no. 20: 239–47. https://doi.org/10.1016/j.dcm.2017.05.005.

Mobilizing Stories of Illness in Digital Contexts: A Critical Approach to Narrative, Voice, and Visibility

Korina Giaxoglou

Open University, United Kingdom

Abstract　Illness stories have been celebrated as a resource for giving patients voice from the active position of the *wounded storyteller*. The proliferating research on illness stories, however, has often reproduced a reductionist approach to narrative as a window to subjective views and experiences based on a largely underdeveloped and essentialized notion of voice. Critics of the over-celebration of narrative have called for caution toward the use of personal stories, pointing to the need to situate constructions of the narrative self in their social, cultural, and political contexts. This article discusses a new type of illness stories that has emerged in digital contexts and that is characterized by the use of illness for producing various forms of economic and social value. Using small stories and affective positioning as its analytic lens, the article examines the specific case of story design, curation, and sharing of the COVID-19 diagnosis of actor Idris Elba in March 2020. As the article argues, the illness experience is mobilized in small stories online as a resource for authenticating the self in line with conventional modes of sharing, blurring the lines between the personal voice and the public visibility of storytelling. The article contributes to the critical study of the mobilization of stories in digital contexts.

Keywords　illness stories, small stories, voice, visibility

1. Illness Narratives: Potential and Risks

In the context of Western, patient-centered medical practice, telling stories of illness has been advocated as a valuable resource for giving voice to patients. Communicating what it feels to be ill arguably empowers patients

Poetics Today 43:2 (June 2022)　DOI 10.1215/03335372-9642623
© 2022 by Porter Institute for Poetics and Semiotics

in medical encounters and can reduce institutional asymmetries of power between doctors and patients. It also allows patients to navigate and negotiate the challenges and identity changes they experience during their illness journey from the active position of the *wounded storyteller* (Frank 1997).

In recognition of these communicative and affective benefits, illness narratives have been extensively used as pedagogical resources for the training of medical students and for physicians' professional development. Specifically, in what is known as *narrative medicine*, physicians are encouraged to develop their *narrative competence*—that is, their ability to acknowledge, absorb, interpret, and act on the stories and plights of others (Charon 2001). The therapeutic functions of illness narratives have also prompted a burgeoning industry of illness memoirs written by patients or their caretakers as an auto/biographical genre in their own right (Vickers 2016). This genre rose to prominence particularly during the AIDS pandemic of the 1980s (Jurecic 2012). Illness narratives now form a well-established object of cross-disciplinary study for scholars concerned with the enhancement of health-care practice or with narratological questions of narrative, experientiality, and identity.

The profusion of talking and writing about illness has, however, tended to privilege a vision of storytelling as inherently ethical and beneficial to both tellers and their audiences. Critiques of what has seemingly turned into an over-celebration of storytelling have been put forward along with calls for caution vis-à-vis the use of personal stories as straightforward reflections of experience (e.g. Atkinson 1997; Atkinson and Delamont 2006; Atkinson 2009; Woods 2011). Instead, the importance of situating constructions of the narrative self in their social, cultural, and political contexts was noted (Schiff 2006). And yet for the most part, such critiques did not make their way into the mainstream of narrative research or practice. More recently, Hanna Meretoja (2018) as well as Meretoja and Colin Davis (2018) have (re)turned attention to this critique of narrative, arguing for the importance of avoiding idealizations of storytelling in favor of recognizing, instead, the ethical potential as well as the risks of different storytelling practices. As Sujatha Fernandes (2017) has shown, for instance, the curation of stories of poverty and mistreatment in different parts of the world as heartfelt accounts ends up detracting attention from structural orders of inequality and undermines the confrontational dynamics of social movements.

In the current *storytelling boom* moment, stories—especially stories of personal experience—are often instrumentalized not only by individuals, but also by businesses and institutions across various spheres of everyday life, resulting in internally contradictory ethics and rhetorics of storytelling

(Mäkelä et al. 2021). Attention to the empowering or disempowering uses of storytelling is acutely relevant in a digital age, where "stories" are being mobilized as a communicative practice and even as a feature on social media platforms such as Snapchat, Facebook, and Instagram (Georgako-poulou 2022b). This is an era of intense (social) mediatization of social interaction as a series of *moments for sharing* (John 2017), whereby practices of design, curation, and uptake of stories are subject to *social media logic*. Social media logic refers to the norms, strategies, mechanisms, and economies that characterize the dynamics of social media infrastructures, namely *programmability*, *popularity*, and *connectivity*, which mediate users' practices, technological platforms, and economic structures (van Dijck and Poell 2013).

In this article, I provide an empirically grounded discussion of the mobilization of illness stories in digital contexts, exploring *practices of story design, curation, and uptake in relation to narrative voice and mediatized visibility*. I use the term *mediatized visibility* to refer to the attention that some stories attract in online contexts on account of their appeal to social media logic. As I will argue, this type of visibility differs in a number of respects to the kind of recognition that can be gained through the use of stories for voicing personal experience.

I start with a brief overview of recurrent findings in the long-standing literature on illness narratives and pinpoint issues relating to emerging modes of telling the illness story on social media that are worthy of critical attention. I then move on to discuss a specific case of sharing a story of COVID-19 in the context of the coronavirus global pandemic in 2020. The contagious disease was first identified in Wuhan, China, in December 2019, and a public health emergency of international concern was issued by the World Health Organization on January 30, 2020, before the disease, labeled COVID-19, was officially declared as a pandemic on March 22, 2020.

Based on the discussion of a COVID-19 story shared on Twitter by British actor Idris Elba and reshared in the media, mainly in the United States and the United Kingdom, I argue that small stories of illness online are associated with the growing commoditization of the "wound," and that the mobilization of the illness experience is a resource for sharing and authenticating the self in highly conventionalized ways. This article contributes to the critical study of the mobilization of stories across domains (Mäkelä 2018; Meretoja 2018; Meretoja and Davis 2018) and the furnishing of critical approaches to storytelling, voice, and visibility.

2. Illness as Narrative

The study of stories documenting the experience of illness occupies an established place in *narrative inquiry* research. This line of research is a qualitatively oriented approach in social research concerned with life experiences, people's identities, and social change, where narratives—often elicited in the context of interviews—are used as a methodological tool with a range of real-world and political applications (Squire et al. 2014). The interest in illness stories has its roots in the narrative turn in the social sciences, which recognized narrative as "one of the most powerful forms for expressing suffering and experiences" (Frank 1997: 51). In addition, this interest arose in the context of a general reaction against medical dominance (Bury 2001) and in the midst of calls for more patient-centered approaches to medicine within which the importance of supporting physicians to develop their narrative competence was acknowledged (*narrative medicine*; see Charon 2001). As a result of these calls, more systematic and sustained intersections among medicine, literature and the arts, and the humanities were sought and are nowadays represented in the interdisciplinary subfield of *medical humanities* (Hurwitz et al. 2004).

The privileging of the patient's life story created a space for bringing to the fore different kinds of patients' experiences. Patients' life stories were viewed as a way of supporting and empowering patients during the subjection of their bodies to medical treatments and rituals (Kleinman 1988). Illness stories are, in this sense, key resources for giving *voice* to those who find they have no voice as their social identities change while their bodies undergo treatment. More recent work has been drawing attention to patients' "bodies" as a source of narrativity as well as to the importance of the story listeners' bodies in shaping narrative interaction (Hydén 2011). Less analytical attention has been paid, however, to the specific links of illness storytelling and voice, given that the positive and beneficial aspects of this relationship seem to have been largely taken for granted.

The notion of voice is intertwined with the concept of *telling rights*—that is, the entitlement to tell a story by virtue of having taken part in an event or having firsthand information about it. Yet as Anna De Fina and Alexandra Georgakopoulou (2011) note, the relationship between ownership rights and performance rights is a complex one, inasmuch as the former doesn't necessarily guarantee the latter. This means that in some cases of asymmetrical participant relationships, the most powerful speaker turns out to be the one who has the right to perform the story, regardless of the story's ownership. Questions of narrative form as well as ownership and performance rights to a story are thus important in any critical investigation of the "voice" afforded to tellers in different contexts, especially when stories get told in "new" contexts—for example, social media contexts.

A focus on narrative in the domain of illness opens up the academic exploration of narrative from a number of vantage points, including the way narrative is socially and culturally constructed; how narrative is embodied and expressed within the analytical context of biomedicine; and last but not least, how it relates to the sufferer's meaning-making practices and world-constructions (Hydén 1997). As Johanna Shapiro (2011) acknowledges, a patient's story is rarely just a story. It is, instead, the conscious and unconscious representation and performance of intricate personal motives and *implicit narrative* influences—that is, cultural narrative models that present tellers with cultural ideals and norms, affecting their sense-making (Meretoja 2021). Such implicit narrative influences become evident in the plot types that have been found to guide the crafting of illness narratives in specific social and cultural formations, at least in Western world contexts, where the bulk of this research has been conducted. According to Arthur Frank (1997: 101), these plot types include: (1) the *restitution* narrative, which focuses on the conclusion of illness, the ultimate victory over illness, an individual's reintegration into society and return to the normalcy of everyday life; (2) the *chaos narrative*, an anti-narrative that highlights the disruptions caused by illness; and (3) the *quest narrative*, which focuses on the temporal enactment of the illness experience and an individual's transformation over time. For Mike Bury (2001), there are three main types of plot: (1) *contingent narratives*, which focus on the details about the disease, its causes, and its implications for everyday life; (2) *moral narratives*, which address questions of illness and social identity; and (3) *core narratives*, which explore deeper layers of meaning related to the experience of suffering and illness.

Despite the recognition of the links of such narrative formats to social and cultural conditions, the study of narrative form in the narrative inquiry and social science research has been mainly based on the analysis of monologic, elicited narratives, privileging one particular type of narrative— namely, the *life story* or *big stories*. This type of story involves the telling of past experience viewed at a distance from the vantage point of the teller's here and now. In the case of the representation of the illness experience, this type of storytelling invites reflection on the biographical disruption brought about by the illness. As a result of this focus, a wide gamut of stories that appear less coherent and hence not entirely amenable to analysis are left out of this line of inquiry.

In applied linguistics—and more specifically in the subfield of health communication—there have been calls for the critical reevaluation of existing narrative approaches to health (Harvey and Kotyeko 2013). This critical reevaluation also needs to take stock of recent research on digital narrativity, affect, and identity if it is to address aspects of the reconfiguration of the personal and the public and its implications for theorizations of storytelling and voice, particularly in the case of illness narratives. A brief overview of relevant research developments is provided below as the main framing of the present discussion.

3. Illness as Sharing

In an age of social media, personal experience is often reconfigured *as sharing*, in the sense that it is being constituted, understood, and constructed in and through particular practices of broadcasting—and curating—significant moments with networked audiences. As Nicholas A. John (2017: 5) notes, sharing is now a metaphor we live by; it involves the entextualization of self—that is, the construction of the self through textual, written, spoken and/or visual means (e.g., messages, videos, and images). Entextualizing the self online is based on the sharing of trivial moments as well as life-changing events and disruptions, including illness, dying, death, and mourning.

Early practices of documenting the contingent experience of illness emerged in blogs, for some time a preferred mode for disclosing intimate stories, given their consideration as safe and empowering spaces. Linguistic research on narratives of illness on blogging platforms has shown the gender-specific patterns structuring these practices and their use primarily for connecting to a community of users (Page 2011). More recently, connection to networked communities has been taking place via video blogs, also known as vlogs, which afford users the possibility to video-document aspects of their lives. In the literature on illness narratives in digital media, observations about the benefits of digital-illness stories as a resource for self-expression, peer-support (Liu et al. 2013), or the creation of support communities via the use of humor and sarcasm (Iannarino 2018) resonate with findings from earlier literature on the benefits of illness stories for patients.

More recent work has pointed to the ways in which such practices of storytelling are shaped by—and in turn shape—social media affordances and sharing norms. For example, in their study of narratives of Danish young people diagnosed with cancer, Carsen Stage, Karen Hvidtfeldt, and Lisbeth Klastrup (2019) argue that younger users approach social media as *vital media* which can help them address their different needs. Their sharing is based on their existing use of social media, meaning that users tend to align to a sense of an expectation to perform vital (that is, positive or life-affirming) approaches to illness. The close links of these performances with the production of social and economic value and visibility has led to the description of these networked illness stories as *entrepreneurial narratives* (Stage 2017).

In my study of the narrativity of a vlogger diagnosed with terminal cancer (Giaxoglou 2021), I showed how this vlogger used small stories to relate details of her *life with illness* (e.g., short medical updates) as well as aspects of her *life despite illness* (e.g., shopping, fashion), cumulatively making up the vlogger's life story in ways that were more aligned to uses of social media as vital and entrepreneurial media and less to the typical plot types identified in the literature on illness narratives. In terms of temporality, the mode of storying in vlogging involved a mix of temporal foci on the vlogger's here and now, the (recent) past, and in some cases also the future. In sum, the storying of illness online aligns with the typical features of digital storytelling, where storying is emergent, multi-semiotic, and participatory (Georgakopoulou 2015), driven by—as much as driving—metrics of popularity and audience engagement (Georgakopoulou, Iverson, and Stage 2020).

In the remainder of this article, I discuss an example of an online illness story in the context of the 2020 coronavirus pandemic, selected as a case that allows the empirical investigation of the interplay of story design, social media affordances, narrative voice, and visibility. I focus more specifically on the Twitter story of Idris Elba (full name: Idrissa Akuna Elba), an English actor, DJ (a.k.a. DJ Big Driis), and musician, known for his roles as Detective Chief Inspector John Luther in the BBC One series *Luther*, for which he won a Golden Globe award, and as Nelson Mandela in the film *Mandela: Long Walk to Freedom* (2013), among many other appearances in series and films. Idris Elba was one of the first celebrities to broadcast a public announcement about his COVID-19 positive diagnosis, on March 16, 2020, shortly after Tom Hanks and his wife Rita Wilson, who made their announcement ten days before the disease was officially declared as a pandemic by the World Health Organization (WHO) on March 22, 2020.

Although there are limits to the insights that the examination of a single story can yield, the present discussion aims to highlight key aspects of story making and sharing online grounded in the selected example.

4. Telling the COVID-19 Story Online: The Case of Idris Elba's Twitter Story

Celebrities' and public figures' announcements about their positive diagnoses and follow-up updates on their health became commonplace during the early days of the spread of the coronavirus. These included announcements by (or on behalf of) political leaders, such as the United Kingdom's prime minister at the time, Boris Johnson, and the then US President Donald Trump, both of whom arguably used their stories of falling ill with COVID-19 as rhetorical strategies for repositioning themselves vis-à-vis their voters as legitimate and heroic leaders (Jones 2021). In addition, stories of COVID-19 as experienced by people around the world also became a regular feature of broadcasts and media reports in the form of *contingent stories* of patients under medical treatment supported by oxygen in hospital rooms, *stories of grief* told by bereaved relatives after an often short and challenging period of illness, and *stories of hope* recounted by recovered patients. Narratives of battles and metaphors of war tended to dominate the telling of the COVID-19 story in ways that advanced a vision of a certain kind of fighting spirit and, in the process, avoided the complexity and particularity of the pandemic crisis (Meretoja 2020). There have also been an increasing number of stories of long COVID, recounting personal experiences of symptoms that persist long after the virus's diagnosis, helping make this new condition visible.

Stories of illness in the media during the period of coronavirus became closely interconnected with political messaging about governments' reactions, the medical search for a better understanding of the symptoms of the disease, and public messaging about socially responsible behaviors in a context of increased public health risks. In this broader context, some celebrities and influencers saw it as their role to contribute to that public messaging by sharing stories of their personal experiences with the disease. Idris Elba was diagnosed with COVID-19 while in the United States preparing to start shooting for a new film. Even though he had no symptoms, he got tested after finding out that a person he had been in contact with had tested positive.

The analysis draws on tweets relating to the actor's COVID-19 story posted from March 16 to March 31, 2020. They include a combination of tweets, photographs, videos and live broadcasts posted by the actor as updates on his health (Elba 2020a; 2020e; 2020f) or as responses to the reactions of his followers (Elba 2020b; 2020c; 2020d).

Idris Elba's updates via his Twitter account are approached here as moments of narrative stance-taking, which Alexandra Georgakopoulou (2022a) defines as follows:

> A moment of position taking where a speaker more or less reflexively mobilizes more or less conventionalized communicative means to signal that the activity to follow, the activity underway or the activity that is indexed, alluded to, deferred, silenced is or can become a story. In doing so, he or she positions

him/herself as a teller: somebody who is in a position to tell and assume a point of view on the telling and/or told.

In my discussion of this example, I draw on an understanding of (small) stories "as discourse engagements that engender specific social moments and integrally connect with what gets done on particular occasions and in particular settings" (Georgakopoulou 2007: 117). As I will argue, stories of illness online mobilize illness for increasing social and economic value and visibility in ways that end up reconfiguring the personal and the public as well as the degree of the tellers' control over their stories. Such practices have important implications for the type of narrative voice and visibility afforded to tellers.

The analysis of the story draws on the concept of *affective positioning*, which is an analytic calibration of *identity positioning* (Bamberg and Georgakopoulou 2008) aimed at addressing dimensions of affect performance as the ground for identity construction. In digital contexts of sharing, social actors are not only faced with a range of identity dilemmas (Bamberg 2012), but they also have to navigate dilemmas that relate to the affective production and authentication of their experientiality—that is, the investment of their telling with credibility and genuineness. These dilemmas include, for example, the ways in which storytellers affectively negotiate the degree of (a) *uniqueness and representativeness of the shared personal experience*, (b) the call for *audience identification or distancing*, and (c) the sharer's *display of emotional control or loss of control* on recounted situations in line with existing templates for storying the self and sharing emotion in different social media platforms. I analyze affective positioning empirically at the three levels posited for the study of identity positioning—namely, the *taleworld*, the *storyrealm*, and the *teller*—with a focus on how a teller emplots degrees of affective proximity or distance from the storyworld, their audiences, and their own emotional selves (Giaxoglou 2021). The small stories and affective positioning framework is apt for capturing aspects of entrepreneurial story design and personal storytelling in digital contexts.

More specifically, the analysis attends to small storying, the sites associated with the telling, and the teller's positioning at different levels and in relation to the above dilemmas. These foci can be articulated into the following questions:

(a) How does the actor's small storying of his experience with COVID-19 affectively construct its uniqueness and representativeness? (*emplotment at the level of the taleworld*)

(b) How does the teller's narrative stance-taking construct different kinds of audience identification or distance? (*story design at the level of the storyrealm*)

(c) How does the actor in question (Elba) affectively position himself vis-à-vis COVID-19, his audience, and his own self through his emotional negotiations of control? (*emplotment and positioning at the level of the teller*)

In what follows, I discuss Idris Elba's COVID-19 *story design, narrative stance-taking activity*, and *affective positioning*, in turn, and discuss the limits of narrative voice afforded in this mode of digital storying.

4. Story Design

The main part of Idris Elba's COVID-19 story is summed up in two tweets: a post made up of a tweet along with an accompanying video shared on March 16, 2020 (Elba, 2020a) and a follow-up tweet posted on March 25, 2020 (Elba 2020e). Additional posts as well as a two-part live video (Elba 2020b; 2020c; 2020d) are supplementary to that main story, picking up elements of the initial post in response to followers' reactions and challenges. In this section I will focus on these two tweets.

The initial tweet from March 16, 2020, is laid out below in numbered lines for ease of cross-referencing in the discussion:

Tweet—March 16, 2020

1 This morning I tested positive for Covid19.

2 I feel ok, I have no symptoms so far

3 but have been isolated since I found out about my possible exposure to the virus.

4 Stay home people and be pragmatic.

5 I will keep you updated on how I'm doing (two oncoming fist emoji)

6 No panic.

The tweet is a *breaking news story* of illness announcing the news of Idris Elba's COVID-19 test outcome, focusing on the very recent event of the diagnosis (line 1, "this morning"). This fifty-two-word post serves as the story's *abstract*—that is, the part of the story that summarizes the point of the story in Labovian terms (Labov 2013). In this case, the abstract also has an interactional function, as it is being used as a metacommunicative device framing the video story that forms the main body of the post (I discuss this framing later on in this section).

Initial diagnoses of illness commonly become the occasion for publicly sharing illness stories. Such diagnoses are critical moments that mark a change or disruption to one's everyday life and plans (Stage, Hvidtfeldt, and Klastrup 2019). In the case of COVID-19, this initial diagnosis carries additional weight and increases its tellability, given the unknown and uncertain outcomes of the course of the illness in each person, especially in the early days of the pandemic. The uncertainty of what a positive diagnosis means motivates the actor's reassuring update on his condition (line 2, "I feel OK, I have no symptoms so far"). The actor then lists the actions he had to take following the positive test, such as going into quarantine (even before the test results were known to him), which here provide the grounds for validating the public health guidelines that the actor reiterates in an advisory tone directly addressing his followers (line 4, "Stay home people and be pragmatic").

An extended version of this story is given in the self-recorded video that accompanies the tweet (see table 1 for the full transcript). The video was posted at 6:18 p.m. on March 16, 2020, and it features Idris Elba in close-up and his wife Sabrina in the background, occasionally nodding. The video allows for a sense of more direct communication and connection with the networked followers.

The actor starts the video with a greeting to his followers (line 1, "hey, what's up guys"), a typical video vlog story-opening strategy that establishes the teller's explicit orientation to a direct connection with his followers (Giaxoglou 2021). He then moves on to break the news of his positive test results (line 2, "so look this morning I got some test results back for coronavirus and it came back positive") and offers a brief, first-order negative evaluation of the implications of this news for him (line 3, "yeah and it sucks"). The video highlights the affordances of video-storying for engaging the viewers through involvement devices (e.g., line 2, "so look"; line 4, "listen"; line 6, "look"), which call attention to the main points of the story. In addition, the possibility for viewers to watch the actor in real time talking about his experience serves as a resource for lending credence to it as an "authentic" and true account. (This doesn't mean, of course, that this account is not subject to challenges for its truthfulness.) In the remainder of the video, Idris Elba assesses the different implications of the test's outcomes through a series of evaluations, either focusing on his personal reaction to the results (line 3), his health condition (line 4), or explanations about why he got tested (line 5), generally maintaining an upbeat and calm tone in reaction to the news of his diagnosis. After having established his experiential angle, he moves on to relate the main point of the story, which is to alert the public to the real health risks of the disease (line 6), the importance of telling others (line 7), being transparent about this despite the potential stigma (line 8), and the significance of being united (line 9). He closes his story by reiterating that he will continue the updates and that both he and his wife are doing okay (line 10), urging his followers to remain positive and calm (line 11).

The follow-up post to this initial announcement, shared on March 25, provides a short update on the couple's health via just a tweet, without an accompanying video.

Table 1   Idris Elba's video story transcript and its narrative sections

1. Hey, what's up guys.	Opening
2. So look this morning I got some test results back for corona-virus and it came back positive.	Abstract and main event of breaking news story
3. Yeah and it sucks.	Evaluation
4. Listen, I'm doing OK. Sabrina hasn't been tested and she's doing OK. I didn't have any symptoms.	Evaluation
5. I got tested because I realized I was exposed to someone who had also tested positive. I found out last Friday that they were tested positive, I quarantined myself and got a test immediately and got the results back today.	Evaluation
6. Look, this is serious, you know, now's the time to really think about social distancing, washing your hands. Beyond that there are people out there who aren't showing symptoms and that can easily spread it, OK. So now's a real time to be really vigilant about washing your hands and keeping your distance, OK.	Evaluation (main point of the story)
7. We've told our families. They're very supportive. We've told our colleagues.	Evaluation
8. And, you know, transparency is probably the best thing for this right now. If you're feeling ill and you feel like you should be tested or you've been exposed, then do something about it. All right, it's really important.	Evaluation (point of the story)
9. Look we live in a divided world right now, we can all feel it, it's been bullshit but now's the time for solidarity, now's the time for thinking about each other. There was so many people whose lives have been affected. From those who have lost people that they love to people that don't even have it have lost their livelihoods. This is real, all right.	Evaluation (point of the story)
10. I just wanted to share my news with you guys and I will keep you updated as how I'm doing but so far we're feeling OK.	Pre-closing
11. All right, man, stay positive and don't freak out.	Closing

Tweet—March 25

1 Hoping everyone is coping with this $@@!!

2 Currently still quarantine.

3 Sab and I still feel ok so far with no changes.

4 Dr told us that after quarantine we will be immune for a certain time since our antibodies fought this.

5 At some point we'd like to go home to London. Bsafe.

This tweet also opens with an explicit orientation to the audience, registering Elba's recognition that the present moment is a difficult time for everyone. There's not much new information to add to the illness story, aside from a reiteration of the couple's ongoing quarantine condition and their unchanged health situation. The final part of the post looks ahead to the immunity after quarantine and their desire to return to London.

In summary, the breaking news story of COVID-19, as it is communicated through a series of text-based and video posts, places little emphasis on the *documentation* of symptoms, given that the story deals with the immediate aftermath of the news of the positive COVID-19 test in the case of someone who had not shown any symptoms. The actor's observance of the requirements in line with public health guidelines forms the main "message" of the update and the key point of the telling. The diagnosis of illness is used here as the necessary experiential ground for convincing people that COVID-19 can happen to anyone and that it needs to be taken seriously.

The lack of any reportable medical updates in this case of an asymptomatic patient makes this *a story of (st)illness*, whose sharing is framed as a story told for the sake of the audience, rather than that of the teller. The story is designed as part of the broader COVID-19 story in the making. This is evident in the actor's reworking of the initial NHS public health messaging "Stay Home, Protect the NHS, Save Lives" (see Giaxoglou 2020) in a more direct address to his followers and with a focus on their emotional well-being (March 16 tweet, line 4, "Stay home, be pragmatic, no panic"; video, line 11, "All right man, stay positive and don't freak out").

The design of the story along an envisaged broader public impact was affirmed by the actor himself, when interviewed by Oprah Winfrey in the first episode of her series "Oprah Talks COVID-19," where he stated, "I think given the context of the video, which was *telling the world what has happened to us*, we weren't thinking about that specifically" (Winfrey 2020, my emphasis). His story was designed as one that would tell the world their experience with the disease and be offered as an *exemplar story* through which the actor and his wife would be seen to be taking a clear and bold stance to what's happening around them. Idris Elba uses this story to affirm his *telling rights* in the public story in the making about COVID-19 and to claim a role in influencing the public to be socially responsible and remain calm.

With respect to the way the uniqueness and representativeness of experience are negotiated in this story, the emphasis is on establishing this personal experience as more broadly representative. However, this claim is challenged by part of the audience on account of the lack of test availability to the wider population. In addition, the uniqueness of his experience ends up requiring additional negotiating, given that the actor is asymptomatic. Finally, parts of the audience also challenge the veracity of his very claim to having tested positive with COVID-19 or express their disbelief in the realness of the disease altogether. The next section turns to the actor's narrative stance-taking activity.

5. Narrative Stance-Taking

Idris Elba's COVID-19 story is embedded in his existing posting activity and presence on Twitter, through which he constructs and maintains a relationship of proximity to his followers. The actor's orientation to this relationship is highlighted in the closing of his posts where he commits to keep everyone updated on how things go (March 16 tweet, line 5, "I will keep you updated on how things are going"; video, line 11, "I just wanted to share my news with you guys and I will keep you updated as how I'm doing but so far we're feeling OK"). His commitment announces the launch of his illness story as a series of updates to come for the sake of his concerned followers rather than in the interest of himself as the teller, and thus builds interactivity at both the level of the story's design and its curation.

In terms of tellership, although the story is told by one teller, it is designed and shared as an interactional story opened up for the validation and scrutiny of the audience. Idris Elba's tweets are shared as narrative stance-taking acts through which he calls for the followers' participation to the story. The response of his followers (March 16 post—286.9K retweets, 81.6 retweets, 1.2M Likes) attests to the popularity of the actor, which ensures that his stories attract a high number of views.

Replies to his breaking news story included expressions of networked stances of support via tweets wishing the actor to get well (e.g., "Be strong brother. I know you'll be awright. Praying for you. Salute," Mokoena 2020) and showing the followers' affective proximity to the actor and identification with his experience. Others saw the actor's disclosure as an opportunity to publicly express their commitment to him as fans—for example, by declaring their will for "heroic sacrifice" (e.g., "Take me instead @god," Blessing 2020) or heroic action (e.g., "Alight, imma kill the virus with my bare hands," G [Taylor's Version] 2020).

The majority of reactions to the story, however, had to do with urgent questions about his symptoms and his wife's health or questions about getting tested. This focus on testing gave rise to a backlash to the story relating to the availability of testing during a time when tests were not widely available, not even for key workers (see tweets 1–3).

1. "Nice how celebs can get tested without reason. Get real people & test NHS staff – this is ridiculous beyond belief" (Jenkins 2020).

2. "I am sorry to hear about your positive result. However how did you get tested with no symptoms? NHS Staff can't get tested even with symptoms! Please use your position to help us instead. Sign the petition and share on change.org" (Houghton 2020).

3. "While I admire you sir, my question continues to be: How does a famous person get a test and results in three days, while the rest of us are begging for resources?" (Angela Clare 2020).

Parallel lines of backlash revolved around the apparent lack of social distancing from his wife on the video (see tweet 4), who had not been tested yet (she tested positive a few days later):

4. "But don't you think you putting your wife at risk? Yoh I know the Corona virus exist but I just feel these celebrities are paid to raise awareness on this. Because how can you quarantine but yet you with your wife?" (Msomi 2020).

There were also users who saw this story as an opportunity to challenge the public alert around the pandemic or altogether deny the existence of coronavirus. Some users suggested that the actor and other celebrities were lying about getting COVID-19 and that they were getting paid to go public about their "fake" diagnoses. There were even a couple of instances of users hijacking the timeline to promote conspiracy theories around COVID-19.

Such reactions illustrate followers' affective distancing and disalignment from the story, and effectively redirect the focus of attention and challenge both the uniqueness and the representativeness of the story, despite its design as both a personal and an exemplary experience. The actor appears to have little control over how his followers read and react to his story; the uptake of the story would seem to matter over and above its interactive story design and curation. Sharing personal moments creates positions of vulnerability for the teller, even—and perhaps even more so—if that teller is a public figure, as people feel entitled to respond and participate to the story often through acts of disalignment. Such reactions trigger additional response posts from the actor, in this case a live video in two parts and a number of posts or direct replies to individual users.

In the live video, Idris Elba repositions himself and adds details to the story to counter some of the reactions and to distance himself from those who circulate conspiracy theories. He also offers information and explanations in response to challenges to the sincerity of his account, the conditions around his testing, and the calculated risk decision he took with his wife Sabrina about social distancing.

The actor's video response highlights the way stories online serve as moments of narrative stance-taking that instigate the development of the story in different directions. This kind of *poly-storying* (Georgakopoulou and Giaxoglou 2018) involves users who get to contribute more or less consciously to the development of the story along different directions by aligning or disaligning to parts of the telling that are most relevant to them or by offering new lines of story development.

As suggested by the above details, Idris Elba's coronavirus story goes some way to mark a difference from "traditional" illness stories, given that it is curated as an *interactive* story in the making, which gets shaped by the public's reactions. Such reactions are not always within the control of the teller, given how parts of his story get picked out as objects of evaluation from followers in ways that Elba himself had not necessarily anticipated.

This poly-storying expands outside social media and in the media. In the case of Idris Elba, media headlines regularly reported on his updates applying a range of frames to their coverage, focusing, for example, on Idris Elba's health (Percival 2020; Welsh 2020) or reporting on the backlashes to his story (see Dicker 2020). In the six months that this story was in the making, it developed from a breaking news story of a positive diagnosis to a recovery story of an asymptomatic patient from coronavirus and a reflection on the mental health impact of the diagnosis on the actor. These diverse cross-storying practices point to the dynamic and distributed nature of this type of storytelling online, which although attributed to a single teller is, in fact, poly-storied.

6. Affective Positioning

In this final section, I will discuss Idris Elba's story in relation to the actor's affective positioning, with special focus on his negotiation of emotional control versus loss of control.

Across his posts, Idris Elba's affective positioning is represented as a balancing act between the challenges, risks, and fears that the positive diagnosis raises for him—especially given that he is asthmatic—and the need to align with expectations for remaining calm, positive, and forward-looking. One way that Elba projects this reassuring affective stance is to move the focus away from himself, marking a distance from the details of his affective negotiation with the implications of having tested positive for the virus and, instead, projecting affective needs to his followers—for example, the need for them to remain calm (live video: "I'm ok, if I'm ok, you'll be ok, *don't panic*"). In this way, the actor assumes control of his emotions and stages an emotionally brave "patient" who can stand up as a role model for others.

The actor's recurring moves from his unique experience to an experience that is to be taken as an exemplar, and from his own feelings to feelings and behaviors assigned to the public, blur the boundaries between the personal and the public. This blurring raises questions about the narrative voice that this story articulates: Is the story articulating the voice of Idris Elba as an "ordinary" patient worried about his positive diagnosis and the way this experience is going to be like for him? Or is it a story representing the voices of other patients who have already tested positive with COVID-19 or are likely to test positive in the future but may not have a similar public forum to tell their stories "to the world"? Or, last, is this the voice of a celebrity and public figure inscribing his experience into the public story in the making and claiming his right to gain visibility as a public health influencer?

These different types of narrative voice appear to be coarticulated in Idris Elba's story of (st)illness, but ultimately the story is designed as a story of a public health influencer, affording the actor his positioning as a socially responsible public figure who can make a change.

Within this kind of digital storytelling, where illness is mobilized as a resource for increasing the sharer's visibility and strengthening their influence, narrative voice becomes even more complicated: story ownership rights and story performance rights intersect with sharing rights. Although everyone in principle has a "right" to share their story, the reach of the shared story is heavily dependent on the sharer's popularity and the metrics associated with it. In other words, narrative voice (which relies on a story being heard and made visible) is displaced by structures of pre-visibility online and their associated pre-distribution of sharing and performance rights based on metrics of popularity and number of followers.

7. Conclusion

Stories of illness are becoming common in digital contexts, drawing on existing digital narrative formats and social media's multi-semiotic affordances. As the discussion above showed, in these contexts, illness is used as a resource for narrative stance-taking that leads to its poly-storying. In the case of COVID-19 storying, the case of Idris Elba's story shows how illness is mobilized for connecting with others through the representation of experience as a unique personal experience that is designed and curated as an exemplary story promoting "appropriate" forms of public behavior and affect. The story's design and curation do not, however, guarantee the positive uptake of the story. Rather, its interactivity invites not only supportive reactions, but also challenges and backlashes that are beyond the teller's control.

The focus on a celebrity's story brings to the fore a shift in the motivation for sharing stories of illness. For Idris Elba, the sharing of his testing positive for COVID-19 served as a statement about the seriousness and realness of the disease that he felt an urgent need to share with the public in a bid to influence that public, rather than functioning as an attempt to document his own experience and connect with others over that experience. This change suggests a shift from the *wounded storyteller* to the persona of a *health influencer storyteller* in digital contexts. Health influencers tend to be public figures with a large following whose popularity ensures not only the visibility of their stories, but also allows them to draw attention to broader public issues.

The case discussed, here, is a specific case of an illness story that represents only a fraction of the uses of illness stories. The reason I chose it for analysis in this article was to draw attention to the increased importance of mediatized visibility over narrative voice especially in digital contexts, where popularity is often a condition for sharing a story that will be heard and/or viewed. Despite the recognition of the inequality revealed by the pandemic (Blundell et al. 2020), for instance, stories from marginal groups remain difficult to find. This differential value of story-sharing "rights" highlights the limits of public illness storytelling and calls for some caution against over-celebrating the uses of social media for drawing attention to diverse experiences. It is thus important to look closer to establish which stories get told, by whom, for whom, and when; which stories get high levels of visibility; and what kind of visibility this is.

To conclude, this article has called for the need to revisit and foreground a critical narrative approach grounded in the empirical investigation of different kinds of illness stories in a range of contexts in line with related endeavors of story-critical orientations in narrative studies (Mäkelä 2018; Meretoja 2018; Meretoja and Davis 2018; Georgakopoulou, Giaxoglou, and Seargeant 2021). This critical viewpoint doesn't look to de-authenticate patients' illness stories, but rather to reauthenticate and revalorize them in digital contexts, so that the voices of patients (and patient groups) reach wider audiences and connections. Looking ahead, it is going to be vital for critical narrative work to address more systematically issues of voice in relation to emerging modes of mediatized visibility, with a view to call out those modes of visibility that contribute to the silencing or the further marginalization of everyday experiences of illness and inequalities.

References

Angela Clare is Moderna Boosted (@AngelaCPMills). 2020. "While I admire you sir, my question continues to be: How does a famous person get a test and results in three days, while the rest of us are begging for resources?" Twitter, March 16, 6:37 p.m., https://twitter.com/AngelaCPMills/status/1239621892031553542.

Atkinson, Paul. 1997. "Narrative Turn or Blind Alley?" *Qualitative Health Research* 7, no. 3: 325–44.

Atkinson, Paul. 2009. "Illness Narratives Revisited: The Failure of Narrative Reductionism." *Sociological Research Online* 14, no. 5: 196–205.

Atkinson, Paul, and Sara Delamont. 2006. "Rescuing Narrative from Qualitative Research." *Narrative Inquiry* 16, no. 1: 164–72.

Bamberg, Michael. 2012. "Narrative Practice and Identity Navigation." In *Varieties of Narrative Analysis*, edited by James A. Holstein and Jaber A. Gubrium, 99–125. London: SAGE.

Bamberg, Michael, and Alex Georgakopoulou. 2008. "Small Stories as a New Perspective in Narrative and Identity Analysis." *Text and Talk* 28, no. 3: 377–96.

Blessing, Adeyoe Jr. (@BlessingJr). 2020. "Thake me instead @god." Twitter, March 16, 6:49 p.m., https://twitter.com/BlessingJr/status/1239624829206024193.

Blundell, Richard, Monica Costa Dias, Robert Joyce, and Xiaowei Xu. 2020. *COVID-19 and Inequalities*. n.p.: Institute for Fiscal Studies. ifs.org.uk/inequality/covid-19-and-inequalities/.

Bury, Mike. 2001. "Illness Narratives: Fact or Fiction?" *Sociology of Health and Illness* 23, no. 3: 263–85.

Charon, Rita. 2001. "Narrative Medicine: A Model for Empathy, Reflection, Profession, and Trust." *JAMA* 286, no. 15: 1897–902.

De Fina, Anna, and Alex Georgakopoulou. 2011. *Analyzing Narrative: Discourse and Sociolinguistic Perspectives*. Cambridge: Cambridge University Press.

Dicker, Ron. 2020. "Idris and Sabrina Elba, Who Both Have COVID-19, Explain Why They Didn't Stay Apart." *HUFFPOST*, March 23, www.huffingtonpost.co.uk/entry/idris-elba-sabrina-oprah-coronavirus_n_5e78c740c5b62f90bc4e7e2e.

Elba, Idris (@idriselba). 2020a. "This morning I tested positive for Covid 19. I feel ok, I have no symptoms so far but have been isolated since I found out about my possible exposure to the virus. Stay home people and be pragmatic. I will keep you updated on how I'm doing. No panic." Twitter, March 16, 6:18 p.m., https://twitter.com/idriselba/status/1239617034901524481.

Elba, Idris (@idriselba). 2020b. "Hope everyone is doing ok and staying on top of this. I'm gonna go LIVE on Twitter in 15 mins and give you update on how we are doing

and see how you are too." Twitter, March 17, 7:06p.m., https://twitter.com/idriselba
/status/1239991405960785920.

Elba, Idris (@idriselba). 2020c [video update: part 1]. Twitter, March 17, 7:20 p.m., https://
twitter.com/idriselba/status/1239995118154702848?lang=en.

Elba, Idris (@idriselba). 2020d [video update: part 2]. Twitter, March 17, 7:30p.m., https://
twitter.com/idriselba/status/1239997526268207105?cxt=HHwWgoCjucXLrbUiAAAA.

Elba, Idris (@idriselba). 2020e. "Hoping everyone is coping with this $@@!! Currently still
quarantine…Sab and I still feel ok so far with no changes. Dr told us that after quarantine we will be immune for a certain time since our antibodies fought this (emoji
thoughtful) At some point we'd like to go home to London. Bsafe." Twitter, March 25,
11:51p.m., https://twitter.com/idriselba/status/1242962428465254400.

Elba, Idris (@idriselba). 2020f. "My peeps." Twitter, March 31, 10:12 p.m., https://twitter
.com/idriselba/status/1245096669483397120?lang=en.

Fernandes, Sujatha. 2017. Curated Stories: The Uses and Misuses of Storytelling. Oxford: Oxford
University Press.

Frank, Arthur. 1997. The Wounded Storyteller: Body, Illness, and Ethics. Chicago: University of
Chicago Press.

Georgakopoulou, Alexandra. 2007. Small Stories, Interaction and Identities. Philadelphia, PA:
John Benjamins.

Georgakopoulou, Alexandra. 2015. "Small Stories Research: Methods—Analysis—Outreach."
In The Handbook of Narrative Analysis, edited by Anna De Fina and Alex Georgakopoulou, 178–93. Hoboken, NJ: Wiley Blackwell.

Georgakopoulou, Alexandra. 2022a. "Sharing the Moment Now as Breaking News."
EGO Media. ego-stg.kdl.kcl.ac.uk/projects/sharing-life-in-the-moment-as-small-stories
-participation-social-relations-and-the-curation-of-selves/sharing-the-moment-now/.

Georgakopoulou, Alexandra. 2022b. "The Social Media Curation of Stories: Stories as
a Feature on Snapchat and Instagram." EGO Media. ego-stg.kdl.kcl.ac.uk/projects
/sharing-life-in-the-moment-as-small-stories-participation-social-relations-and-the
-curation-of-selves/the-social-media-curation-of-stories-stories-as-a-feature-on-snapchat
-instagram/.

Georgakopoulou, Alexandra, and Korina Giaxoglou. 2018. "Emplotment in the Social
Mediatization of the Economy: The Poly-Storying of Economist Yanis Varoufakis."
Language@Internet 16, no. 6: 1–15.

Georgakopoulou, Alexandra, Stefan Iversen, and Carsten Stage. 2020. Quantified Storytelling: A Narrative Analysis of Metrics on Social Media. London: Palgrave Macmillan.

Georgakopoulou, Alexandra, Korina Giaxoglou, and Philip Seargeant. 2021. "Stories in
everyday life: from Instagram to electoral politics." Presentation (online) at Contemporary Cultures of Writing Seminar Series 2021: The Personal as Political, March
30, The Open University, UK, https://www.open.ac.uk/arts/research/contemporary
-cultures-of-writing/node/56.

Giaxoglou, Korina. 2020. "Public Health Communication during a Pandemic." Open-
Learn, last updated June 1. www.open.edu/openlearn/languages/linguistics/public
-health-communication-during-pandemic.

Giaxoglou, Korina. 2021. A Narrative Approach to Social Media Mourning: Small Stories and Affective Positioning. New York: Routledge.

G (Taylor's Version) (@ocdfangirl). 2020. "Alight, imma kill the virus with my bare hands."
Twitter, March 16, 7:21 p.m., https://twitter.com/ocdfangirl/status/12396329954825
13410.

Harvey, Kevin, and Nelya Koteyko. 2012. Exploring Health Communication: Language in Action.
London: Routledge.

Houghton, Sophie Jane (@Sophietweets123). 2020. "I am sorry to hear about your positive result. However how did you get tested with no symptoms? NHS Staff can't get
tested even with symptoms! Please use your position to help us instead. Sign the peti-

tion and share on change.org." Twitter, March 17, 10:39 p.m., https://twitter.com
/Sophietweets123/status/1240045029722374144.

Hurwitz, B., T. Greenhalgh, and V. Skultans, eds. 2004. *Narrative Research in Health and Illness*. Oxford: Blackwell.

Hydén, Lars-Christer. 1997. "Illness and Narrative." *Sociology of Health and Illness* 19, no. 1: 48–69.

Hydén, Lars-Christer. 2011. "Broken and Vicarious Voices." In *Health, Illness, and Culture*, edited by Lars-Christer Hydén and Jens Brockmeier, 36–53. London: Routledge.

Iannararino, Nicholas T. 2017. "'My Insides Feel Like Keith Richard's Face': A Narrative Analysis of Humor and Biographical Disruption in Young Adults' Cancer Blogs." *Health Communication* 33, no. 10: 1233–42.

Jenkins, Prys (@grandscarlet). 2020. "Nice how celebs can get tested without reason. Get real people & test NHS staff—this is ridiculous beyond belief." Twitter, March 18, 3:08 p.m., https://twitter.com/grandscarlet/status/1240293943851593731.

John, Nicholas A. 2017. *The Age of Sharing*. Cambridge: Polity.

Jones, Rodney. 2021. "The Wounded Leader: The Illness Narratives of Boris Johnson and Donald Trump." *Discourse, Context and Media* 41: 1–11.

Jurecic, Ann. 2012. *Illness as Narrative*. Pittsburgh: University of Pittsburgh Press.

Kleinman, Arthur. 1989. *Illness Narratives: Suffering, Healing, and the Human Condition*. New York: Perseus Books Group.

Labov, William. 2013. *The Language of Life and Death: The Transformation of Experience in Oral Narrative*. Cambridge: Cambridge University Press.

Liu, Leslie, Jina Huh, Tina Neogi, Kori Inkpen, and Wanda Pratt. 2013. "Health Vlogger-Viewer Interaction in Chronic Illness Management." In *CHI '13: Proceedings of the SIGCHI Conference on Human Factors in Computing Systems*, 49–58. New York: Association for Computing Machinery. https://doi.org/10.1145/2470654.2470663.

Mäkelä, Maria. 2018. "Lessons from the *Dangers of Narrative* Project: Toward a Story-Critical Narratology." *Tekstualia* 4: 175–186.

Mäkelä, Maria, Samuli Björninen, Laura Karttunen, Matias Nurminen, Juha Raipola, and Tytti Rantanen. 2021. "Dangers of Narrative: A Critical Approach to Narratives of Personal Experience in Contemporary Story Economy." *Narrative* 29, no. 2: 139–59.

Meretoja, Hanna. 2018. *The Ethics of Storytelling: Narrative Hermeneutics, History, and the Possible*. Oxford: Oxford University Press.

Meretoja, Hanna. 2020. "Stop Narrating the Pandemic as a Story of War." *openDemocracy*, May 19. www.opendemocracy.net/en/transformation/stop-narrating-pandemic-story-war/.

Meretoja, Hanna. 2021. "A Dialogics of Counter-narratives." In *The Routledge Handbook of Counter-narratives*, edited by Marianne Wolff Lundholt and Klarissa Lueg, 30–42. New York: Routledge.

Meretoja, Hanna, and Colin Davis. 2018. *Storytelling and Ethics: Literature, Visual Arts, and the Power of Narrative*. London: Routledge.

Mokoena, Fana K. (@fanamokoena). 2020. "Be strong brother. I know you'll be awright. Praying for you. Salute." Twitter, March 16, 7:42 p.m., https://twitter.com/fanamokoena/status/1239638176844722186.

Msomi, Velile (@msomi_velile). 2020. "But don't you think you putting your wife at risk? Yoh I know the Corona virus exist but I just feel these celebrities are paid to raise awareness on this. Because how can you quarantine but yet you with your wife?" Twitter, March 16, 6:50 p.m., https://twitter.com/msomi_velile/status/1239627019647946753.

Page, Ruth. 2011. "Blogging on the Body: Gender and Narrative." In *New Narratives: Stories and Storytelling in the Digital Age*, edited by Thomas Brownen and Ruth Page, 220–38. Lincoln: University of Nebraska Press.

Percival, Ash. 2020. "Idris Elba Reveals He's Tested Positive for Coronavirus." *HUFFPOST*, March 16, www.huffingtonpost.co.uk/entry/idris-elba-coronavirus-positive-test_uk_5e6fc42fc5b60fb69ddbe28b.

Schiff, Brian. 2006. "The Promise (and Challenge) of an Innovative Narrative Psychology." *Narrative Inquiry* 16, no. 1: 19–27.

Shapiro, Johanna. 2011. "Illness Narratives: Reliability, Authenticity, and the Empathic Witness." *Medical Humanities* 37, no. 2: 68–72.

Squire, Corinne, Mark Davis, Cigdem Esin, Molly Andrews, Barbara Harrison, Lars-Christer Hydén, and Margareta Hydén. 2014. *What Is Narrative Research?* London: Bloomsbury.

Stage, Carsten. 2017. *Networked Cancer: Affect, Narrative, and Measurement.* London: Palgrave Macmillan.

Stage, Carsten, Karen Hvidtfeldt, and Lisbeth Klastrup. 2020. "Vital Media: The Affective and Temporal Dynamics of Young Cancer Patients' Social Media Practices." *Social Media + Society* 6, no. 2: 1–13.

van Dijck, José, and Thomas Poell. 2013. "Understanding Social Media Logic." *Media and Communication* 1, no. 1: 2–14.

Vickers, Neil. 2016. "Illness Narratives." In *A History of English Autobiography*, edited by Adam Smyth, 388–401. Cambridge: Cambridge University Press.

Welsh, Daniel. 2020. "Idris Elba Describes Traumatic Impact Coronavirus Diagnosis Had On His Mental Health." *HUFFPOST*, July 15, www.huffingtonpost.co.uk/entry/idris-elba-coronavirus-mental-health_n_5f0e6230c5b63b8fc11012af.

Winfrey, Oprah. 2020. "Idris Elba and Sabrina Dhowre." Episode 1 of *Oprah Talks COVID-19*, aired March 21, on Apple TV + Press (UK).

Woods, Angela. 2011. "Post-narrative—an Appeal." *Narrative Inquiry* 21, no. 2: 399–406.

From Swallowing the Red Pill to Failing to Build the Wall: Allusive Cognitive Metaphors in Advocating Political and Extremist Views

Matias Nurminen
Tampere University

Abstract   The article analyzes how allusive cognitive metaphors (ACMs) function as a persuasive narrative strategy in contemporary social media–fueled storytelling cultures. The ACM is a concise way of combining intertextual and metaphorical meaning-making for use in viral storytelling. Well-known works of fiction function as a shared baseline that can be easily alluded to. This narrative-metaphorical strategy has been adopted especially frequently by populists and online groups advocating extreme ideologies, one of the prominent and influential cases being "the red pill," coined by the antifeminist manosphere. The popularity of ACMs suggests that the interpretive contexts and target texts that narrative scholarship has grown accustomed to are changing, and that scholars of narrative and fiction need to adapt to the new challenges stemming from the ever-expanding digital sphere.

Keywords   allusion, cognitive metaphor, storytelling boom, viral storytelling, manosphere

During the first few decades of the new millennium, a storytelling boom has been integrating narrative into the Western way of life. What might have seemed to be the start of narrative empowerment, with social media enabling the endless telling and sharing of stories, has turned sour in the

I am grateful for the helpful comments and suggestions from Samuli Björninen, Matti Hyvärinen, the appointed reviewer, and both the special issue and the journal editors.

Poetics Today 43:2 (June 2022)   DOI 10.1215/03335372-9642637
© 2022 by Porter Institute for Poetics and Semiotics

context of post-truth, fake news, and the recent hype over conspiracy theories. The storytelling boom has given rise to critical voices (Salmon 2010; Fernandes 2017; Meretoja 2018; Mäkelä et al. 2021), but academics have been slow to recognize the boom's impact on narrative and narrative scholarship. This article analyzes intertextual, allusive narratives that exploit metaphorical intrigue and virality. I suggest that a rhetorical narrative strategy, the *allusive cognitive metaphor*, is effective in conveying viral ideological content in contemporary storytelling environments. The allusive cognitive metaphor (ACM) has been adopted in recent years in cultural and political debate to advocate and spread views efficiently in a meme-like fashion. This strategy presents a challenge for the study of narrative: the ACM represents a broader cultural shift of how people understand and utilize storytelling. Narrative studies must revise its methods to tackle new forms of storytelling ensuing from this shift in the forms, uses, platforms, and tellers of influential narratives.

The ACM is simultaneously the pinnacle and the antithesis of the storytelling boom: ACMs are encapsulated in concise phrases and memes that evoke vast amounts of narrative matter using both allusions and metaphors; they are persuasive but confuse discourses as they insinuate much, yet often enunciate little, thus handing responsibility and power to the interpreter; they are easily distributed as phrases or visual cues that can be adjusted to suit different ideological purposes; and they have been adopted in recent years especially by political populists and extremists. In ACMs, allusions to fiction become associated with real-world events and evoke a deterministic, metaphorically loaded *masterplot* (Abbott 2008) to guide the perception of reality. The ACM of the "red pill" is a case in point.

In May 2020, billionaire entrepreneur Elon Musk urged his then thirty million Twitter followers to "take the red pill," ending the tweet with a rose emoji. The media was perplexed, assuming that Musk, who had been attacking and defying the US government due to the COVID-19 restrictions on businesses, was insinuating a leftist conspiracy (see, e.g., Rao 2020). This interpretation required explanation—but none was offered by Musk. Many recognized, to be sure, that the "red pill" alludes to the sci-fi film *The Matrix* (dir. the Wachowskis,[1] 1999) and its now iconic scene of epiphany about the actual state of the world behind the simulation. In the film, the protagonist becomes aware of a conspiracy in which intelligent machines have subjugated humankind as slaves living in a blissful virtual

---

1. Lilly and Lana Wachowski are siblings who work as film directors and producers. They are trans women who have later said that *The Matrix*, their first box-office success and directed when they were still known as "the Wachowski brothers," is a trans allegory (see López 2020).

reality. The protagonist is made to choose between two different pills representing different destinies: to take the red pill means to realize the dreadful truth; to take the blue pill is to keep on living a lie. The protagonist chooses the red pill and frees himself from the virtual reality to become a messianic figure who challenges the conspiracy. It is a story we have heard time after time, a recurring masterplot of the underdog rising to greatness and becoming the "chosen one" to fight for truth and justice, but the ACM of the "red pill" crystallizes the masterplot into a single compact discursive item that works as a verbal or visual metaphor for an epiphany.

The alleged culprit of Musk's conspiracy is hidden in the rose emoji. On Twitter, the rose has come to signify allegiance to left-wing politics and especially to the Democratic Socialists of America. The rose connects the conspiracy narrative to left-wing politics without making explicit claims. Musk signals that people are aware of the alleged conspiracy and capable of unmasking this foul play, and Musk challenges others to accept there actually is a conspiracy. One of the most influential people in the world thus poses as the one who understands a hidden truth, implying that all who do not accept the premise are mindless slaves. Then again, Musk did not explicitly say as much, which makes disputing or even explicating the claims especially challenging.

Using the red pill as an ACM is not one of Musk's inventions but a common figure in far-right activism—in particular the far-right activism that takes the form of radical masculinity movements known collectively as *the manosphere*. What is meant by the red-pill ACM differs. For the manosphere, taking the red pill signifies the revelation of a feminist conspiracy against men; the alt-right has adapted it to accuse conspirators of the liberal left. For white supremacists, the red pill functions as a metaphor for their anti-Semitism; also, conspiracy theorists in general have started to use the red pill to explain the struggle for their perceived truths (Marwick and Lewis 2017; Nagle 2017; Brigley Thompson 2020). The red pill is an embodied metaphorical image that everyone can experience and relate to but also an empty vessel to be filled with the ideology of one's choice. Thus, the discourse of the red pill, such as it is, poses a dilemma for the study of narrative: how should one study emergent narratives, their unexpected hybrid forms, and their implied meanings in a field of crisscrossing communicative and rhetorical affordances when we actually have no narrative to analyze, just a heavily charged discursive fragment?

In this article, I analyze how narrative allusion[2] and cognitive meta-

---

2. By using the term *narrative allusion*, I wish to emphasize the way allusion activates other texts and, in the case of ACMs, masterplots and the narrativization process, as well. I will discuss the terminology of intertextuality more thoroughly in the next section.

phors can work together to evoke masterplots and other narrativization processes in the viral storytelling environment. I study what is novel about this collaboration and how separate devices create a hybrid narrative strategy that entices audiences into narrative meaning-making. I propose three arguments:

1. The allusive cognitive metaphor is a persuasive and efficient narrative strategy that spreads virally and is easily adapted to suit different purposes.

2. Allusive narrative strategies such as the ACM thrive in the ongoing storytelling boom, when the affordances of narrative, metaphor, and viral storytelling blend successfully into new hybrid forms of storytelling and narrative.

3. Narrative scholars cannot analyze the storytelling boom and fully contribute to the ongoing cultural debate about, for example, post-truth and digital citizenship without adapting their own methods to the interpretation of these new hybrid forms.

This article will consider narrative allusions and cognitive metaphors and the synergy of their affordances in the contemporary viral storytelling environment. I will analyze the red pill as an archetypical ACM, and examine other prominent contemporary cases as well, from leftist online hacktivism to Donald Trump's rhetoric. Finally, the article will address some of the methodological and ethical challenges of modern narrative theory: the affordances of viral storytelling bring forth hybrid narrative strategies that complicate the processes of narrative interpretation and analysis while also creating the need for a skilled and informed interpretation of contemporary political phenomena.

Allusion and Cognitive Metaphor and Their Affordances

In delineating the concept of the ACM, my aim is not to revolutionize our understanding of intertextuality or cognitive metaphors but to analyze how these discursive phenomena find synergy in hybrid forms. To understand why the ACM has vast potential to distribute ideological meanings, I want to begin with a brief analysis of the ACM's components and natural habitat—the viral storytelling environment.

Intertextuality, a term originally coined by Julia Kristeva in 1966 (see Kristeva 1980) to explain the complex rhetorical dynamics between texts, is often understood as synonymous with *allusion*, despite Kristeva's rejection of the association (Machacek 2007: 523–24). In everyday language use, we "allude" when referring to something indirectly, sometimes only by hinting or through omission. In traditional allusion studies, allusion is considered a reference and a concrete link between two texts, allowing the study of inter-textuality and bidirectional meanings. When one text alludes to another, both texts are simultaneously activated. Simultaneous activation enables elements and meanings from the earlier text to enrich and amplify the cur-rent text (Ben-Porat 1976: 116–17; Perri 1978: 289–90). Naturally, allusions work as a two-way dynamic, the current text also influencing the earlier text, but classic allusion studies tend to disregard the reinterpretation of these earlier works in the light of new meanings made by the alluding text (Hebel 1991: 139). From the perspective of narrative studies, an allusion in a text is not in itself exciting, but the meanings created in simultaneous acti-vation are. How is the text that makes the allusion changed by the presence of another text? How does the interpretation of the text alluded to change when that text is called out into a new textual domain?

I suggest that a concise allusion is enabled to guide the narrativization of a phenomenon through this simultaneous activation of texts, as the alluded text may activate a *masterplot* to (re)structure the alluding text. H. Porter Abbott (2008: 46–47) describes masterplots as the "skeletal and adaptable" narrative models that are the basis for much of our identity work and value base but "often work in secret, influencing us without our wholly realizing it." Abbot's archetypical case of a masterplot is Cinderella: "Its variant can be found frequently in European and American cultures. Its constit-uent events elaborate a thread of neglect, injustice, rebirth and reward that responds to deeply held anxieties and desires. As such, the Cinderella masterplot has an enormous emotional capital that can be drawn on in constructing a narrative" (46). While some masterplots can become uni-versal, there are also competing masterplots that offer a range of takes on life and promote different values (Abbott 2008: 47–48). The ACM could be described as a synecdoche for a masterplot where a single utterance summons through allusion a masterplot to describe the world around us. On the other hand, allusions and how they are interpreted simultaneously work back on the masterplot and laden it with new meanings.

In the influential article "Allusion," Gregory Machacek (2007) condemns the theoretical use of allusion for its lack of clarity. Machacek finds the ter-minology used insufficient to describe the variety of types and uses of allu-sion. Terms like *borrowing, echo,* and *source* create non-reciprocity between texts, reducing alluding works to mere repetitions. Machacek (2007: 525) proposes to divide allusion into *learned* or *indirect reference* and *phraseologi-cal adaptation,* with both concepts highlighting the ways in which shared cultural kinship must be activated (see also Page 2018: 22). Allusions can enable the experience of unity when the reader shares the cultural references made by the author, or they can be a method of differentiation when common ground is not found. Intertextual references can help to build communities as a shared cultural backdrop and align the communities "with the political implications and connotations of the references themselves" (Nguyen 2021: 99). Allusions can thus become collective guidelines for communities of like-minded individuals.

Machacek (2007: 526) explains the curious way phraseological adaptations work: "An integrated verbal repetition treats pre-existing phraseology almost as a sort of physical raw material that can be cut, reworked, and incorporated into a new setting—like scraps of paper glued to a collage or fragments of stone set into a mosaic." For Machacek, the dividing factor between learned references and phraseological adaptations is in the way these forms of allusion are experienced, if they are experienced at all. Learned references are more visible, and if the alluded text is not known to the readers, those readers are likely to feel acutely that they are missing out on something. Phraseological adaptation, on the other hand, can be more easily missed as the adapted phrase blends into the alluding text (525). The ACM, as I define it, resembles more a learned reference than phraseological adaptation insofar as it often utilizes well-known works of popular culture. The prominent status of the works alluded to makes them accessible even if we are not acquainted with the works intimately, allowing for vague allusions. In the service of analytical contrast, I will also analyze an example of an ACM resembling more a phraseological adaptation in its precise way of alluding to a certain phrase. It also seems that metaphorical elements, like embodiment, allow readers to enjoy the more obscure references, even when not fully understanding their contexts. The ACM oscillates between Machacek's allusion types, which is why I use the term *allusive*. Moreover, I use the concept *narrative allusion* to emphasize the way the ACM activates the particular texts alluded, the shared cultural masterplots, as well as the narrativization process in general.

Metaphors can be understood as essential prerequisites for abstract thought (Goatly 2011: 261). The history of metaphor is broad and multifaceted (see Ricoeur 2003) but in this article, I focus on the *cognitive metaphor* proposed by George Lakoff and Mark H. Johnson (1980) in *Metaphors We Live By* and further developed by Elena Semino (2008) and Zoltán Kövecses (2017). Lakoff and Johnson explain how human experience can be used as a concrete domain that allows people to understand the more abstract phenomena in life through metaphor.[3] To describe this process,

---

3. Even if disregarded by Lakoff and Johnson, their theory shares similarities to Max Black's (1962) *interaction theory*.

Lakoff and Johnson proposed the term *conceptual metaphor*, alternatively referred to as *cognitive metaphor*. I find the latter term more precise and connected to the cognitive study of narrative. In cognitive metaphor theory, the static vehicle and tenor of classical metaphor theories are replaced by a broader source domain and target domain (Fludernik 2011: 3; see also Kövecses 2017: 13).

Metaphors, narratives, and allusions between narratives are intertwined in human discourse. Richard Garner (1990) notes that allusion and metaphor share a similarity in their mechanics, which would suggest the concepts coincide naturally. Jens Brockmeier (2015: 84–85) suggests that metaphor is always surrounded by stories and thus is "embedded in a narrative milieu": metaphors have narrative potential as they generate narratives in their wake, and they additionally call on narratives to explain their meanings. Also, the potential interplay of intertextuality and metaphors has been identified: Jörg Zinken (2003: 509) suggests that *intertextual metaphors* are particularly original and "motivated by the speaker's adaptation to a certain cultural structure or substructure, which provides specific imaginative resources." Marco Caracciolo, Andrei Ionescu, and Ruben Fransoo (2019: 223; see also Caracciolo 2017) propose that creative metaphors derived from literature often have the potential to have a greater impact on their audiences in contexts in which "the combination of source and target domain is novel and emotionally impactful; readers' viewpoint on the target is more likely to be affected." Intertextuality and fiction can give weight to a metaphor and deepen its reach. I argue that both narrative allusions and cognitive metaphors are narrative-cognitive devices that activate narrativization and undercurrent masterplots.[4] But the ACM is not something that can be purely explained by looking at the separate pieces of the puzzle—they must be looked at as a unit.

4. *Metaphor scenario*, coined by Andreas Musolff, shares similarities with the ACM. Musolff explains:

> [Metaphor] Scenarios are mini-narratives that include a "conclusion" or "solution" that seems to be ethically correct, self-evident and practicable at the source level, and is presented analogically as equally "good" in all respects at the target level. Its inferences are suggested to the hearers or readers as convincing topic explanations, on account of their seeming evidentiality, and thus "naturally" lead to recommendations for specific problem-solving actions. Such inferences deriving from metaphoric scenarios are in the first place context-specific, "emergent" conclusions, which over time can become crystallized into figures of thought that are taken for granted in a discourse community. (Musolff 2016: 312)

Musolff's "metaphor scenario" is kindred to the ACM, but allusive qualities strengthen the element of narrative guidance in the ACM: alluded works are like instructions on how to understand the cognitive metaphor. Narrative allusion enables a more comprehensive but at the same time precise meaning-making.

In recent years, populist rhetoric has been a vital domain for cognitive metaphors. As is the case in political discourse, such rhetoric "both direct[s] and constrain[s] the audience's understanding by drawing on certain metaphorical themes" (Pilyarchuk and Onysko 2018: 99). Metaphors can be easily used both in teaching new concepts and "to deceive or manipulate an audience" (Breeze 2020: 13).[5] The way narrative allusions activate texts can be described by drawing from the work of Caroline Levine (2015: 6–7), who notes that different *forms* afford "both the particular constraints and possibilities," allowing them to somewhat supersede context situatedness (see also Hutchby 2001). Elsewhere, I have analyzed along with my colleagues from the Dangers of Narrative research project how understanding the affordances of form "could result in a more ethical and rhetorically sound storytelling," and that different narrative forms—especially when cooperating with other (for example, social or institutional) forms—may carry latent risks irrespective of the storyteller's intentions (Mäkelä et al. 2021: 141–43). In the ACM, we see different forms—cognitive metaphor and narrative allusion—cooperating, and their affordances amplifying one another, summoning masterplots and ushering in narrativization processes.

Allusive Cognitive Metaphor in the Viral Storytelling Environment

Many mechanics of the ACM are not novel: something similar to how the ACM works as a synecdoche for a masterplot can already be seen, for instance, in medieval heraldry, where the family crest would tell the story of a nation or its ruling house. Also, literary history is filled with cooperations of allusion and metaphor, like "tilting at windmills" or "the White Whale," which would activate a masterplot upon use. Nevertheless, contemporary viral storytelling gives the combination of narrative allusion and cognitive metaphor meme-like qualities that make them easier to use and share and quicker to grasp. Instead of the elaborate insinuation we see in heraldry, the ACM in the viral storytelling environment is about reaching the masses. This is why the ACM usually alludes to popular culture, such as blockbuster films and other works of fiction that are globally well known and easily recognizable.

As insinuated, the ACM is in many ways similar to an internet meme. Limor Shifman (2014: 7–8) defines the internet meme "as (a) a group of digital items sharing common characteristics of content, form, and/or stance; (b) that were created with awareness of each other; and (c) were circulated,

---

5. Naturally, a new concept taught can also be dubious or even dangerous.

imitated, and/or transformed via the Internet by many users." Memes, an important visual method of online communication since the 1990s, have been described as being "like a funhouse mirror for culture and society, reflecting and refracting the anxieties and preoccupations of a variety of social groups across a series of national contexts" (Miltner 2017: 413). Internet memes can be used just for amusement, but they have proven their worth also in politics, activism, and advertising (Miltner 2017; Literat and Kligler-Vilenchik 2019). A useful, crystallized definition of Internet memes that helps us to understand how ACMs differ from memes has been made by Asaf Nissenbaum and Shifman (2018: 29): "In short, memes allow the individual to use a collectively created template to deliver a personalized message."

ACMs share many qualities with internet memes, but instead of working simply as a template, ACMs are more heavily tied to the alluded work. Even though memes use popular culture just as avidly as ACMs, this often US-centered pop culture serves simply as a background—"merely as wallpapers"—for memes (Nissenbaum and Shifman 2018: 306). With the ACM, the alluded work guides the interpretation, enriching it with meaning. In fact, the ACM seems to share the same kind of affordances as the hashtag: by using the same hashtag, people can "imply a will to speak with each other, but they do not necessarily say the same thing" (Literat and Kligler-Vilenchik 2019: 1991). Whereas "viral" content is something that is shared unchanged and the "meme" is changed or altered before posting it (Shifman 2014), the ACM seems to fall somewhere between these categories.

Having discussed two essential elements of the ACM, what is still missing is the way of distributing the allusive narrative strategy efficiently, so I turn to social media and its affordances as a viral storytelling environment. Online social media platforms allow potentially millions of people to join in on producing, consuming, and reproducing a story (Page 2018: 2). The digital public sphere has the capacity for quick but often uncontrollable distribution that might work in unanticipated ways when something is posted or shared (see Sampson 2012). Paul Dawson and Maria Mäkelä (2020: 22) suggest that social media narratives differ from those studied in narrative fiction: "Rather than structured aesthetic artefacts, narratives on social media are the product of self-organizing networks without a central design: they emerge from the logic of connective action." Storytelling on the internet challenges the conception of narrative and calls for a methodological revision for us to fully understand strategies like the ACM.

Ruth Page (2018) sees new avenues for intertextuality in social media forms—like hyperlinks and hashtags—and multimodal forms—like memes that combine images and captions. Page (2018: 22; see also Dawson and Mäkelä 2020) explains how interpretation and the power of the reteller are highlighted in online storytelling and sharing: "For example, as an intertextual referent is recontextualized, it can open up many different kinds of new interpretations for the tellers and their audiences. The recontextualization can involve greater or lesser creative input from the co-tellers, who may leave the referent relatively unchanged or may alter it significantly." This recontextualization is prevalent in the ACM, which can fluctuate between contexts and be altered for different audiences while remaining connected to the undergirding masterplot activated by it. To illustrate this complex dynamic, I return to an exemplary social media ACM case, the red pill.

"The Red Pill" as Allusive Cognitive Metaphor

Despite initial high hopes that the emergent digital world might be an egalitarian space, constructed hierarchies, like gender, race, class, and sexuality are reproduced in digital platforms (Vickery and Everbach 2018: 10; see also Nissenbaum and Shifman 2018). Debbie Ging and Eugene Siapera see "a new and uniquely toxic turn in gender politics" (Ging and Siapera 2018: 2) that is supported by men's rights activists relying on social media affordances, like anonymity and echo chambers, in a similar fashion to the alt-right (Ging 2019). The culmination of men's rights activism that rests upon social media affordances is the *manosphere*, and it uses the ACM of the red pill.

The manosphere is an online ecology that consists of fragmentary men's rights advocacy groups across the internet (Ging 2019). The term *manosphere*, coined in a singular blog post in 2009 and gaining traction over the past decade,[6] is vague: in its broadest interpretation, it encompasses all masculine-related online activities—support groups, hobby-related forums, and also feminist male communities—but what are often referred to in public parlance are radical, vocally antifeminist groups.[7] These dif-

6. The original blogpost is not available anymore, but the origin story has been recorded to many academic and popular sources (see Nagle 2017; Ging 2019).
7. Debbie Ging's (2019: 644) analysis shows the manosphere consists of five different interest groups: Men's Rights Activists, the Men Going Their Own Way movement, the Pick-Up Artist Community, traditional Christian conservatives, and gamer/geek culture. As Ging notes, this classification is partly artificial due to overlaps between the different groups, and it has several weaknesses: for example, only part of gamer and geek culture shares manosphere views. This classification also seems to associate different tier groups: the Men Going Their Own Way movement is a rather clear-cut group encouraging men to delve into developing themselves instead of marrying or sometimes even dating women,

ferent groups' hostility toward feminism is particularly highlighted in their specialized, shared vocabulary (Marwick and Caplan 2018). Demographically, the manosphere is populated by young, white heterosexual males (see, e.g., Zuckerberg 2018). Its participants are known to employ discourses of sexual violence, rape threats, and online harassment campaigns (Gotell and Dutton 2016; Jane 2017; Marwick and Caplan 2018), but beyond that, many of the groups are avid storytellers. I have analyzed elsewhere the manosphere's attempts to reinterpret the Western canon of literature (Nurminen 2019) and how manosphere groups use counternarratives to justify their misogynistic worldviews (Nurminen 2020). Leaning on the affordances of social media and digital culture (see, e.g., Ging 2019) has led the manosphere to adopt sophisticated narrative strategies to recruit new members.

The social media site Reddit's subreddit /TheRedPill hosts over 1.7 million registered users. This largest manosphere community, quarantined by Reddit with warnings of shocking content, is named after the manosphere's core philosophy shared by the radical groups. As explained earlier, the red pill alludes to the science fiction film *The Matrix*: the red pill signifies a conspiracy that a person has gained exclusive knowledge of. While in the film the conspiracy is led by devious machines exploiting humankind, the manosphere insists that feminism is a conspiracy aiming to subjugate men—especially conservative, white, heterosexual men.

The red pill has become the manosphere's symbol and underlying philosophy insofar as it is used to interpret real-world events and create a common ground for its loyalists. On different sites, users tell stories about their "red pill moments." Ging (2019: 653) calls red-pill narratives "mobilizing and reifying narratives of personal suffering to build affective consensus about an allegedly collective, gendered experience, namely men's position in the social hierarchy as a result of feminism." As Dawson and Mäkelä (2020: 23) have suggested, emergent storytelling is created on social media by individuals, but virality makes it possible for such stories to become "macro-level narrative distinct from the narrative elements observable at the micro-level." The individual red-pill narratives shape both the red-pill metaphor and the masterplot it activates: every individual narrative on the micro-level contributes to a macro-level narrative, lending the abstract

---

but Men's Rights Activism is a complex cluster of groups. I am willing to accept Ging's conclusion that the various groups of the manosphere are almost identical in their ideology and that they exaggerate "their differences in displays of infight posturing" to jockey for power (644). I propose, however, that the manosphere should be defined more clearly to avoid clustering all masculinity-related online activities as part of the same online ecology.

notion of the red pill a concrete form, delineating its usual plot and loading it with cultural weight. But what makes the red pill highly transmittable is how it acts as an ACM.

The ACM of the red pill alludes to an iconic moment of a well-known work of fiction that is known also to people who have not seen the film: in the early 2010s, the "What if I told you?" Internet meme alluding to *The Matrix* and its revelation of conspiracy scene became popular across the internet. The allusion activates *The Matrix* essentially as a classic underdog story, which is a universal masterplot in its own right: a ragtag bunch of rebels righteously defying an evil enemy and the unlikely geeky hero rising from a white-collar desk job to become the leather-coated savior of humankind with superhuman kung fu skills. Having analyzed underdog stories in relation to terrorism, Lois Presser (2018: 87) suggests that this type of story "arouses us because it put us in mind of a deep sense of wrongful vulnerability in the world only to assuage that sense through triumphant, transcendent action. The story tells us that we are both more powerful and less alone than we imagined ourselves—to be less alone, but also special." To claim to have taken the red pill is to claim to be special—someone who sees the truth behind a claimed conspiracy. Naomee-Minh Nguyen (2021: 112) has noted in studying Asian American activists that intertextual references enable people "to infuse their stance with the implications of the references themselves, which has the effect of elevating the authority of their stances." *The Matrix* makes the digital inhabitants of the manosphere feel like righteous rebels in their crusade against feminism and allows them to act in morally questionable, misogynistic ways.

While working as a powerful narrative allusion, the red pill simultaneously has qualities of a cognitive metaphor. Małgorzata Waśniewska (2020: 68) connects the red pill to the TRUTH IS MEDICINE cognitive metaphor that appears most commonly in the phrase "a hard pill to swallow." The red pill is thus also an embodied metaphor that emphasizes the need for a new concept like the ACM. For example, Zinken (2003: 509) claims that intertextual metaphors commonly do not invite bodily experience. Yet the red pill is indeed heavily embodied: the red pill enables one to experience what the protagonist in *The Matrix* feels: what it feels like to see, take, and swallow the bright red pill; what it feels to be "unplugged"—another widely used manosphere metaphor—from the comforting simulation to a cold harsh reality; but also what it feels like to be a nearly omnipotent rebel, who hurts and even kills without consequence. The narrative allusion allows the ACM to access a common narrative backdrop for the manosphere in ways that activate a bodily storyworld immersion (see Ryan 2001; Caracciolo 2014). Storytelling can use a set of shared beliefs to create a sense of loyalty and administer emotions as part of the readerly experience—even create "a constraining collective myth" (Salmon 2010: 74). The red pill signifies a righteous resistance, but also encourages the members of the community to see their chosen adversaries as evil and thus deserving of merciless attacks. It also signals an impending victory for their cause: as Abbott (2008: 58) explains, masterplots can be seen as "coded narrative formulas that end with closure."

As I explained earlier, the ACM oscillates between the learned reference and phraseological adaptation proposed by Machacek. I understand this oscillation to be the result of its hybrid form, since the metaphorical elements diminish the need for its users to fully understand the intertextual reference made. The ACM also acts similarly to phraseological adaptations in its fluidity between different settings: for example, "the red pill" that has been adopted and adapted at least by alt-right white nationalists and conspiracy theorists to support their identity work and recruitment processes (see Marwick and Lewis 2017; Nagle 2017; Kelly 2017; Brigley Thompson 2020). Partly this spreading is due to the overlap in ideologies and memberships between the diverse groups, but the red pill is also an effective tool of persuasion and argumentation. This particular ACM carries exceptional narrative potential to be applied for different purposes—as we saw in the case of Elon Musk's personal battle against COVID-19 restrictions.

The ACM is able to harness the affordances of narrative allusions, cognitive metaphors, and viral storytelling: the term describes the intersecting cooperations and collusions of these affordances that generate effects which no one piece of the puzzle could explain on its own. The ACM is easy to distribute, laden with meanings, and deceptively simple but difficult to argue against: much is insinuated and alluded to, but little is actually said. In the case of the red pill, the discovery of such a potent strategy by the manosphere is part luck, part determinate effort and interest in narrative meaning-making. In fact, the radical manosphere has taken its interest in narrative so far—and claims its adversaries have too—that it talks about waging "narrative warfare" (see Nurminen 2019). The ACM can be seen as a weapon in this war, but the ACM is, however, also used in other contexts, as the following examples demonstrate.

Partial Successes and Misfires in Using the ACM

While the red pill is an archetypical ACM, it is not an isolated incident but rather a particularly successful occurrence. Through the following case studies, I will analyze the ACM and its affordances.

The ACM Is Context-Specific, Concise, and Uses Popular References to Gain Virality

A defining national moment of the Finnish political scene was the historic 2011 victory of the right-wing populist Finns Party, formerly the True Finns, in the parliamentary election, a victory that transformed a previously marginal party into the third biggest in the country. The experienced party chair Timo Soini showcased his renowned rhetorical skills when addressing party supporters and encapsulated the shocking chain of events into a single phrase: "Dear friends, there came a big thump!" (Hyvät ystävät, tuli iso jytky). "The thump," or *jytky* in Finnish, became a catchphrase for the Finns Party's success. The phrase was adopted by the media and others to transmit a broad range of information and emotions—positive or negative depending on the political standpoint—cost-efficiently, in the space of a single word.

Soini consolidated the political party's foundation by infiltrating the Finnish language, but chose not to utilize an available intertextual opportunity. The word *jytky* is referred to in the title of Finnish expressionist artist Tyko Sallinen's painting *Jytkyt* (1918; *The Barn Dance*), which depicts a barn dance and the thumping of feet hitting the floor. Curiously, the allusion was not explicitly activated by Soini, despite the fact that the Finns Party had vowed in their election program to only support nationalistic art rather than the work of artsy postmodernists.[8] Sallinen's painting would have been a fitting work to allude to, but "the thump" seemed to work well on its own. The original Finnish word *jytky* connotes both the rural and the archaic, qualities in obvious accord with conservative populist party claims to be the voice of the people. The word, like its English translation, is onomatopoetic, conveying a rough and dull sound that is metaphorically fitting for the shocking success of the party. Even without the allusion to the painting depicting a dance, "the thump" signals motion and noise, but also activates the cognitive metaphor CHANGE IS MOVEMENT. But why not lean more heavily on the Sallinen painting that would complement these qualities?

"The thump," I want to argue, has ACM qualities not fully actualized, because the Sallinen painting lacks public legibility among the general Finnish population. "The thump" of the Finns Party was a context-situated success that leaned heavily on the phrase's metaphorical meanings but also its onomatopoetic and archaic appeal. These effects could never be fully translated, making "the thump" an exclusively Finnish phenome-

---

8. This stance on art can be found in the extended Finnish version of the Finns Party's Election Programme for the Parliamentary Election 2011 (Finns Party 2011).

non. Even if it were to evoke the Sallinen painting as a reference point, the painting's international obscurity would limit the appeal of "the thump" abroad. "The thump" has been successful without a narrative allusion, as it is highly metaphorical, but this invites the question whether with a different intertextual reference point, there could have been a wider success in signaling the rise of right-wing conservative populism globally.

ACMs are context-specific, but they expand their reach by alluding to well-known works of fiction and popular culture. This broad allusiveness allows the ACM to be concise: the red pill often needs no explanation. The ACM is so concise that a range of tellers with opposing aims can use it while both the source narrative alluded to and the masterplot activated remain the same. As a narrative strategy, the red pill can thus be easily used by both the manosphere and Elon Musk, each for their own purposes. The "thump" remains isolated in a specific context because of the language barrier, but more importantly, it has no well-known work to allude to and no clear masterplot to turn to. Its potential for wider audiences must be left untapped.

The User of the ACM Is Required to Have Intimate Knowledge of the Alluded Work

Donald Trump's use of metaphor in political speech has been analyzed thoroughly: Kateryna Pilyarchuk and Alexander Onysko (2018: 100–19) have found Trump using, for example, animal metaphors to evoke fear and distrust toward immigrants, while also depicting himself metaphorically as a constructor. This latter metaphorical meaning-making is connected to Trump's wall project, a project that became famous during the 2016 presidential election when Trump pledged, if elected, to expand the existing Mexico–United States barrier—the wall. The wall is a meaning-laden word metaphorically and intertextually. It alludes to historical walls from the Great Wall of China and the Berlin Wall to the Western Wall in Jerusalem, and it has fictive reference points in works such as the album *The Wall* by the psychedelic rock group Pink Floyd. Trump's wall turned out to be a project he had little success in advancing, yet Trump kept rallying support for his pet project. One of the more confusing attempts was seen in January 2019, when a picture was posted on Trump's (2019) Instagram account of the president hovering above a section of the wall and the text "The wall is coming."[9]

Trump's post uses a phraseological adaptation that alludes to George

9. This Instagram post can be found via this link: https://www.instagram.com/p/BsMBe LbFLxd/.

R. R. Martin's fantasy novel series *A Song of Ice and Fire* (1996–) and its television adaptation *Game of Thrones* (2011–19). The cycle depicts the power struggles of different families trying to claim the throne of the continent of Westeros and fend off the looming supernatural threat of the Others. This threat is ominously echoed in one of the main families' motto, "Winter is coming," which became a catchphrase for the fans of the television adaptation in particular. On the other hand, "the Wall" is an important structure in Westeros, separating the known world from the wild lands and the Others. This is surely "the Wall" many would think of when coming across recent allusions to a wall.

By alluding to the phrase "Winter is coming," and even adopting the font used in the series, Trump ends up dabbling with an ACM, with poor results. News outlets and *Game of Thrones* fans greeted Trump's adaptation with ridicule (e.g., Heritage 2019). "The wall is coming" is awkward, as it lacks even the basic knowledge about the alluded work. The ACM replaces the word *winter*, which in the world of Westeros is something to be dreaded, not to be anticipated. In advocating for the wall, Trump uses implicit cognitive metaphors like COMMUNITIES ARE CONTAINERS and IMMIGRATION IS FLOOD (Pilyarchuk and Onysko 2018), but when we consider how miserably the Wall in *Game of Thrones* tumbles down in the seventh season because winter has finally come, Trump is dooming the wall before it is even finished.

When members of an audience are confronted by a narrative allusion they are not familiar with, they might still enjoy the ACM as a metaphor. On the other hand, one can become familiar with a widely used reference without being familiar with the original text—many understand what "the White Whale" signifies without having read Herman Melville's *Moby-Dick* (1851). But when the user of an ACM demonstrates a lack of knowledge of the work alluded to, this obvious ignorance might entice counter-reactions from audiences familiar with the work. I suggest that Trump's demonstrated lack of familiarity with the work alluded to prevents the effective use of the ACM. Trump's "The wall is coming" attempts to carry the inevitability of the original statement and use its catchiness to gain popularity for the widely criticized wall project. It would seem that Trump—or maybe more accurately, his social media team—treats the picture and phrase as a meme, and therein lies its downfall. This ACM fails to create metaphorical continuity, as it contradicts the original work and seems to fail to understand it, bringing out affordances of viral storytelling in an unwanted way: as social media allow ACMs to spread effectively, they also enable just as decisively people to contest and ridicule a haphazard ACM. If I were to speculate, Trump would have fared better using the phrase

"Winter is coming," with or without the photo of the wall, and leaving the people to do the narrativization.

The ACM Can Also Be Visual Instead of Textual

Another example of an ACM is the Guy Fawkes mask, alluding to Alan Moore and David Lloyd's graphic novel *V for Vendetta* (1982–89) and its film adaptation (dir. James McTeigue, 2005), but made famous by its use by anti-establishment activists. *V for Vendetta* tells the story of a dystopian, totalitarian Britain and an eloquent revolutionary clad in a Guy Fawkes mask named V, who incites an uprising against the corrupt government. Guy Fawkes was a conspirator of the Gunpowder Plot, a famous assassination attempt on James I of Great Britain in 1605. Having ACM qualities, the mask has become a frequent emblem of left-leaning political activism, most notably as used by the hacktivist group Anonymous.

Anonymous is a global hacker movement with no centralized leadership, known for cyberattacks on organizations the movement deems somehow morally dubious. The movement began its actions already in 2003, but it became famous around 2008 following a series of pranks and cyberattacks against the Church of Scientology. Since then, Anonymous has launched activities against governments, companies, child porn distributors, copyright-advocating entities, terrorist groups, and various other organizations. Anonymous's actions have led to the arrests of activists in several countries. After having slowly faded into the background in the late 2010s, the organization was revitalized in 2020 by the wide public reaction to the murder of George Floyd. Anonymous members often wear Guy Fawkes masks when posting video messages about their actions, and they also use the recurring phrase: "We are Anonymous. We are Legion. We don't forgive. We don't forget. Expect us." While the masks and the way the videos often imitate a news broadcast allude to *V for Vendetta*, the recurring phrase is original. Textual allusion is not needed in the wake of such an iconic visual cue.

In studying *V for Vendetta*'s allusions to other fictive works, Wojciech Lewandowski (2020: 97–98) notes that intertextuality can transmit "political and social ideologies or agendas" that both enhance the work's message and give it context. *V for Vendetta* is a way for Anonymous to signal a righteous rebellion against corrupt establishments, although this stance is questionable, at least when it comes to attacking copyright-protecting organizations. The ACM of the Guy Fawkes mask has similarities to "the red pill," but the works alluded to differ: in *The Matrix*, innocent bystanders are hurt nonchalantly in the name of a greater good, while in *V for Vendetta* the attacks are directed more clearly against evil-doers. These two narrative allusions import differing actantial roles: in *The Matrix* the red pillers are the chosen ones, while in *V for Vendetta* the emancipation belongs to "all of us." The cognitive metaphor behind the Guy Fawkes mask is thus POWER IS PEOPLE.

An allusion helps to map out a literary work's genre (Machacek 2007: 531), and it can be seen as working analogously when referring to events in the actual world: the Guy Fawkes mask symbolizes resistance, and it has been adopted by different activist movements oriented especially toward the left-wing politics. The ACM of the Guy Fawkes mask actualizes the masterplot of people resisting corrupt leaders. It also epitomizes how the ACM requires no words at all to spread. Then again, the Guy Fawkes mask is not a perfect ACM: it has metaphorical continuity, as it signals resistance to corruption and authority; it has a well-known work of popular culture to allude to, but it still lacks coherence in its target. I suggest that the lack of phraseological adaptation makes it more difficult to designate the use of the ACM. Who is using it and to what end? I would argue that a visual cue is maybe even more easily adaptable to different causes than a phraseological adaptation, but it is not as precise as a tool for meaning-making: while often used in left-leaning anti-establishment rallies, Guy Fawkes masks were also present in the 2021 attack on the United States Capitol instigated by right-wing extremists. Based on this specific example, I hypothesize visual symbols to be more fluid in meaning-making, perhaps connecting them more closely to memes and their affordances, but more in-depth inquiry on this aspect is required.

ACMs have found particular success in their use by populists and movements of the radical far right, but as a narrative strategy, the practice has no necessary ideological allegiance. One example of this mobility is the at least partly actualized ACM of the "fight club," which alludes to David Fincher's film *Fight Club* (1999), adapted from Chuck Palahniuk's novel of the same name (1996). The satire that is clearly present in the novel has been lost as the film has inspired alt-right and neo-Nazi groups but also anti-fascist movements to establish "fight clubs." When author Chuck Palahniuk was asked in an interview what he thought about the sporadic online culture of sexually frustrated young men called involuntary celibates—or incels—quoting *Fight Club*, he noted that the book was first adopted by the online pickup artist community:

> It's fascinating that the group that can't get laid is now adopting the same language. It shows how few options men have in terms of metaphors: a skimpy inventory of images. They have *The Matrix*—there's a lot of red pill, blue pill stuff—and they have *Fight Club*. The only other thing is *Dead Poets Society*, where

men go into a cavern and say poems to each other, and they're not going to adopt that. (Beaumont-Thomas 2018)

But if we believe Palahniuk that *Dead Poets Society* will not do, from what narrative sources might we expect the next ACMs to emerge? The ACMs seem to allude to popular Hollywood films, many of which could be categorized as works of speculative fiction. Todd Phillips's thriller film *The Joker* (2019), which offers an origin story for the well-known *Batman* villain, comes to mind: the film was received with both plaudits and grave concern as people recognized in it yet another potentially harmful inspirational model for angry young men. Could and should narrative scholarship participate in analyzing potentially dubious narrative uses of the ACM? This is one of the pertinent challenges and opportunities presented for us by the viral storytelling environment.

Narrative Studies' Methodological Challenges amid the Storytelling Boom

The past decade has been defined by oscillation between modes of hopeful belief in the power of narratives and the troubling climate of post-truth. Scholars have called this contemporary interest in narratives *a storytelling boom* (e.g., Salmon 2010; Fernandes 2017; Mäkelä et al. 2021). This boom is manifested especially well on the internet and in its storytelling environment, which is a double-edged sword: the internet offers us seemingly endless amounts of data, but these data are also forced upon us. As our realities are flooded with constant flows of information, interpretation becomes a pressing matter: who really understands what is going on, or at least claims to do so, like Elon Musk with the ACM of the red pill?

The affordances of fast-paced, viral storytelling make easy explanations of complicated social phenomena more and more enticing: intriguing narratives and interpretations are easier to digest and share than the boring and complex reality—especially when the status quo contradicts one's views. Andreas Musolff (2019: 8) comments on one-sided framing in political discourse: "Complaints about 'lies' or about wrong, exaggerated or misleading representations of 'facts' are, as we have seen, futile if they assume that the political public is chiefly interested in receiving ever more facts." This is why the president of one of the most powerful nations could make up alternative facts that his followers want to hear, and why conspiracy theories, like QAnon, find supporters explaining an otherwise chaotic reality using scapegoats. The border between the storytelling boom and storytelling doom seems to be fragile, and this is also the slippery storytelling environment where the ACM thrives.

As I explained earlier, the ACM is not a new form of allusion or cognitive metaphor; it is rather an intersection of these structures' affordances that thrives in a viral storytelling environment. I have elsewhere argued that "the omnipresent urge to tell and share experiential stories results in collisions between the narrative form and other forms, such as those of the social media," creating "unwanted or unsolicited effects" (Mäkelä et al. 2021: 141). To illustrate my analysis of the ACM, I turn to an analogy derived from physics. The superposition principle's classic example explains how two waves equal each other's sum when overlapping in space. The overlapping waves develop individually, but nevertheless they have a hidden potential in working together. It is possible that the waves move in different phases, dampening each other out in *destructive interference*—a principle used in sound-canceling headphones to fight sound with sound. However, if the waves have similar phases, they achieve *constructive interference*, creating a large wave instead of two small ones. This somewhat simplified explanation showcases the way allusion and cognitive metaphor can amplify each other's affordances and have a greater impact in their overlapping than they do when kept distinct. This is not to say that the cooperation of allusion and cognitive metaphor is unheard of—we have had our "white whales" and such in the past—but affordances of the viral storytelling environment give the ACM extra leverage. If allusions and cognitive metaphors are the waves that combine their efforts, the internet has taken over the space that surrounds these waves and allows their movement. The viral storytelling environment and its affordances give the ACM the momentum that is required for it to spread. The ACM in its prime, like in the case of the red pill, is a big wave, and it moves fast.

It has been noted that literature has globally lost "its role as a major source of ideas and directives for sociocultural activity and consciousness," and this loss of cultural authority necessitates changes in literary studies' methods and perspectives (Even-Zohar, Torres Feijó, and Monegal 2019: 27). One of the main pressure points seems to be how the internet, social media, and viral storytelling are taking over much of the narrative space traditionally reserved for literature. Nevertheless, narrative scholarship has the competence to explain the storytelling boom and its narrative strategies, and to contribute actively to societal discussions, but this requires adopting some of the perspectives outlined in this and other affiliated essays.

As the analysis of the ACM suggests, contemporary narrative strategies are often known to us but repurposed within new contexts with unexpected consequences. While, for example, narratology most often presumes stable and limited target texts like novels and short stories, the viral storytelling environment hosts narratives and narrative strategies that can quickly mutate and expire. In addition, the storytelling boom has meant that businesses, organizations, and media are increasingly interested in stories, and social media has given storytelling a sense of empowerment that we would do well to meet with critical analysis and reservation. Yet narrative scholarship operates upon its own presumptions as well. For example, social scientific narrative scholars, while well versed in understanding everyday storytelling, have unintentionally treated *counternarratives* as benevolent, even though narrative strategies do not discriminate among types of goals (Hyvärinen 2020; Meretoja 2020; Nurminen 2020). In tackling the viral storytelling environment, narrative scholarship would do well to venture into even more comprehensive collaborations among its various schools.

But does scholarly intervention on the use of narratives also require ethical—or even political—positioning? For example, the majority of the cases studied in this article are derived from groups aligned with right-wing politics, which could be interpreted as a political statement. Are we to go about categorizing interest groups into storytelling boomers and storytelling doomers? Hanna Meretoja (2017: 91–92) writes: "There is nothing in stories to guarantee that their possible ethical potential will be actualized. Narrative form does not make a narrative either inherently harmful or beneficial; instead, its ethical value is contextual: that is, dependent on how the narrative is interpreted and put to use in a particular social, historical, and cultural world."

Now interpretation is a pressing matter when we try to understand the storytelling boom, and our data-filled, fast-paced reality can be misused by individuals—be they radicals, politicians, marketers, or maybe even social media influencers—to gain authority for their agenda. This is where the analytical interpretative skills of narrative scholarship could balance the scales. Sometimes it can be an ethical choice for a narrative scholar to not take a political stance but simply force the magician to reveal the trick. People can still become radicals, but they are not unknowingly wooed into extremism with smoke, mirrors, and ACMs.

Conclusion

When Elon Musk controversially tweeted the red pill as an ACM, Ivanka Trump, businessperson and senior adviser to their father, then US President Donald Trump, was one of the more famous supporters of Musk's tweet. Supporters responded enthusiastically to Musk's demand by tweeting: "Taken!" By claiming to have taken the red pill, Ivanka Trump embraced the position of the witty one who understands the alleged hid-

den undercurrents of power. Ivanka Trump—along with other supporters rushing to red pill themselves—also made Musk's claim become more
credible. By borrowing the ACM of the red pill from online extremists,
Musk was able to cultivate uncertainty and doubt against the government,
but in an elaborate, pass-the-buck way that seems to require a whole article
to fully explain. Lilly Wachowski, one of the directors and writers of *The
Matrix*, tweeted a vexed response to both Elon Musk and Ivanka Trump:
"Fuck both of you." Yet in many ways, the damage was done, as literary theorists understand well: narratives are shaped by their interpreters,
and narratives create our reality. The ACM allows people to interpret and
experience a whole conspiracy narrative in a simple phrase.[10]

This article has analyzed the use of ACMs and offered notions of how
this allusive narrative strategy utilizes colliding affordances that in collaboration gain synergy and become more than the sum of their individual
parts. The ACM is a concise way of combining intertextual and metaphorical meaning-making to be transmitted in the viral storytelling environment in a meme-like fashion. It is easily shared and adapted, as it often
uses well-known works of fiction to create common conceptual ground. As
we have seen with the case of the red pill, this narrative strategy has been
adopted especially by populists and online groups advocating extreme
ideologies.

Through this analysis, I have offered perspectives for narrative scholarship facing methodological challenges in the flux of the ongoing storytelling boom and—as I have playfully put it—doom. The viral storytelling environment requires scholarship to analyze its own predispositions:
the interpretative contexts and target texts we have grown accustomed to
have gained challengers from the ever-expanding digital sphere. Extensive
scholarship and collaboration among different schools of narrative study
can offer coherence for the chaotic nature of the storytelling boom and
contribute to social discussions. When contemporary narrative strategies
at their worst disregard scientific knowledge and use fictions to bend facts
in order to encourage hatred and violence, scholarship has the opportunity and obligation to rise to the challenge of limiting the persuasiveness
of these forms.

Daring a last glance at *The Matrix*, when the protagonist is asked to
choose between the red and the blue pill, a narrative is hinted at by Mor-

---

10. However, the long-waited fourth film in the Matrix-universe, *The Matrix Resurrections*
(dir. Lana Wachowski, 2021), has been analysed as an attempt to "un-redpill America"
(Robertson 2021). Time will tell if the new installment will affect the use of the red pill
ACM in any way, but I remain skeptical.

pheus, the protagonist's future mentor. It is of consequence that Morpheus uses an allusion from Lewis Carroll's *Alice's Adventures in Wonderland* (1865) to leverage the choice: "You take the red pill, you stay in Wonderland and I show you how deep the rabbit hole goes." The rabbit hole is in a sense an ACM filled with the promise of adventure and intrigue, so the protagonist's choice is obvious. The question remains as to whether a scholarly intervention, interpretation, and understanding of the ACM would make the choice fair.

References

Abbott, H. Porter. 2008. *The Cambridge Introduction to Narrative.* 2nd ed. Cambridge: Cambridge University Press.

Beaumont-Thomas, Ben. 2018. "*Fight Club* Author Chuck Palahniuk on His Book Becoming a Bible for the Incel Movement." *Guardian*, July 20. www.theguardian.com/books/2018/jul/20/chuck-palahniuk-interview-adjustment-day-black-ethno-state-gay-parenting-incel-movement.

Ben-Porat, Ziva. 1976. "The Poetics of Literary Allusion." *PTL* 1, no. 1: 105–28.

Black, Max. 1962. *Models and Metaphors: Studies in Language and Philosophy.* Ithaca, NY: Cornell University Press.

Breeze, Ruth. 2020. "Introduction: Approaching Metaphor in Political Discourse." In *Metaphor in Political Conflict: Populism and Discourse*, edited by Ruth Breeze and Carmen Llamas Saíz, 11–26. Pamplona: Ediciones Universidad de Navarra (EUNSA).

Brigley Thompson, Zoë. 2020. "The (Alt)right to rape: Violated White Masculinities in the Alt-right, and the Film *Nocturnal Animals*." *Feminist Media Studies* 20, no. 1: 104–18. https://doi.org/10.1080/14680777.2018.1550432.

Brockmeier, Jens. 2015. *Beyond the Archive: Memory, Narrative, and the Autobiographical Process.* Oxford: Oxford University Press.

Caracciolo, Marco. 2014. *The Experientiality of Narrative: An Enactivist Approach.* Berlin: de Gruyter.

Caracciolo, Marco. 2017. "Creative Metaphor in Literature." In Semino and Demjén 2017: 206–18.

Caracciolo, Marco, Andrei Ionescu, and Ruben Fransoo. 2019. "Metaphorical Patterns in Anthropocene Fiction." *Language and Literature* 28, no. 3: 221–40.

Dawson, Paul, and Maria Mäkelä. 2020. "The Story Logic of Social Media: Co-construction and Emergent Narrative Authority." *Style* 54, no. 1: 21–35.

Even-Zohar, Itamar, Elias J. Torres Feijó, and Antonio Monegal. 2019. "The End of Literature; or, What Purposes Does It Continue to Serve?" *Poetics Today* 40, no. 1: 7–31.

Fernandes, Sujatha. 2017. *Curated Stories: The Uses and Misuses of Storytelling.* Oxford: Oxford University Press.

Finns Party. 2011. *Suomalaiselle sopivin. Perussuomalaiset r.p:n eduskuntavaaliohjelma 2011.* Finns Party website. www.perussuomalaiset.fi//wp-content/uploads/2013/04/Perussuomalaisten_eduskuntavaaliohjelma_2011.pdf.

Fludernik, Monika. 2011. Introduction to *Beyond Cognitive Metaphor Theory: Perspectives on Literary Metaphor*, edited by Monika Fludernik, 1–16. New York: Routledge.

Garner, Richard. 1990. *From Homer to Tragedy: The Art of Allusion in Greek Poetry.* London: Routledge.

Ging, Debbie. 2019. "Alphas, Betas, and Incels: Theorizing the Masculinities of the Manosphere." *Men and Masculinities* 22, no. 4: 638–57.

Ging, Debbie, and Eugenia Siapera. 2018. Introduction to "Online Misogyny," edited by

Debbie Ging and Eugenia Siapera. Special issue, *Feminist Media Studies* 18, no. 4: 515–24. https://doi.org/10.1080/14680777.2018.1447345.

Goatly, Andrew. 2011. "Conventional Metaphor and the Latent Ideology of Racism." In *Beyond Cognitive Metaphor Theory: Perspectives on Literary Metaphor*, edited by Monika Fludernik, 258–80. New York: Routledge.

Gotell, Lise, and Emily Dutton. 2016. "Sexual Violence in the 'Manosphere': Antifeminist Men's Rights Discourses on Rape." *International Journal for Crime, Justice, and Social Democracy* 5, no. 2: 65–80.

Hebel, Udo J. 1991. "Towards a Descriptive Poetics of *Allusion*." In *Intertextuality*, edited by Heinrich F. Plett, 135–64. Berlin: de Gruyter.

Heritage, Stuart. 2019. "The Wall Is Coming: Trump Becomes World's Worst *Game of Thrones* Fan." *Guardian*, January 9. www.theguardian.com/tv-and-radio/2019/jan/09 /the-wall-is-coming-how-donald-trump-became-the-worlds-worst-game-of-thrones -fan.

Hutchby, Ian. 2001. "Technologies, Texts, and Affordances." *Sociology* 35, no. 2: 441–56.

Hyvärinen, Matti. 2020. "Toward a Theory of Counter-narratives: Narrative Contestation, Cultural Canonicity, and Tellability." In Lueg and Lundholt 2020: 17–29.

Jane, Emma. 2017. "Systemic Misogyny Exposed: Translating Rapeglish from the Manosphere with a Random Rape Threat Generator." *International Journal of Cultural Studies* 21, no. 6: 1–20.

Kelly, Anne. 2017. "The Alt-right: Reactionary Rehabilitation for White Masculinity." *Soundings* 66, no 1: 68–78.

Kristeva, Julia. 1980. "Word, Dialogue, and Novel." Translated by Thomas Gora, Alice Jardine, and Leon S. Roudiez. In *Desire in Language: A Semiotic Approach to Literature and Art*, edited by Leon S. Roudiez, 64–91. New York: Columbia University Press.

Kövecses, Zoltán. 2017. "Conceptual Metaphor Theory." In Semino and Demjén 2017: 13–27.

Lakoff, George, and Mark H. Johnson. 1980. *Metaphors We Live By*. Chicago: University of Chicago Press.

Lueg, Klarissa, and Marianne Wolff Lundholt, eds. 2020. *The Routledge Handbook of Counternarratives*. New York: Routledge.

Levine, Caroline. 2015. *Forms: Whole, Rhythm, Hierarchy, Network*. Princeton, NJ: Princeton University Press.

Lewandowski, Wojciech. 2020. "Intertextuality and the Depiction of Ideological Conflicts: The Case of *V for Vendetta*." *Copernicus Journal of Political Studies* 1, no. 2: 85–100.

Literat, Ioana, and Neta Kligler-Vilenchik. 2019. "Youth Collective Political Expression on Social Media: The Role of Affordances and Memetic Dimensions for Voicing Political Views." *New Media and Society* 21, no. 9: 1988–2009.

López, Canela. 2020. "*The Matrix* Is an Allegory for Being Transgender, According to Director Lilly Wachowski." *Insider*, August 10. www.insider.com/the-matrix-trilogy-is -an-allegory-for-being-transgender-wachowski-2020-8.

Machacek, Gregory. 2007. "Allusion." *PMLA* 122, no. 2: 522–36.

Mäkelä, Maria, Samuli Björninen, Laura Karttunen, Matias Nurminen, Juha Raipola, and Tytti Rantanen. 2021. "Dangers of Narrative: A Critical Approach to Narratives of Personal Experience in Contemporary Story Economy." *Narrative* 29, no. 2: 139–59.

Marwick, Alice E., and Robyn Caplan. 2018. "Drinking Male Tears: Language, the Manosphere, and Networked Harassment." *Feminist Media Studies* 18, no. 4: 543–59.

Marwick, Alice E., and Rebecca Lewis. 2017. *Media Manipulation and Disinformation Online*. Data and Society Research Institute. www.datasociety.net/library/media-manipulation -and-disinfo-online.

Meretoja, Hanna. 2017. "On the Use and Abuse of Narrative for Life: Toward an Ethics of Storytelling." In *Life and Narrative: The Risks and Responsibilities of Storying Experi-

ence, edited by Brian Schiff, A. Elizabeth McKim, and Sylvie Patron, 75–98. Oxford: Oxford University Press.

Meretoja, Hanna. 2018. *The Ethics of Storytelling: Narrative Hermeneutics, History, and the Possible*. Oxford: Oxford University Press.

Meretoja, Hanna. 2020. "A Dialogics of Counter-narratives." In Lueg and Lundholt 2020: 30–42.

Miltner, Kate M. 2017. "Internet Memes." In *The SAGE Handbook of Social Media*, edited by Jean Burgess, Alice E. Marwick, and Thomas Poell, 412–28. Los Angeles: SAGE.

Musolff, Andreas. 2016. "Metaphor and Persuasion in Politics." In Semino and Demjén 2017: 309–22.

Musolff, Andreas. 2019. "Metaphor Framing in Political Discourse." *Mythos-Magazin: Politisches Framing* 1, no. 1: 1–10.

Nagle, Angela. 2017. *Kill All Normies: Online Culture Wars from 4chan and Tumblr to Trump and the Alt-right*. Winchester, UK: Zero Books.

Nguyen, Naomee-Minh. 2021. "'This Is Similar to Vincent Chin': Intertextuality, Referring Expressions, and the Discursive Construction of Asian American Activist Identities in an Online Messaging Community." *Discourse and Society* 32, no. 1: 98–118.

Nissenbaum, Asaf, and Limor Shifman. 2018. "Meme Templates as Expressive Repertoires in Globalizing World: A Cross-Linguistic Study." *Journal of Computer-Mediated Communication* 23, no. 5: 294–310.

Nurminen, Matias. 2019. "Narrative Warfare: The 'Careless' Reinterpretation of Literary Canon in Online Antifeminism." In "Real Fictions: Fictionality, Factuality, and Narrative Strategies in Contemporary Storytelling," edited by Sam Browse, Alison Gibbons, and Mari Hatavara. Special issue, *Narrative Inquiry* 29, no. 2: 312–31.

Nurminen, Matias. 2020. "'The Big Bang of Chaotic Masculine Disruption': A Critical Narrative Analysis of the Radical Masculinity Movement's Counter-narrative Strategies." In Lueg and Lundholt 2020: 351–62.

Page, Ruth E. 2018. *Narratives Online: Shared Stories in Social Media*. Cambridge: Cambridge University Press.

Perri, Carmela. 1978. "On Alluding." *Poetics* 7, no. 3: 289–307.

Pilyarchuk, Kateryna, and Alexander Onysko. 2018. "Conceptual Metaphors in Donald Trump's Political Speeches: Framing His Topics and (Self-)Constructing his Persona." *Colloquium: New Philologies* 3, no. 2: 98–156. https://doi.org/10.23963/cnp.2018.3.2.5.

Presser, Lois. 2018. *Inside Story: How Narratives Drive Mass Harm*. Oakland: University of California Press.

Rao, Sonia. 2020. "How the Red Pill Got to Elon Musk: A Brief Look Back at Public Figures Co-opting *The Matrix*." *Washington Post*, May 18. www.washingtonpost.com /arts-entertainment/2020/05/18/elon-musk-ivanka-trump-matrix-red-pill.

Ricoeur, Paul. 2003. *The Rule of Metaphor*, translated by Robert Czerny, Kathleen McLaughlin, and John Costello. London: Routledge.

Robertson, Derek. 2021. "'The Matrix Resurrections' Tries to Un-Redpill America." *Politico*, December 23. www.politico.com/news/magazine/2021/12/23/matrix-resurrections -review-red-pill-america-526038.

Ryan, Marie-Laure. 2001. *Narrative as Virtual Reality: Immersion and Interactivity in Literature and Electronic Media*. Baltimore, MD: Johns Hopkins University Press.

Salmon, Christian. 2010. *Storytelling: Bewitching the Modern Mind*, translated by David Macey. London: Verso Books.

Sampson, Tony D. 2012. *Virality: Contagion Theory in the Age of Networks*. Minneapolis: University of Minnesota Press.

Semino, Elena. 2008. *Metaphor in Discourse*. Cambridge: Cambridge University Press.

Semino, Elena, and Zsófia Demjén, eds. 2017. *The Routledge Handbook of Metaphor and Language*. New York: Routledge.

Shifman, Limor. 2014. *Memes in Digital Culture.* Cambridge, MA: MIT Press.

Trump, Donald (@realdonaldtrump). 2019. "The Wall Is Coming." Instagram photo, January 3, www.instagram.com/p/BsMBeLbFLxd/.

Vickery, Jacqueline Ryan, and Tracy Everbach. 2018. "The Persistence of Misogyny: From the Streets, to Our Screens, to the White House." In *Mediating Misogyny: Gender, Technology, and Harassment*, edited by Jacqueline Ryan Vickery and Tracy Everbach, 1–27. London: Palgrave Macmillan.

Waśniewska, Małgorzata. 2020. "The Red Pill, Unicorns, and White Knights: Cultural Symbolism and Conceptual Metaphor in the Slang of Online Incel Communities." In *Cultural Conceptualizations in Language and Communication*, edited by Barbara Lewandowska-Tomaszczyk, 65–82. Cham: Springer.

Zinken, Jörg. 2003. "Ideological Imagination: Intertextual and Correlational Metaphors in Political Discourse." *Discourse and Society* 14, no. 4: 507–23.

Zuckerberg, Donna. 2018. *Not All Dead White Men: Classics and Misogyny in the Digital Age.* Cambridge, MA: Harvard University Press.

Social Networking Sites as Contexts for Uses of Narrative: Toward a Story-Critical Approach to Digital Environments

Hanna-Riikka Roine
Tampere University

Laura Piippo
Tampere University

Abstract Narrative theorists have identified the role of social networking sites as elementary in the contemporary story economy. This article argues that they have, however, neglected to treat the sites as part of the digital infraculture which creates blind spots in current analyses of the digital as a context for narrative. The aim is to construct tools for a semiotics of the imperceptible, an approach to analyze the ways in which the digital shapes human agency in dimensions the users cannot directly perceive but which nevertheless affect users' sense of what is possible for them. The article first reevaluates affordance and affect as concepts to demonstrate digital environments as a new type of context for uses of narrative. It then shows how these concepts can be applied to readings of experientiality and narrativity in digital environments which shape users' narrative agency on multiple layers. Finally, the article examines how different agencies on these layers can be analyzed within the wider affective logic of the social networking sites. Finally, the article's findings are summarized as a story-critical approach to digital environments, one

Hanna-Riikka Roine cowrote this article in the context of her postdoctoral project, "Drawing the Possible into the Future: Entanglements of Human and Computer in Speculation," funded by the Academy of Finland (grant no. 333768). Laura Piippo cowrote this article in the context of her postdoctoral project, "The Places, Forms, and Value of a Book (Codex) in Digital Environments," funded by the Finnish Cultural Foundation.

Poetics Today 43:2 (June 2022) DOI 10.1215/03335372-9642651
© 2022 by Porter Institute for Poetics and Semiotics

which accounts for the entanglement of individual agents in collectivities and points the way toward recognizing the ethics of shared responsibility.

Keywords   digital environments, social media, affordance, agency, affect, assemblage

Narrative theorists have identified the role of social networking sites such as Facebook, Instagram, and Twitter as elementary in the contemporary story economy (see Mäkelä and Meretoja, in this issue). So far, existing narratological research on such sites has focused on users as storytellers and "consum[ers] of others" (Fernandes 2017: 2), and thus on narrative as a form and practice for users to share their experiences and connect with each other. This research has focused, for instance, on the sharing of everyday life as stories (Georgakopoulou 2017), on stories produced by multiple tellers and promoting shared attitudes between them (Page 2018), and on the connective logic of broader social media collectives (Dawson and Mäkelä 2020). While these approaches do discuss the ways in which the affordances of these sites may shape "the communicative *how*" of stories told (Georgakopoulou 2017: 312) and do consider stories shared as "mediated by various technological resources used in the contexts of production and reception" (Page 2018: 3), they primarily see the sites as platforms hosting human agents and encouraging or constraining their actions as users. This neglect to treat the sites as digital environments creates blind spots in current theories of online narratives.

Here, we set out to analyze social networking sites as contexts for the uses of narrative. We suggest that because these sites are produced by computation, they differ in nature from contexts that have been studied by narrative theory so far: digital environments do not surround us "like a culture but rather like a kind of *infraculture*" (Lindberg and Roine 2021a: 10).[1] As infraculture, they have formed a new, algorithmically organized base of facilities, services, and installations for social and cultural contexts and also for producing meanings and values. Although such an algorithmic base is often seen simply as an effective structure to organize basic facilities and services, it is rather a sprawling assemblage. It involves not only many forms of human labor and material resources (see Finn 2017: 7), but also a

---

1. Algorithmically organized culture has given rise to concern in numerous fields of research: for instance, "algorithmic governmentality," a term coined by Antoinette Rouvroy and Thomas Berns (2013: X), refers "broadly to a certain type of (a)normative or (a)political rationality founded on the automated collection, aggregation and analysis of big data so as to model, anticipate and preemptively affect possible behaviors." Shoshana Zuboff's (2019) theorization of "surveillance capitalism" then describes how the very application of big data, such as personal data about us collectively, has presented lucrative business opportunities for various actors.

meshwork of agencies, "collectivities through which information, interpretations, and meanings circulate," as N. Katherine Hayles (2021: 37) puts it. While these collectivities do involve a multitude of human agents pursuing different interests, most of the agencies operate on scales beyond human awareness (e.g., satellite-based systems like GPS) and below it (e.g., micro-temporal operations of code). Digital infraculture can thus be described as *environmental* (see Hörl 2018), a term implying not only the ubiquitous presence of digital media in contemporary society, but also the ways in which virtually every aspect of human experience is now entangled in and conditioned by digital technologies.

In this article, we begin the work of conceptualizing narrative theory within digital infraculture. This calls for a reconsideration of some narratological concepts, whose core is still predominantly based on the view of narratives as "passive," human-made artifacts (see Roine 2019: 314) and on an understanding of reading as "strictly derived from book reading" (Andersen, Kjerkegaard, and Pedersen 2021: 139). Digital environments, however, are not book-like artifacts organized through and for human sense perception and experiential memory (see Hansen 2015: 40), but a meshwork of procedural and unfolding agencies. Most of this environment is imperceptible to users, and that which users can perceive is constantly (re) organized, updated, and evolved by the meshwork. Our aim is to construct tools for what one might call a semiotics of the imperceptible, an approach to analyze and account for the ways in which digital environments shape human agency in dimensions human users cannot directly perceive but which nevertheless affect users' sense of who they are and what is possible for them. The fact that human actions such as reading, writing, telling, and sharing occur within assemblages whose effects cannot be located in any singular object or agent makes it quite complex for users to imagine the potential consequences of their actions, especially in a narrative dimension, which is at play both in processes of self-interpretation and more broadly as "a constitutive aspect of moral agency" (Meretoja 2018: 11).[2] The understanding that is required from narrative theorists cannot be limited to the practicalities of how, for instance, reading works in the digital age, but must be extended to the *literacy* of complex technologies and our entanglement with them (see Bridle 2018: 8).

---

2. Assemblage is how *agencement* is usually translated in Gilles Deleuze and Félix Guattari's (1987) work *A Thousand Plateaus*: for them, it connotes a kind of agency without individual actors, a flow that temporarily creates a provisional and highly flexible arrangement capable of agency. Hayles's (2017) discussion of digital, cognitive assemblages differs from Deleuze and Guattari's in describing connections through which information flows as technically precise and often knowable.

In what follows, we first reevaluate the concepts of affordance and affect in the framework of relational materialism in order to be able to both demonstrate and analyze digital environments as a new type of context for uses of narrative. We then show how these concepts can be applied to readings of experientiality and narrativity in digital environments, and focus on the ways in which the entanglement in the assemblages shapes users' narrative agency on multiple layers. We move on to examine how the intersecting and conflicting agencies on these layers can be analyzed in relation to the wider affective logic of the social networking sites. Throughout our discussion, we take up examples that draw out the dangers in narrowing the focus of narratological analysis on human intentional action and, instead, put forward ways to locate the traces of the imperceptible through empirical analyses of social media content as well as (para)textual marks left by a site itself. Finally, we summarize our findings as a story-critical approach to digital environments, one which accounts for the entanglement of individual agents in collectivities and points the way toward recognizing the ethics of shared responsibility.

From Fixed to Relational: Affordance and Affect

We first sketch out the nature of digital environments as fundamentally different from the more traditional understanding of the contexts for uses of narrative. As meshworks, they should be seen as *relational*: as the core principle of relational materialism has it, "objects are no mere props for performance but parts and parcel of hybrid assemblages endowed with diffused personhood and relational agency" (Vannini 2015: 5). Taina Bucher (2018: 5) continues this idea to note that as the concepts such as sociotechnical and sociomateriality express, human and nonhuman actors (or the "social" and "technical") are seen as composite entities whose enactive powers cannot merely be reduced to their constituent parts. From this point of view, we argue that narrative theorists should review critically their current emphasis on activity *by* humans and perceptible *to* humans at the expense of the imperceptible and nonhuman.[3] In existing narratological analysis, agency, understood here as the capacity to act with effectivity (Raipola 2019: 263), is seen as the property of discrete human subjects instead of being distributed, including "interplays between complex cognitive components, the

---

3. The emphasis on the human individual has recently been challenged, for instance, by material ecocriticism and its focus on the capacity of nonhuman matter to participate in the construction of stories (see Raipola 2019), as well as by econarratology, with its approach to the "pairing" of narrative and the environment (see James and Morel 2020).

information they can and cannot access, the constraints on their actions, and resultant actions that the assemblage as a whole will enact" (Hayles 2021: 39). These passive characteristics are then shown to affect, sometimes in an almost deterministic sense, how humans tell and share their stories as well as how these stories are read and perhaps shared again. The focus of narrative theorists, described by Maria Mäkelä (2021: 52) as "not specializing in algorithms but narrative structure and its uses," can be described, on the one hand, as upholding an illusion about how digital technologies function, but, on the other, as being deliberately limited to the examination of that illusion: the illusion of narrative structure and its uses being a territory of intentional human agents only.[4] We now begin to unpack this illusion for the purposes of a story-critical approach through reevaluating the key concepts of affordance and affect.

Adopting a relational approach to the concept of affordance offers a useful way for narrative theorists to understand digital environments as contexts where a human subject or even a collective of such subjects is not alone in producing meanings, values, and interpretations. Current literary studies of affordances notably lack relationality: among the most influential ones, Caroline Levine's (2015: 6) *Forms* defines affordance as "a term used to describe potential uses or actions latent in materials or designs." Her interest is thus restricted to "the ways that affordance allows us to think about both constraint and capability—that is, what actions or thoughts are made possible or impossible by the fact of a form" (152). Levine rather straightforwardly follows Donald Norman's approach to affordance that has increasingly been applied to digital artifacts and objects too. Norman (1999: 39) contends that objects should be designed to indicate how a user is to interact with them: a user cannot act upon an affordance if it cannot be perceived, and thus, "all affordances are 'perceived affordances.'" This lies in stark contrast with James J. Gibson's (1979: 129) original idea of the affordance that "cuts across the dichotomy of subjective-objective" and "points both ways, to the environment and to the observer." For Gibson, then, affordance emerges in relational constellations of environment and agent, while Norman focuses on the designer who, through design choices, can enable or constrain certain possibilities for action (Scarlett and Zeilinger 2019: 12; Bucher and Helmond 2017: 236).

Lacking relationality, Levine's approach as well as those following her come to describe both forms and their affordances as fixed, despite Levine's (2015: 7) notion that the "meanings and values" of a pattern or shape may

---

4. Mäkelä uses the expression herself, arguing that "contemporary narrative didacticism is based on the *illusion* of immediate, personal experience" (57; emphasis added).

change as they travel and that "specific contexts . . . matter."[5] Moreover, this approach dismisses the importance of the environment. Peter Nagy and Gina Neff (2015: 2) illustrate this in the framework of communication theory: they argue that the affordance concept typically refers "to what users and their sociality get from a technology," and thus the technologies and their design (along with the black boxes, the algorithms, the automatic) is ignored. Their concept of "imagined" affordances attempts to describe the ways in which what people believe and expect technologies to be able to do shapes "how they approach them and what actions they think are suggested" (4). In this sense, the actions and thoughts enabled by the affordances arise both from a specific environment and from the user. If narrative is understood as a form that is used, instrument-like, within a context of social networking sites, we must account for both users' perceptions of the digital technologies as well as the ways in which these perceptions are shaped.

Building on Gibson's original conception, where affordances exist independently within the environment but nevertheless cannot materialize without human interaction, we suggest that the built-in assumption of the centrality of *human intention* in most accounts of the affordance concept must be reevaluated.[6] Following Nancy Ettlinger's (2018: 3) discussion of the intersection between affordance and algorithm, we want to emphasize that as contexts for human behavior, digital environments "encompass a diverse assemblage of both animate and inanimate actors," and they thus actively adapt to human behavior. Although technologies since the invention of writing have shaped our thinking, digital technologies engage in what Ed Finn (2017: 55) has called "a mutual hermeneutic pro-

---

5. The fixedness is partly due to Levine's tendency to evoke the affordance perspective to describe phenomena that more closely reflect *a feature* of a form or *an outcome* of an affordance (see Evans et al. 2017). As an example of the latter, Levine (2015: 6) suggests that narratives "afford the connection of events over time," which surely is an outcome of the affordance of sequentiality.
6. Understanding affordances as relational instead of perceived has always allowed thinking of them as independent of human perception. William Gaver's (1991: 80) concept of technology affordances, for instance, suggests that affordances can be both perceptible and hidden—put in simple terms, "a cat-door affords passage to a cat but not to me." Furthermore, the concept of communicative affordance promoted by sociologist Ian Hutchby (2001: 30) has similarly attempted to find a "third way" between technological determinism and social constructivism, defining affordances as "possibilities for action that emerge from . . . given technological forms." The communicative affordance concept emphasizes that affordances are both functional and relational: functional "in the sense that they are enabling, as well as constraining," and relational in terms of drawing "attention to the way that the affordances of an object may be different for one species than for another" (Hutchby and Barnett 2015: 151).

cess."[7] Digital environments are not only surrounding contexts for users' interpretations and acts of sense-making, but also interpret and make sense of the users, and as such participate in constituting the users as subjects and anticipate what they desire when they use forms such as narrative. The loop constantly tightens: what users believe, expect, and desire to follow from "telling a story" in social networking sites shapes their behavior, and this behavior is bolstered by the sites themselves, influencing what, in turn, becomes the object of the users' desire (see also Kangaskoski 2021: 94). From the perspective of users, this loop mostly occurs beneath human consciousness or is even inaccessible to it, remaining on the level of non-conscious cognition (Hayles 2017: 27). This is an important insight for our analysis, as invisibility can be seen as one of the key affordances of digital technologies in general.[8]

This invisibility as well as the capacity to change in consequence of an encounter also characterize the digital as affective environments. Although affects are often connected to easily distinguishable emotions or their manifestations that spread virally through the network in the form of, for instance, a meme (see Payne 2018: 282), they should not be confused with feelings of the lived body. Rather, affects should be seen as that which permits feelings to be felt. In Zizi Papacharissi's (2015: 21) terms, affect can be thought of as the movement—such as the "rhythm of our pace as we walk"—that may lead to a particular feeling. While Papacharissi's approach focuses on human activity and the emergent structures of feeling on social networking sites (such as collective discourses organized around hashtags on Twitter), we want to shift the discussion toward the coexistence of human and non-human agents. Bucher (2018: 116) points out that while we cannot "ask the algorithm about its capacity to affect and be affected," it is important to understand "the affective encounters that people have with algorithms not as isolated events that are somehow outside the algorithm but as part of the same mode of existence." Following Claire Colebrook (2014), we see affect as creating a relation between two bodies, each affecting and being affected by the other. This way, we may

7. Meretoja's discussion of narrative agency provides another way of thinking about such a hermeneutic process. She writes that "culturally mediated narrative (self-)interpretations take part in constituting us as subjects capable of action, while simultaneously recognizing that as agents of narrative interpretation we are both constituting and constituted" (Meretoja 2018: 12).

8. Ingrid Hoetzl and Rémi Marie (2015: 101), for instance, argue that invisibility is in many ways that which facilitates the collection, surveillance, and commoditization of user data, while Wendy Hui Kyong Chun (2011: 2) has even argued that software embodies "a powerful metaphor for everything we believe is invisible yet generates visible effects, from genetics to the invisible hand of the market, from ideology to culture."

better understand not only the ways in which algorithms learn and adapt to their surroundings through encounters with users, but also how they may become generative of the user's sense of agency. Framing all affective commotion on social networking sites as of human origin (which is often seen in the media coverage of Twitter, for instance) thus hides the complexity of digital environments as meshworks.

Articulating the concept of affect as a relation of affecting and being affected provides a precise way of thinking about the nonconscious loop between users and algorithm-based environments, or the invisible creating visible effects. It helps theorists understand the relations between people and algorithms as *recursive*: as Bucher (2018: 115–16) explains, users' movements or reactions (such as commenting more frequently on some of their friends' posts to support their visibility, or emphasizing positively charged words) are not just affected by the algorithms, but these practices also have the ability to affect the very algorithms that helped generate these responses in the first place. Understanding this is important for narrative theorists, as such recursivity is also at play in narrativizations of all sorts of commotion on the social networking sites, in making sense of the commotion by means of a narrative form. Although concepts such as "viral exemplum" (e.g., Mäkelä 2019a, 2019b) and "emergent storytelling" (Dawson and Mäkelä 2020) are useful tools for examining the ways in which such narrativizations may be placed within wider social and cultural contexts, they do not account for the fact that the majority of content users interpret as stories on these sites are generated according to principles that are "anything but organic" (Payne 2018: 287; see also Roine and Piippo 2021: 63). Alexandra Georgakopoulou (2017: 327) takes steps toward analyzing this side of digital environments in her discussion of story facilities such as Instagram Stories, noticing the "branding and rhetoric of 'stories' as an app feature" and thus arguing that stories, "however small, are an algorithmically preferred participation mode in terms of hallmarks of the participatory subject" (329). In our view, Georgakopoulou's observation of stories as "app features" is important, as it draws out the very basic sense in which the algorithms can create "the force of movement" (Bucher 2018: 99), prompting the users to react—also emotionally—in a manner preferred by the algorithms.

In order to become aware of the users' coexistence with agents that are anything but organic, narrative theorists should not merely focus on the surface layer that is readily offered to human perception, but also attempt to analyze the ways in which narrative is used in calling a "participatory subject" into being by the dynamics of the meshwork. This way, it becomes possible to examine the ways in which different subject positions for nar-rativizing both content and commotion emerge as well as the possibilities and limits such positions involve in terms of narrative agency. Further-more, we argue that while mediated experientiality as the basis of nar-rative sense-making in the sense theorized by Monika Fludernik (1996) is still valid, its emergence as situated in the lived or imagined experience of an individual must be reevaluated. In our view, experientiality on social networking sites is relational as well, born out of the ways in which the digital environments, constantly adapting to users, make it possible for humans to make sense of the content as being rooted in human experience despite being produced, organized, and framed by a meshwork of human and nonhuman agencies. To get a grip on how a sense of experientiality emerges from the assemblic relation of a user and an environment and how commotion both small and site-wide gets narrativized, narrative theorists must break the illusionary or imagined quality of content as originating from human actions only.

Recognizing the relationality of affordances—that they are not merely qualities or features but depend on the interaction between agents and their environments—points the way toward grasping digital environments as meshworks. Instead of being a "passive" context surrounding human activity, the digital offers a multitude of possibilities to act with effectivity for agents such as algorithms. Furthermore, a similarly relational under-standing of affects helps us to open up the ways in which such a meshwork contributes to an emergence of different subject positions as well as expe-rientiality despite not following the logic of intentional human action. As a result, we are better equipped for our next step, the analysis of digital environments as multilayered, as a way for narrative theory to account for "the myriad visible and nonvisible mechanisms making content available and guiding interpretations of it, human and nonhuman" (Mäkelä 2021: 53). Our story-critical method unravels loops and entanglements of digital environments for analytical purposes: first, we discuss how these environ-ments' nature as contexts operating on both perceptible and imperceptible scales shapes and determines uses of narrative, and second, we focus on the intersecting and sometimes conflicting agencies and interests that function on these scales.

Analyzing the Scales and Layers of Digital Environments

Although quite a few aspects of digital technology operate outside the users' view, beneath the surface, these imperceptible layers affect what users perceive in a manner that is much more fundamental in nature than the loop that always exists between the surfaces of literary artifacts and readers.[9] Being recursive, this logic, in turn, affects what users consider desirable or valuable as well as how they understand the possibilities and limits of their conscious actions, such as communicating their experiences to others in narrative form. The relationship of the surface to other layers of the digital environment can be understood through the three scales suggested by Sy Taffel (2019: 14): content, software, and hardware, which "are not distinct and separable layers, but entangled meshworks that cannot be functionally isolated from one another." Of these three, only content can be directly perceived by human users through interfaces. The other two include various imperceptible dimensions of computation, all of which have their own affordances that unfold and come into existence through processual operations despite being hidden from human users. As we argued above, the affordances of the digital should thus be seen not only through the formal opportunities and constraints users identify in the environment, but also through the environment adapting to the users' behavior.

The classic distinction between story (*fabula*, content) and discourse (*sujet*, form), called by James Phelan (2011: 58) "the mother's milk of narratology," is an illustrative example of how narratological analyses are limited to the surface for two reasons.[10] First, despite being analytical, this distinction has often resulted in the understanding of story as the intended or natural course of the events "behind" the representation. Such an understanding, then, has caused confusion in the discussions of narratives in digital artifacts, as they can be actively navigated and manipulated by the user, resulting in various different courses of events.[11] This problem, concerning the understanding of narrative based on explicitly stated causal relations, has been addressed, for instance, by Richard Walsh (2007: 66), who sug-

9. Previous theorizations of this loop in the context of digital media include Espen Aarseth's (1997) notion of *textual dynamics* and Lev Manovich's (2001) concept of *transcoding*. Both of them acknowledge the fact that the sides of this loop are not distinct, but separating them from each other for analytical purposes can help us understand it.
10. The approach to storytelling on social media platforms as "quantified," focusing on the ways in which storytelling intertwines with the "measurement regime" of social media (Georgakopoulou, Iversen, and Stage 2020: 19), is one recent, welcome example of the expansion of narratology from this previous limitation.
11. Gameplay and stories were seen as a complicated combination especially by the so-called ludologists, who argued quite forcefully that digital games in particular display a unique formalism that defines them as a different genre from narrative, drama, and poetry (e.g., Eskelinen 2001). Thus, they argued that the "proper" analysis of games must focus on the analysis of their formal qualities, such as their rules. Perhaps the great emphasis on these qualities led ludologists to form an alliance with classical narratology in viewing narrative as a mode of presentation defined by certain textual features. See Roine 2016: 69.

gests that the story is rather a function of interpretation than a reconstruc-
tion of the author's "original" story that serves as the basis for the selec-
tions and arrangements of the realized discourse (see also Roine 2016).
Second, and more importantly for the purposes of this article, the distinction between story (or the "what" of narrative) and discourse (or the "how"
of narrative) is more than shaky in digital environments. If the "what" is
understood as a function of human interpretation, how should one discuss
algorithm-based environments where the "how" adapts to the "what," first
beginning to anticipate it and finally even predetermining it? The question
is further complicated by the inaccessibility of the algorithmic operations
to human users. We must thus account for the fact that while it is possible
to access the narratives partly emerging from the ways in which algorithms
affect human users and prompt them to certain directions, it is impossible
to access everything that shapes and informs these narratives. In what follows, we sketch out a framework for approaching the loop between users'
actions and the adaptable environment through the analysis of the digital
as not only functioning on different scales (content, software, hardware) but
also being available to users through multiple, entangled layers.

In terms of scales, the digital is always based on hardware of some sort,
which from the users' perspective means *a device or technology*, such as a
mobile phone or laptop. The content, in turn, is instantiated and generated
on digital *platforms* which are software, making use of the aforementioned
technologies. Social media platforms owned by big tech companies such as
Google and Facebook are illustrative examples of these platforms, which are
then available to end users through another layer of software, the (usually
graphic) user *interfaces*.[12] In everyday language and use, platform and interface often merge, although interface—in other words, everything through
which the user accesses different and differently organized content—
is not all that a platform includes. Platforms can rather be understood as
environments where certain algorithms function or where their logic is
valid, including their own affordances for various agents. As an interesting
comparison, a printed book (or a codex), the previously dominant object
of narratological research, is both a technology and interface of literature,
but in the codex these layers have blended together so deeply that it is difficult to separate one from another. Furthermore, there is no platform to
be distinguished in the sense of a distribution channel of content, as the

---

12. For the sake of brevity, we focus here on the layers of content and software, but it is
important to keep in mind that hardware has its own affordances that enable and constrain
user action and also shape the layers of content and software. For more on the layer of hardware, see, e.g., Kirschenbaum 2012.

"software" of the codex has seamlessly merged with the "hardware." This, by contrast, illustrates the dynamic nature of digital objects.[13] In a printed book, the text remains static regardless of the acts of reading or interpretation it encounters.

Interface is often used as an analytical tool to open up the dynamic or loop between the perceptible "surface" and those operations that lie hidden beneath it. The digital interface can simply be understood as the point of interaction between the components of hardware and software. Lori Emerson (2014: x) describes it even more expansively as a "threshold" or "the point of transition between different mediatic layers within any nested system," suggesting that it functions as a mediator between the user and the surface-layer, human-authored writing as well as, in the case of digital devices, the imperceptible machine- or algorithm-based writing. For Emerson, what is new about digital interfaces is not that they create and limit creative possibilities, but that both the interfaces and their affordances have become more and more difficult to perceive—or, as Alexander Galloway (2012: 25) argues, the nature of the interfaces as a threshold has become more and more invisible and thus more inoperable to the users. The invisibility of interfaces is one of the consequences of digital environmentality, but at the same time, their imperceptibility results from a conscious work in design, where the aim has been to create user interfaces that do not call attention to themselves, but "let us direct our attention to the task" (Murray 2011: 10).

The ways in which interfaces as well as platforms "direct our attention" should be made visible also in the narratological analysis. We mean "attention" here in the sense suggested by Bucher (2012: 1–2): not as a type of human spectatorship, but rather as a mode of participation governed by technical rationalities, realized in the automated, anticipatory, and personalized aspects of platforms such as Facebook or Twitter. The task especially suited for narrative theory is to isolate and analyze what one could call the "voice" of the platform: human users create, read, and share content as entangled with the cascading agencies encompassed by the digital environment. This also connects platforms and various agents on it with affective relations—affections—that make up the assemblages where information, interpretations, and meanings circulate (see Hayles 2021: 37). It is precisely the affections produced by the sense of this assemblic coex-

---

13. In Aarseth's (1997: 62) terms, both the *textons* and *scriptons* of a text can respond to a user's interactions with it. Scriptons refer to the "string of signs" constituting the text as "they appear to readers"—for instance, on a screen—and textons "as they exist in the text, since these may not always be the same."

istence and cocreation that determine which affordances of the platform emerge as affordable, usable, or desirable from the users' point of view, since they are always perceived through this affective experience. Emerson's (2014: 163–64) concept of *reading-writing* describes the imperceptible feedback loop between user and environment in terms of blurring between reading and writing, the practice of writing through the network, which as it tracks, indexes, and algorithmizes every click and every bit of text users enter, constantly reads their writing and writes their reading. Matti Kangaskoski (2021) has similarly discussed the "automatization" of literature in digital cultural interfaces where quick, affective signaling about what users desire has started to resemble an almost automatic reaction to stimuli. The idea of automatization aptly captures the ways in which digital environments adapt to users' actions, the scale of software remaining under the scope of users' conscious perception and blending in with the scale of content. On social networking sites, the constant organizing, reframing, and recycling of content, based on the algorithmic infrastructure underlying it, controls the ways in which users make sense of the "what," thus directing their attention in specific ways.

An illustrative example of interfaces and platforms directing the ways in which users make sense of the "what" is provided by Kristen Roupenian's fictional short story "Cat Person," published on the website of the *New Yorker*, a story which dominated social media feeds at the end of 2017 in a way that pieces of fiction rarely do. Most of the story focuses on a miserable sexual encounter from the perspective of Margot, a twenty-year-old college sophomore, who realizes too late that she would rather not have sex at all with Robert, a man fifteen years her senior. In their social media shares, quite a few readers associated "Cat Person" with a personal essay and viewed it as weighing in on a timely issue, most obviously the #MeToo movement. As a result, despite not being structurally, rhetorically, or ideologically unambiguous in the sense that content favored by social networking sites typically is (see Mäkelä 2019b: 459), "Cat Person" was quickly being received and shared as such content. Robert is not simply presented as "a bad guy" although he ends up sending bitter and poisonous texts to Margot toward the end of the story; Margot is shown to happily get on with her life; and there are no clear moral guidelines given. Still, the afterlife following the publication of "Cat Person" was bent on transforming it, in Mäkelä's (2018: 184) terms, into the form of an exemplum, a story asking everyone in its audience to be convinced by its maxim through emulating the protagonist's righteous affective responses, or to avoid the protagonist's moral failure. In a more confusing twist, a smaller but still significant portion of readers not only associated the story with a personal essay, but outright mistook it to be "a piping hot thinkpiece" (Miller 2017) and framed it as such when discussing it.

In our view, the case of Roupenian's story being "transformed" into an exemplum and giving rise to "unsolicited narrative effects" (Mäkelä et al. 2021: 154) demonstrates the ways in which social media users' perception of content, or their attention in the sense of a mode of participation, is entangled in the rationalities of the platform. These rationalities are materialized in the platform's affordances, which, for their part, direct the users' perception of what the uses of narratives such as "Cat Person" can and should be. This directing, in turn, shapes the users' understanding of the affordances of narrative in these environments: in the case of the afterlife of "Cat Person," the most valuable affordance can be perceived as universality—as unifying people through evoking shared human emotions, myths, cultural reference points, and values. This is clearly visible in the ways the short story was used: it enabled users sharing it to appeal to it as a shared, representative example of contemporary dating culture, and its moral ambiguity (perhaps the most "valuable" aspect of it in terms of literary aesthetics) was turned into an example of "how men (or women) are." In other words, the users' mode of participation was directed toward a subject position which allowed the users to make sense of the "what" of "Cat Person" in a manner that was deemed favorable, valuable, or desirable by the platforms.

For narrative theorists, it is crucial to pay attention to the fact that since digital environments as contexts for uses of narrative are algorithm-based, what is valuable or desirable in content is not determined only through social or cultural value systems (such as what is true or provable, as opposed to what is not). Instead, valuability and desirability are governed by that which engages or attracts users, or creates affective commotion, and this commotion is bolstered through the environment adapting in order to increase engagement or traffic. It is noteworthy that although "Cat Person" was published both in the printed and digital versions of an esteemed magazine, it largely gained its reputation through the social media shares and likes which tied it with other linked online phenomena such as the aforementioned #MeToo movement. In this side of the circulation of publications, as certain uses of narrative (or narratives in general) increase engagement, the possibilities for users to create and interpret content in this form increase correspondingly. This can be observed further in the ways in which "Cat Person," to a degree, lost its fictionality, as in digital environments no special value is bestowed upon originality. When a media text or other such content is shared, its "original point" can easily be ignored at the expense of more desirable uses, and the reframings and recontextualizations are equally persistent and exist within the same environment as the original text.[14] The relevance or value of the original is made even more inconsequential by the replicability of digital content: made out of bits, it can be duplicated, and there is thus no way to differentiate the original bit from its duplicate when content is, for instance, copied and pasted (see boyd 2011: 47).

The erosion of the relevance of the original demonstrates the quality of social networking sites as environments where the author of a text, image, or other content cannot control its afterlife, which may consist of reframing and reuse (see Mäkelä 2019b: 460). This also applies to the ways in which content such as "Cat Person" produce ambiguous and complex affections, which are then reshaped, streamlined, and flattened in social media circulation. In our view, such a development as well as the exponential growth in stories geared toward unifying people cannot be situated only within the "omnipresent urge to tell and share experiential stories" (Mäkelä et al. 2021: 142), but also within the digital platforms directing and conditioning users' modes of participation. Focusing on the universal and sometimes "dangerous" appeal of stories keeps social networking sites out of sight as adaptable to users' actions, bolstering content and the ways in which it can be used and reused according to the amount of affective commotion they create. Although algorithms do not dictate users' behavior in the sense of technological determinism, they shape an environment in which certain subject positions—such as the one from which to make sense of "the what" as experience-based—are made more real and available to users (see Bucher 2018: 156).

A story-critical approach to digital environments must attempt to analyze both the ways in which such positions emerge and the ways in which some positions become dominant at the expense of others. Understanding these environments as contexts that are based on the logic of algorithms instead of human value systems thus helps us to follow how the abstract rationalities of digital platforms may be concretized in interpretations of works of fiction such as Roupenian's short story. Being able to follow such rationalities may, furthermore, enable the human users to better understand the nature of their entanglement within the assemblage. As the digital value systems are implemented by numerous agents operating on

14. Persistence is one of the platform affordances originally discussed by danah boyd (2011: 46): in brief, it means that as online expressions are, by default, recorded and archived, what remains may lose its essence when consumed outside of the context in which it was created. It is also one contributor to the collapse of contexts, the lack of spatial, social, and temporal boundaries in digital environments that makes it difficult to maintain distinct social contexts (49).

both perceptible and imperceptible scales of digital environments, in the remainder of our article we attempt to draw out their functioning as well as their intersecting and conflicting nature.

Agencies and Interests

Besides individual users making sense of "the what" on social networking sites, journalists as well as other "influencers" mentioned by Mäkelä and Meretoja in their introduction play an important role in guiding and shaping our perception of the commotion on social networking sites. Such sense-making is often part of contemporary journalistic storytelling, and it typically focuses on narrativizing the surface-layer phenomena of digital environments while ignoring their wider affective logic and nonhuman agencies. In narrative theory, a similar emphasis can be seen in discussions of social networking sites such as Twitter enabling and facilitating "narrative interpretation" (Sadler 2018: 3272) as well as producing "new narrative phenomena" (Dawson and Mäkelä 2020: 21). We suggest, however, that while social networking sites such as Twitter can be described as mediators, they do not simply mediate between human users and content. Taina Bucher and Anne Helmond (2017: 244) note that as platforms, social networking sites are characterized by the combination of their nature "as programmable and extendable infrastructures, and their economic model of connecting end-users to advertisers." Twitter, for instance, affords different things to different user types, which are predefined by addressing them through distinct interfaces, including the end-user interfaces and various application programming interfaces for developers, advertisers, and researchers alike (246). Following this, social networking sites must be recognized as diverse assemblages drawing together and negotiating between different groups and individuals, all of which have their own goals and agendas (243; see also Gillespie 2010; Gerlitz 2016). Furthermore, while their possibilities to act with effectivity differ from group to group significantly, these differences in agency are not only based on their social or cultural prominence, but also the fact that they are situated on different scales of the digital.

In this final section of our article, we argue that to understand the ways in which the surface comes to be narrativized both by individual users and various "influencers," narrative theorists must account for the actions, affections, and associations related to social networking sites. In other words, while it is interesting to examine the ways in which users are able to "read Twitter as narrative" (Sadler 2018: 3268), it is even more pressing to consider what a reading of this sort ignores. The most fundamental of the agencies are hidden to human users, those that make use of the selection of affordances "enacted within the algorithmic underbelly of digital computation" (Scarlett and Zeilinger 2019: 6). In addition to this, as most sites are owned by big tech companies such as Google, Amazon, and Facebook, there are powerful economic interests and the guidance of human end users toward a more profitable direction for the companies involved, such as gearing toward systematic collection, algorithmic processing, circulation, and monetization of user data (van Dijck, Poell, and de Waal 2018: 4; see also Srnicek 2017).[15] While it is important to bear in mind that the interests of different agents are not always explicit or voiced openly—and are therefore an object of speculation in some respects—theorists can still identify interests of different kinds intersecting on the sites, shaping both content and the ways in which it is engaged with.

Media scholars Elena Pilipets and Susanna Paasonen (2020) have shown the usefulness of identifying different kinds of interests in their thorough analysis of the user critiques of nonhuman, algorithmic interventions in Tumblr subcultures, addressing the relational, networked, and affective qualities of the critique. Tumblr, a social networking site, algorithmically implemented a blanket ban on all "adult content" in 2018, shortly after their app was removed from the Apple App Store—an action which is widely regarded as gatekeeping and content-policing and which demonstrates the fundamental differences in sizes of agency. Prior to the ban, Tumblr had developed into a relatively safe and user-friendly space for sexual and gender minorities to come together and, for instance, create and share sexually explicit content (such as visual fan fiction), which was not possible on other sites. The ban, however, effectively meant that material produced by these minorities and their communities was, more often than not, removed. In other words, human users, acting on the scale of content, found their possibilities to act severely restricted while the restrictions themselves were implemented on the scale of software through the means of algorithms. This sparked criticism both on and off the site and highlighted the fact that while the algorithms in question were directed by human designers in the form of coded instructions, the scale of the algorithmic functioning allowed unanticipated effects to emerge. These effects included the way in which Tumblr's ban fell on specific minorities and communities as well as on content that was mislabeled as sexually explicit.

15. Alexandra Georgakopoulou, Stefan Iversen, and Karsten Stage (2020: 5–6) analyze in depth the various new ways in which storytelling on social media platforms is currently being "metricized" and "quantified," and pay attention to, for instance, the opaque nature of metrics that make it possible to "measure and count how often, for how long, and in what order and in what location communication takes place."

In our view, Pilipets and Paasonen's experimental approach, built on visual and digital methods, illuminates three key aspects of digital environments as diverse assemblages in terms of intersecting and conflicting interests. They focus on drawing out "networked resistance" on Tumblr through: (1) examining the embeddedness of the networks of visual and textual associations in "the attentional dynamics of commenting, tagging, and receiving notes, as afforded by the platform"; (2) analyzing their situated relevance by looking at how users repurpose this textual and visual material; and (3) looking into the ways in which platforms filter and circulate this material to highlight shifts "in relations of relevance that shape the communicative and affective dynamics of social media" (Pilipets and Paasonen 2020: 3). In what follows, we use Pilipets and Paasonen's empirical analysis of social media content to identify key aspects of various intersecting and conflicting interests for narrative theory: experienced locatability, situated relevance, and the algorithmic framing and circulation of content. These aspects have remained a blind spot for narrative theory, although it has, more often than not, exceled in perceiving the structures of its objects of research clearly.

For narratologists attempting to analyze the role of different interests underlying the narrativized surface, resisting or creative uses of platform affordances are good places to turn to. One illustrative example is provided by the (mis)use of the check-in feature of Facebook, designed to share one's presence in a certain physical location, such as a restaurant or museum. The feature thus makes use of the affordance of *locatability*, a condition originally enabled by mobile technologies (Schrock 2015: 1235). In late 2016, over one million people checked in to the location of the Standing Rock Indian Reservation on Facebook. This was a response to a viral Facebook post claiming that this action would help the activists in North Dakota protesting against an oil pipeline. It was claimed that the police would monitor the activists through their digital presence (again making use of the affordance of locatability) and that checking in would hinder the cyber surveillance of the area. The digital support of the protest received wide media coverage and thus also contributed to the media exposure of the on-site demonstration, but also sparked criticism of cyber activism for a lack of commitment and participation. Furthermore, it remains unclear whether the check-in protest actually had any effect on the actual cyber surveillance on-site, or if it was just slightly misguided speculation on police tactics and the functions of the Facebook site.

What is interesting from our perspective, however, is the way in which different interests and subject positions for making sense of the protests at Standing Rock both emerge and entangle in the affordance of locatability. Andrew Schrock (2015: 1238), too, notes that individuals interpret the affordance of locatability more heterogeneously than an industry-sponsored vision, and concludes that this affordance "can be leveraged in a wide variety of ways." Furthermore, since any type of commotion on the platform fuels the economy of social networking sites that operate with user data, it is more profitable for the site—also in a financial sense—to afford and allow various simultaneous usages than to restrict them (cf. Gerlitz 2016; Pilipets and Paasonen 2020). In the case of Standing Rock, it is possible to identify a number of different ways of leveraging locatability, aligning with partially conflicting interests: those of the on-site protesters and their online supporters, those that were supposed to be the interests of the police, those of the press, and those of the pipeline company. Apart from these more or less obvious interests, there are also the underlying agencies and interests of, for example, the software developers and programmers.

All of the interests listed above are in some way present on the surface-layer phenomena, in the forms of content shared and actions performed on the site, and their presence is what a story-critical approach to digital environments attempts to make visible. For narrative theory, unraveling all interests and associated agencies from one another is, of course, an impossible task, but an aspect it can address is *the experienced locatability*, emerging from the transactions between users and the sites. The tendency of the surface-layer narrativizations by both individual users and influencers to flatten the commotion of different agencies and interests into an experience of an individual or a clearly defined group is fed by the sites constantly adapting, hiding the ways in which experientiality arises from the assemblic relation of a user and an environment. Theorists must consider what kind of subject (or subject position) is produced, and thus analytically separate a user's experience of the site, its platform, and the interface from, for instance, the (supposed) on-site experiences. In other words, narrative theorists should not only point out that as content to be reframed, copied, and pasted, narratives "will be susceptible to multiple uses and abuses, interpretations and reinterpretations" (Mäkelä et al. 2021: 146), but also examine the conditions set by social networking sites as assemblages to the production and circulation of information, interpretations, and meanings. As Pilipets and Paasonen (2020: 17) argue, networked contributions (such as images in their analysis of Tumblr) are "at once machinic, affective, cognitive, and somatic," and thus they "rearrange themselves around and contribute to novel pathways of experience." Instead of narratives, it is the agencies that are in contest (cf. Phelan 2008)—or perhaps different positions for narrativizing content at the expense of other positions. The ways in which they emerge and gain dominance over others should be seen through the wider affective logic of the sites.

Another, partly opposite yet similar example of the intersecting and conflicting interests is the ways in which the affordance of *searchability* enabled by, for instance, hashtags was put to different and sometimes resisting uses during the Black Lives Matter protests in 2020. In brief, searchability points out that content on social networking sites can be accessed through search, thus radically reworking the ways in which information is received compared to previous forms of media (boyd 2011: 46, 48). The widespread protest started after George Floyd, a Black man from Minneapolis, was murdered by a white police officer. The hashtag #blacklivesmatter soon became a hub of intersecting interests, exemplifying the ways in which the shifting dynamics of the digital assemblage call users into being through circulating and reacting to online material, as suggested by Robert Payne (2018: 286). This hashtag became not only a rallying cry for the protests, but also a site of sharing on-site information on the protests between the activists as well as a gesture of solidarity for internet users all over the world.

In their discussion of emergent storytelling and the #MeToo movement, Paul Dawson and Maria Mäkelä (2020: 26) suggest approaching hashtags as a rhetorical resource: "the emergent subject" called into being by #MeToo or #blacklivesmatter could thus be seen as allowing individual users to "rely upon the connective logic of social media to give narrative shape to their own shared stories." In other words, while Dawson and Mäkelä acknowledge the subject position as produced by and as a part of the assemblage, they see it as a resource for a human individual, the end user, to make use of. They consequently see that the conflicting interests manifest on the level of cultural scripting (for instance, in the debates of what "the narrative" of the #MeToo movement should be about) instead of being situated within what Pilipets and Paasonen (2020: 3) call "the attentional dynamics of social media platforms." As affective networks, these dynamics on specific platforms are informed by what Carolin Gerlitz (2016) has called "grammars of action." In such grammars, hashtags like #MeToo and #blacklivesmatter are not so much rhetorical resources as a way to streamline or flatten ambiguous and complex affections and experiences for social media circulation: they technically embed ambiguity and complexity into reproducible action formats. Furthermore, they enact platform activities through which content resonates and spreads (Pilipets and Paasonen 2020: 4). As such, they manifest the ways in which the social networking sites themselves turn various forms of media practices into value on different registers (see Georgakopoulou, Iversen, and Stage 2020: 140). In other words, it is profitable for them to let hashtags like #blacklivesmatter host as many affective meanings and uses as possible, such as a rallying cry, a hub of on-site information, an act of solidarity, or various uses that counter or dispute them. Affective encounters consequently "translate into valuable engagement" (Pilipets and Paasonen 2020: 4), not only in the sense that content may come to matter to end users, but also in much more complicated and diverse forms of value production, highlighting the multivalent nature of social media communication.

While Pilipets and Paasonen's approach shows that drawing out the intersecting and conflicting interests requires visual and empirical methods, narrative theorists can aim for recognizing them through the analysis of the traces and marks they leave on the layer of content. To do this, we suggest accounting for *the situated relevance* of content in the shifting dynamics of circulating, sharing, and reacting to online material. The traces and marks include, for instance, the overall on-screen presentation of the material, such as the icons indicating likes, shares and replies, as well as the amount of these reactions. These can be read as paratexts, which "in reality control one's whole reading of the text," as suggested by Gérard Genette (1997: 1–2) after Philippe Lejeune. Paratexts of social networking sites include, for instance, the hashtags, the user handles or usernames, and the user interface, which conditions and enables both the reading and writing of a single post. It should also be noted that an individual post as well as the entire user interface "both construct their own paratextual elements" (Roine and Piippo 2021: 69). Following Pilipets and Paasonen's (2020: 13–14) analysis, one must also be mindful of the different tones and meanings associated with the usage of, for instance, hashtags. Following the ban of "adult content" on Tumblr, humor was a noticeable mode of engagement, as well as a detached and sarcastic metacommentary. These features of online culture call for a nuanced reading of different situated meanings and connotations, and the polyphony of the aforementioned traces and marks. Another example of this phenomenon is the case of Black Lives Matter protests, where hashtags relating to it evolved into different variations diverging from the original. The affordance of searchability was also used to disrupt groups and individuals promoting white supremacy or downplaying the problems related to racism under their own hashtags, such as #whitelivesmatter and #alllivesmatter. These hashtags were, for instance, flooded with unrelated imagery and posts by artists and fans from the large international community surrounding the South Korean pop stars and groups collectively known as K-pop.

These examples illustrate not only that agencies of various sizes constantly intersect in digital environments, but also the ways in which the affordances of social networking sites, emerging in the transactions between users and sites, can be leveraged in different ways. Such leveragings can then both accelerate and hinder the algorithmic functions of the said site, generating different kinds of meaning-making chains. In their examination of "the engaging potential of user contributions and the ways in which platforms filter and circulate them, highlighting the shifts in relations of relevance," Pilipets and Paasonen (2020: 3) develop data-analytical methods for identifying the ways in which the users' actions together with the platform agencies both raise and diminish the visibility of content, thus resulting in a constant adapting of the environment. The ongoing shifts and adaptations are perhaps the most difficult aspect for narrative theory to tackle, but they nevertheless cannot be ignored, as they manifest, for instance, in the *scalability* of content, the possibility for content to scale in tremendous visibility on digital platforms (boyd 2011: 47). In the case of #blacklivesmatter and #MeToo, such scalability drew out both the role of the journalistic media and the imagined quality of the sites and their affordances: in the narrativizations of the intersections of various agencies and interests, multiple layers are flattened and, often, the importance of those with a large following or prominent position gets emphasized alongside human intentionality (such as in the case of #MeToo getting noticed only after it was tweeted by the actor Alyssa Milano). These mediated narrativizations also enhance and build up the size and scale of the phenomena they pledge to describe, simultaneously ignoring and bolstering *the algorithmic framing and circulation* of content.

So, while the capacity to recognize, name, and frame certain constellations and activities as specifically "narrative" (see Dawson and Mäkelä 2020: 28) is based on the actual agencies within the meshwork, their binding to narrative logic neither accurately represents the complexity of the assemblage (Roine and Piippo 2021: 64) nor acknowledges the diversity and adaptability of the digital environments. Moreover, accounting for the entanglement of agencies shows that narrative ethics in digital environments is not uncontrollable only due to "the confluence of narrative and the forms aiding its social distribution" or collisions "between storytelling related forms and the social forms" (Mäkelä et al. 2021: 146), but also because the functioning of the diverse assemblage encompassed by the environments largely remains both beyond and beneath human awareness. In other words, as different interests interact and intersect with one another in unexpected and often strange ways, and as human users are entangled with them, it is not always clear whose ethicality is being judged and from which position or situation (see also Bridle 2018: 8). This underlines the importance of finding ways to act in a responsible manner despite the fact the users cannot determine the consequences of their acts.

In this section, we have outlined an approach for taking the wider affective logic and intersecting agencies of digital environments into account in the analyses of the narrativization of surface-layer phenomena by both individual users and the so-called influencers. Building on the key aspects identified by the experimental method of Pilipets and Paasonen, we suggested a threefold focus on uses and contextualizations of narratives in digital environments, in conjunction with the three fundamental affordances of social networking sites (locatability, searchability, and scalability), also pinpointed by a wealth of earlier research. The focus on the experienced locatability, the situated relevance, and the algorithmic framing and circulation of content means applying narratological tools in locating and unraveling the (supposed) experientiality, on- and off-site intertextuality, and the textual traces and marks left by a social networking site itself (such as the features of a user interface), contextualizing the narratives shared or fashioned in digital environments.

Conclusions

In this article, we have sketched out a story-critical approach to digital environments as a new type of context for uses of narrative, based on the meshwork of agencies that actively participates in creating our objects of research. Our aim has been to contribute to literacy of complex technologies and our entanglement with them, outlining an approach to account for the agencies and those layers of the digital that cannot be directly perceived but which nevertheless affect the human side of agency. Analyses of literary theory have always been geared toward detailed readings of what lies "behind" the individual narrative or a work of art as well as of multiple viewpoints representing different agendas within such works. However, in digital environments theorists must specialize in equally detailed analysis of the ways in which narrative structure and its uses are entangled with the diverse assemblage of intersecting and conflicting agencies. Simply acknowledging this is not enough: in order to be story-critical, theorists must also be mindful of their own impulses to frame all commotion on the sites as narrative, often serving to conceal the ways in which the environments, for instance, bolster certain forms and uses of narrative in order to keep the users engaged. As theorists, we must look beyond the prioritizing of human action and downplaying everything that is not human. Such prioritization is not unlike the appeals to the universal campfire of storytelling obscuring the nature of contemporary narratives of the public sphere as carefully curated and instrumentalized (see Mäkelä 2021: 49). If we do not understand the imperceptible functioning and mechanisms of digital assemblages, we surrender ourselves to be curated and instrumentalized by them.

In sum, the story-critical approach we have developed in this article aims to better account for the nature of digital environments as relational contexts. Narrative theorists need to be able, for instance, to draw out how human entanglement in collectivities affects the ways in which information, interpretations, and meanings are produced and circulated. Through the analysis of social networking sites and the ways in which they shape users' engagement as well as their perception of content, our approach attempts to make the sense in which human users can and cannot do something in digital environments perceptible instead of letting it operate out of view. This allows us to disseminate critical practices for the analyses of forms and contexts of narrative in digital environments, but also illustrates the pleasurable and empowering side of agency: of making something happen in a dynamically responsive world (Murray 2011: 410). Attending to this side of agency is vital for both building and understanding humanly sustainable digital environments and narratives online.

Furthermore, the story-critical approach emphasizes the shared ethical responsibility which, in our view, is sorely needed in understanding digital environments as contexts for uses of narrative. While many important analyses on the ethics of digital storytelling have been made on the scale of content (such as asking whose story is being shared on social networking sites), narrative theorists also need to engage with ethical readings that account for the entanglement of agencies as well as the dimensions that remain both beyond and beneath human sense perception. This applies to the conceptualization of the affect as well: in addition to the accounts of social networking sites as echo chambers of—often negative—emotions, narrative theory needs more detailed analyses of the role affective relations play in both creating the "voice" of the platform and shaping human agency, calling a "participatory subject" into being by the dynamics of the meshwork. In digital environments, narrative ethics are entangled in assemblages which not only have the capacity to act as a whole, but also include algorithm-based agencies that possess the potential to initiate a cascading series of relational actions. These capacities and agencies must be made visible and available for narrative analysis: theorists need to recognize not only that "form and content are inseparable and interdependent" and that "storytelling is ethically loaded precisely because it is a way of making sense of our being in the world," as Meretoja (2018: 27) argues, but also engage with ethics that, following Mark Fisher (2012)—himself inspired by Jacques Derrida—can be called hauntological. This means an ethics that does not merely concern that which can be said to be present and immediate, or which refers to that which has not yet happened, but also concerns that which is already effective in the virtual (see Fisher 2012: 19). Therefore, the critical analysis of social networking sites as contexts for uses of narrative must involve not only that which is readily available to human perception and organized through its logic, but also the imperceptible and unanticipated in digital environments with multiple scales and agencies.

References

Aarseth, Espen. 1997. *Cybertext: Perspectives on Ergodic Literature*. Baltimore: Johns Hopkins University Press.

Andersen, Tore Rye, Stefan Kjerkegaard, and Birgitte Stougaard Pedersen. 2021. "Introduction: Modes of Reading." *Poetics Today* 42, no. 2: 131–47.

boyd, danah. 2011. "Social Networking Sites as Networked Publics: Affordances, Dynamics, and Implications." In *Networked Self: Identity, Community, and Culture on Social Network Sites*, edited by Zizi Papacharissi, 39–58. London: Routledge.

Bridle, James. 2018. *New Dark Age: Technology and the End of Future*. London: Verso Books.

Bucher, Taina. 2012. "A Technicity of Attention: How Software 'Makes Sense.'" *Culture Machine* 13: 1–23.

Bucher, Taina. 2018. *If . . . Then: Algorithmic Power and Politics*. Oxford: Oxford University Press.

Bucher, Taina, and Anne Helmond. 2017. "The Affordances of Social Media Platforms." In *The SAGE Handbook of Social Media*, edited by Jean Burgess, Thomas Poell, and Alice Marwick, 233–53. SAGE Publications Ltd.

Chun, Wendy Hui Kyong. 2011. *Programmed Visions: Software and Memory*. Cambridge, MA: MIT Press.

Colebrook, Claire. 2014. *The Death of the PostHuman*. Vol. 1 of *Essays on Extinction*. London: Open Humanities.

Dawson, Paul, and Maria Mäkelä. 2020. "The Story Logic of Social Media: Co-construction and Emergent Narrative Authority." *Style* 54, no. 1: 21–35.

Deleuze, Gilles, and Félix Guattari. 1987. *A Thousand Plateaus: Capitalism and Schizophrenia*, translated by Brian Massumi. Minneapolis: University of Minnesota Press.

Emerson, Lori. 2014. *Reading Writing Interfaces: From the Digital to the Bookbound*. Minneapolis: University of Minnesota Press.

Eskelinen, Markku. 2001. "The Gaming Situation." *Game Studies* 1, no 1. gamestudies.org /0101/eskelinen.

Ettlinger, Nancy. 2018. "Algorithmic Affordances for Productive Resistance." *Big Data and Society* 5, no. 1: 1–13.

Evans, Sandra K., Katy E. Pearce, Jessica Vitak, and Jeffrey W. Treem. 2017. "Explicating Affordances: A Conceptual Framework for Understanding Affordances in Communication Research." *Journal of Computer-Mediated Communication* 22, no. 1: 35–52.

Fernandes, Sujatha. 2017. *Curated Stories: The Uses and Misuses of Storytelling*. Oxford: Oxford University Press.

Finn, Ed. 2017. *What Algorithms Want: Imagination in the Age of Computing*. Cambridge, MA: MIT Press.

Fisher, Mark. 2012. "What Is Hauntology?" *Film Quarterly* 66, no. 1: 16–24.

Fludernik, Monika. 1996. *Towards a "Natural" Narratology*. New York: Routledge.

Galloway, Alexander. 2012. *The Interface Effect*. Malden, MA: Polity.

Gaver, William. 1991. "Technology Affordances." In *CHI '91: Proceedings of the SIGCHI Conference on Human Factors in Computing Systems*, 79–84. New York: Association for Computing Machinery.

Genette, Gérard. 1997. *Paratexts: Thresholds of Interpretation*, translated by Jane E. Lewin. Cambridge: Cambridge University Press.

Georgakopoulou, Alexandra. 2017. "Sharing the Moment as Small Stories: The Interplay between Practices and Affordances in the Social Media-Curation of Lives." *Narrative Inquiry* 27, no. 2: 311–33.

Georgakopoulou, Alexandra, Stefan Iversen, and Karsten Stage. 2020. *Quantified Storytelling: A Narrative Analysis of Metrics on Social Media*. London: Palgrave Macmillan.

Gerlitz, Carolin. 2016. "What Counts? Reflections on the Multivalence of Social Media Data." *Digital Culture and Society* 2, no. 2: 19–38.

Gibson, James J. 1979. *The Ecological Approach to Visual Perception*. London: Routledge.

Gillespie, Tarleton. 2010. "The Politics of 'Platforms.'" *New Media and Society* 12, no. 3: 347–64.

Hansen, Mark B. N. 2015. *Feed-Forward: On the Future of Twenty-First-Century Media*. Chicago: Chicago University Press.

Hayles, N. Katherine. 2017. *Unthought: The Power of the Cognitive Nonconscious*. Chicago: University of Chicago Press.

Hayles, N. Katherine. 2021. "Three Species Challenges: Toward a General Ecology of Cognitive Assemblages." In Lindberg and Roine 2021a: 27–46.

Hoetzl, Ingrid, and Rémi Marie. 2015. *Softimage: Towards a New Theory of the Digital Image*. Chicago: University of Chicago Press.

Hörl, Erich. 2018. "Introduction to General Ecology: The Ecologization of Thinking." In *General Ecology: The New Ecological Paradigm*, edited by Erich Hörl and James Burton, 1–74. London: Bloomsbury.

Hutchby, Ian. 2001. *Conversation and Technology: From the Telephone to the Internet*. Cambridge: Polity.

Hutchby, Ian, and Simone Barnett. 2015. "Aspects of the Sequential Organization of Mobile Phone Conversation." *Discourse Studies* 7, no. 2: 147–71.

James, Erin, and Eric Morel. 2020. "Introduction: Notes toward New Econarratologies." In *Environment and Narrative: New Directions in Econarratology*, edited by Erin James and Eric Morel, 1–24. Columbus: Ohio State University Press.

Kangaskoski, Matti. 2021. "The Logic of Selection and Poetics of Cultural Interfaces: A Literature of Full Automation?" In Lindberg and Roine 2021a: 77–97.

Kirschenbaum, Matthew. 2012. *Mechanisms: New Media and the Forensic Imagination*. Cambridge, MA: MIT Press.

Levine, Caroline. 2015. *Forms: Whole, Rhythm, Hierarchy, Network*. Princeton, NJ: Princeton University Press.

Lindberg, Susanna, and Hanna-Riikka Roine. 2021a. *The Ethos of Digital Environments: Technology, Literary Theory and Philosophy*. New York: Routledge.

Lindberg, Susanna, and Hanna-Riikka Roine. 2021b. "Introduction: From Solving Mechanical Dilemmas to Taking Care of Digital Ecology." In Lindberg and Roine 2021a: 1–21.

Mäkelä, Maria. 2018. "Lessons from the *Dangers of Narrative* Project: Toward a Story-Critical Narratology." *Tekstualia* 4: 175–86.

Mäkelä, Maria. 2019a. "Disagreeing with Fictionality? A Response to Richard Walsh in the Age of Post-truth Politics and Careless Speech." *Style* 53, no. 4: 457–63.

Mäkelä, Maria. 2019b. "Literary Facebook Narratology: Experientiality, Simultaneity, Tellability." *Partial Answers: Journal of Literature and the History of Ideas* 17, no. 1: 159–79.

Mäkelä, Maria. 2021. "Viral Storytelling as Contemporary Narrative Didacticism: Deriving Universal Truths from Arbitrary Narratives of Personal Experience." In Lindberg and Roine 2021a: 49–59.

Mäkelä, Maria, Samuli Björninen, Ville Hämäläinen, Laura Karttunen, Matias Nurminen, Juha Raipola, and Tytti Rantanen. 2021. "Dangers of Narrative: A Critical Approach to Narratives of Personal Experience in Contemporary Story Economy." *Narrative* 28, no. 2: 139–59.

Manovich, Lev. 2001. *The Language of New Media.* Cambridge, MA: MIT Press.

Meretoja, Hanna. 2018. *The Ethics of Storytelling: Narrative Hermeneutics, History, and the Possible.* Oxford: Oxford University Press.

Miller, Laura. 2017. "The *New Yorker*'s 'Cat Person' Story Is Great. Too Bad the Internet Turned It into a Piping Hot Thinkpiece." *Slate,* December 11. slate.com/culture/2017/12/too-bad-twitter-turned-the-new-yorker-s-cat-person-story-into-a-piping-hot-thinkpiece.html.

Murray, Janet. 2011. *Inventing the Medium: Principles of Interaction Design as a Cultural Practice.* Cambridge, MA: MIT Press.

Nagy, Peter, and Gina Neff. 2015. "Imagined Affordance: Reconstructing a Keyword for Communication Theory." *Social Media + Society* 1, no. 2: 1–9.

Norman, Donald. 1999. "Affordance, Conventions, and Design." *Interactions* 6, no. 3: 38–43.

Page, Ruth. 2018. *Narratives Online: Shared Stories in Social Media.* Cambridge: Cambridge University Press.

Papacharissi, Zizi. 2015. *Affective Publics: Sentiment, Technology, and Politics.* Oxford: Oxford University Press.

Payne, Robert. 2018. "'Je suis Charlie': Viral Circulation and the Ambivalence of Affective Citizenship." *International Journal of Cultural Studies* 21, no. 3: 277–92.

Phelan, James. 2008. "Narratives in Contest; or, Another Twist in the Narrative Turn." *PMLA* 123, no. 1: 166–75.

Phelan, James. 2011. "Rhetoric, Ethics, and Narrative Communication; or, From Story and Discourse to Authors, Resources, and Audiences." *Soundings* 94, no. 1–2: 55–75.

Pilipets, Elena, and Susanna Paasonen. 2020. "Nipples, Memes, and Algorithmic Failure: NSFW Critique of Tumblr Censorship." *New Media and Society,* December 15. doi.org/10.1177/1461444820979280.

Raipola, Juha. 2019. "Unnarratable Matter: Emergence, Narrative, and Material Ecocriticism." In *Reconfiguring Human, Nonhuman, and Posthuman in Literature and Culture,* edited by Sanna Karkulehto, Aino-Kaisa Koistinen, and Essi Varis, 263–79. New York: Routledge.

Roine, Hanna-Riikka. 2016. "How You Emerge from This Game Is Up to You: Agency, Positioning, and Narrativity in *The Mass Effect Trilogy.*" In *Narrative Theory, Literature, and New Media: Narrative Minds and Virtual Worlds,* edited by Mari Hatavara, Matti Hyvärinen, Maria Mäkelä, and Frans Mäyrä, 67–86. London: Routledge.

Roine, Hanna-Riikka. 2019. "Computational Media and the Core Concepts of Narrative Theory." *Narrative* 27, no. 3: 313–31.

Roine, Hanna-Riikka, and Laura Piippo. 2021. "Authorship vs. Assemblage in Computational Media." In Lindberg and Roine 2021a: 60–76.

Roupenian, Kristen. 2017. "Cat Person." *New Yorker,* December 4. newyorker.com/magazine/2017/12/11/cat-person.

Rouvroy, Antoinette, and Thomas Berns. 2013. "Algorithmic Governmentality and Prospects of Emancipation: Disparateness as a Precondition for Individuation through Relationships?," translated by Elisabeth Libbrecht. *Réseaux* 177, no. 1: I–XXXI.

Sadler, Neil. 2018. "Narrative and Interpretation on Twitter: Reading Tweets by Telling Stories." *New Media and Society* 20, no. 9: 3266–82.

Scarlett, Ashley, and Martin Zeilinger. 2019. "Rethinking Affordance." *Media Theory* 3, no. 1: 1–48.

Schrock, Andrew. 2015. "Communicative Affordances of Mobile Media: Portability, Availability, Locatability, and Multimediality." *International Journal of Communication* 9: 1229–46.

Srnicek, Nick. 2017. *Platform Capitalism.* Cambridge: Polity.

Taffel, Sy. 2019. *Digital Media Ecologies: Entanglements of Content, Code, and Hardware.* New York: Bloomsbury Academic.

van Dijck, José, Thomas Poell, and Martijn de Waal. 2018. *The Platform Society: Public Values in a Connective World.* Oxford: Oxford University Press.

Vannini, Phillip. 2015. *Non-representational Methodologies: Re-envisioning Research.* London: Routledge.

Walsh, Richard. 2007. *The Rhetoric of Fictionality: Narrative Theory and the Idea of Fiction.* Columbus: Ohio State University Press.

Zuboff, Shoshana. 2019. *The Age of Surveillance Capitalism: The Fight for a Human Future at the New Frontier of Power.* London: Profile Books.

III. STORY-CRITICAL AFFORDANCES OF CONTEMPORARY LITERARY FICTION

Lists, Vignettes, Enumerations: Contemporary Life Writing and the Gesture of Refusal toward Narrative

Anne Rüggemeier
University of Freiburg, Germany

Abstract Focusing on Maggie Nelson's *Bluets* (2009) and Han Kang's *The White Book* (2016), this contribution explores how contemporary life writers critically engage with the causally and temporally bound form of narrative through the use of story-critical forms such as lists, vignettes, and meditations. While scholars of narrative agree that we witness a new dominance of the generic conventions of traditional autobiography— especially its trope of redemption and conversion narratives—among storytellers on digital platforms as well as in advertisement, marketing and political campaigns, the literary genre of autobiography, this article argues, starts to reinvent itself. The life writers Nelson and Kang turn toward the essayistic rather than the affirmative, the enumerative rather than the narrative, and the unity of form rather than the linear and causal cohesion of storytelling. *Bluets* and *The White Book* show their authors as deeply involved in imagining alternative acts of literary representation that exceed the scripts and protocols that are usually activated and called up through the story-ing of the self. As Nelson and Kang explore the story-critical affordances of fragmentary literary forms and test the limits of experientiality (sensu Fludernik), they highlight the opaqueness of life and ask for non-subsumptive readings (sensu Meretoja).

Keywords narrativity, essayistic life writing, story-critical affordances, lists, enumerations

This article is part of the research conducted in the project Lists in Literature and Culture (LISTLIT), funded by the European Research Council Starting Grant no. 715021.

Poetics Today 43:2 (June 2022) DOI 10.1215/03335372-9642665

Life resumes when narrativity ceases.
Robert Scholes, *Semiotics and Interpretation*

1. Personal Storytelling and the Conflicted Role of Narrative

It is especially since the emergence of what has been called a "post-truth mentality" (Mäkelä et al. 2021: 147) which manifests itself in the fact that compelling stories of personal experience win "the story wars" (cf. Sachs 2012) against scientific data and research-based facts, that narrative scholars have realized it is time to develop critical approaches to what Hanna Meretoja and Colin Davis (2018a: 8) have described as the "ever-more important, ever-more conflicted" role of narrative. What has once been interpreted as proof for narrative's unique capacity to capture and convey human experience (cf. Bruner 2001; Brockmeier and Carbaugh 2001; Ritivoi 2008), is now also recognized as a possible danger: in today's story economy, personal stories, especially those situated in the contexts of social media, the self-help industry, and political campaigns, have an immense potential to be instrumentalized in dubious ways—either by their narrators or by their affected audiences (Mäkelä et al. 2021).

What makes narratives so attractive (or so seductive) is that they evoke a reduction of contingency. When Jerome Bruner (1991: 4) claimed that we "organize our experience and our memory of human happenings mainly in the form of narrative," he framed narrative as "an epistemic structure that renders reality intelligible to us" (Neumann and Nünning 2008: 5). This intelligibility relies on the establishment of temporal and causal connections (cf. Ritivoi 2008: 231): "While lived experience can be amorphous . . . narratives have plots that mediate between disparate states" (Neumann and Nünning 2008: 5). Put differently, narratives frame, order, and connect isolated experiences and events that could otherwise be perceived as random.

Although philosophers of selfhood as well as social psychologists have repeatedly emphasized the importance of narrative for the perception and also for the representation of selfhood, it has also been noted that narrative form not only shapes but also constrains. The process of giving narrative form to events, impressions, or experiences for the purpose of making them intelligible is connected with the danger that the actualized narratives end up having less to do with the original "raw material" (Ryan 2008a: 347), but with a certain conventionalizing alignment to culturally preestablished narrative schemata (cf. White 1981). This alignment to preestablished narrative templates works like a mold that preforms, limits, or at least influences what is ultimately conveyed. Jens Brockmeier and

Donal Carbaugh (2001), for example, have shown that the personal stories which we tell about ourselves are the result of selection processes that rely on criteria which derive from culturally available building blocks—that is, conventionalized schemata as well as established generic conventions that preform the act of telling a personal story.

Furthermore, this narrativization of "raw material" not only happens in the act of telling stories, but also in the way we process, listen to, and read texts or everyday discourse. Relying on Jonathan Culler's (1975: 134–60) concept of naturalization, Monika Fludernik (1996) has argued that we process texts (written and oral) by recourse to a set of naturalizing principles that allow us to "explain away" recalcitrant parts. However, this synthesizing of possible inconsistencies by recourse to naturalizing and ultimately often conventionalizing schemata eventually implies a top-down reading model in which our already established cognitive frames and expectations would determine what we ultimately understand. Eventually, it might be precisely these recalcitrant elements that challenge us to overcome preestablished views or even to problematize and make visible the pitfalls of narrative sense-making.

The question of how far narrativization ultimately conventionalizes experience has driven writers to experiment with highly fragmentary literary forms to foster an awareness for the procedures of narrativization and also to capture and communicate a fundamentally nonnarrative experience of reality (Meretoja 2014: 14–15). Especially avant-garde writers such as James Joyce, Virginia Woolf, or Alain Robbe-Grillet chose fragmentation and collage as they worked toward and explored the possibilities of an understanding of reality that is more "episodic"[1] than "narrative." As they refuse to organize their "raw material"—that is, characters, events, settings, impressions, and thoughts—into a determinate story (Ryan 2008a: 347), they challenge their readers to come to terms with the possibility that the world might be less intelligible than nicely bound and coherent narratives tend to suggest. The texts discussed in the following, Maggie Nelson's *Bluets* (2009) and Han Kang's *The White Book* (2016), tie in with this

1. According to the philosopher Galen Strawson (2004), there are "diachronics" or "narrativists" who understand their lives as temporally structured, and "episodics" who do not seek to give a sequential record of the course of their lives. Although Strawson's objection to the narrative identity thesis is important, it rests on problematic presuppositions. These concern both his biological determinism (i.e., the claim that our genes would determine if we are diachronics or episodics) and his normative claims regarding the harmful consequences of narrative self-understanding ("The more you . . . narrate yourself, the further you risk moving away from accurate self-understanding, from the truth of your being"; Strawson 2004: 447).

tradition. With their lists, vignettes, and enumerations, both writers resist narrative sense-making and perform a different sort of "form-finding tendency" (Strawson 2004: 8).

Yet, as David Herman (2009: 14) points out, a writer's refusal to form their discourse into a causally or temporally bound narrative does not mean that the texts do not *cue* the construction of such a sequence on the side of the reader. According to Fludernik (1996: 30) a text can be regarded as narrative as long as it produces the impression that it represents "experience"—that is, human consciousness and its sometimes chaotic experience of being in the world. As soon as we can assign a (possibly chaotic) discourse to a specific speaker's consciousness, the process of narrativization begins. Fludernik calls this "recuperation on the basis of the speaker function" (277) and further explains that "the prominence of an *I* guarantees the hierarchical framing of other discourses as the *I*'s memories, fantasies or textual inventions, perceptions or thoughts" (278). If we apply this view from cognitive narratology, ultimately both texts discussed in this article, even though they largely dispense with narration (in the sense of a sequence of events) and rely on associative reflections, quotations, and the description of sensory impressions, cannot prevent narrativization on the part of the reader. The mere presence of a speaker function, an *I*, can cue narrativization.

Nevertheless, it seems to me that Kang and Nelson try to further inhibit the cuing of narrativization. *Bluets*, for example, is situated in the tradition of the meditation which "turns the attention away from what an 'I' has done in the world and toward the meaning of a precise moment in larger spiritual history" (Smith and Watson [2001] 2010: 246)—which in this case equals the larger relational history of people who fell in love with the color blue. And *The White Book* likewise tries to circumvent the notion of an "I" that would perform the speaker function as it repeatedly leaves behind linguistic discourse for the sake of photography.

Focusing on Nelson's *Bluets* and Kang's *The White Book*, I will explore the story-critical affordances of literary forms that rely on textured fragmentation, the forming devices of enumeration and list-making, and a poetics of essayistic incompleteness. It is through the texts' constant hints at their own incompleteness that readers are inspired to always consider a story's madeness and to critically interrogate the selection of the individual set pieces and the motivations and intentions that guide their composition. As they use and rely on vignettes, lists, and enumerations, these texts highlight the arbitrariness on which the seemingly causal connections and conclusions that are performed through acts of storytelling are ultimately based. The way in which these works balance the communication and the withholding of the expected stories which they constantly imply serves as a means to save personal experience from the appropriating and conventionalizing scripts that would otherwise be uncritically activated in the processes of narrativization. This happens not only on the grounds of disrupting narrative coherence, but also in the sense that the life writings discussed in the following work toward shifting the focus of personal storytelling away from experientiality. They avoid referring to their real life experience, but rather embed their acts of life writing in associative networks of quotations, descriptions, and photographs.

I in no way want to suggest that episodic understandings of being in the world are in any way better, less harmful, or more true than narrative sense-making. My aim is rather to explore how contemporary life writers (try to) achieve unity, pattern, and form via alternative methods of production that allow them to inhibit, frustrate, and bypass the naturalizing interpretive powers of narrativization. For this purpose it is not only necessary to illuminate the processes of narrativization as such, but especially to explore how contemporary life writing[2] rewrites and engages with the problematic generic heritage of autobiography whose traditional master-plot relied heavily on the story-ing of the self and the narrativization of personal experience. The following section will further demonstrate the nature of this generic influence and complicity.

2. Autobiography and Its Shaping of the Prototypical Story of Personal Experience

As the French literary critic Philippe Lejeune ([1971] 1989: 4) exemplarily made clear in his widely cited definition of autobiography as a "retrospective narrative in prose that someone makes of his own existence when he puts the principle accent upon his life, especially upon the story of his own personality," the notion of narrative looms large in autobiographical theory. According to Paul John Eakin (1999) this conspicuous predominance of narratives in the field of autobiographical writing is either nothing more than a "literary convention" (99), or, it derives from the fact that narrative is "an integral part of a primary mode of identity experience, that of the extended self, the self in time" (137). Eakin's assumption is not only in line with the

---

2. I use the term *life writing*, like Sidonie Smith and Julia Watson (2010: 4), as an open and inclusive umbrella term "for written forms of the autobiographical." The term implies a critical awareness of the genre conventions of autobiography and their ideological implications (such as teleological development, autonomous selfhood, and self-transparency) and distances itself from them without fundamentally cutting the connection.

theories of narrative identity outlined above, but also resonates with the claims of the founding texts of autobiography criticism.

Georg Misch in his early standard work *A History of Autobiography* ([1907] 1950) understands the genre of autobiography as "the supreme form of 'understanding a life'" (Schwalm 2014: 19). This process of understanding involves both selection ("as the autobiographical self takes from the infinite moments of experience those elements that, in retrospect, appear relevant" [Schwalm 2014: 19]) and the fitting of the individual parts into a coherent and meaningful whole: a life story. This coherence comes at a price. Forming personal experience via bound narrative triggers conventional schemata that reduce complexity for the sake of creating sense out of lived experience (cf. Smith and Watson 2010: 33). Since the early critical understandings of autobiography, these discursive schemata have included the expectation that the life described must be exceptional and exciting. In traditional autobiographical discourses, this exceptionality was guaranteed either by "individuality and greatness" (203) or by particularly compelling stories that were characterized by a radical transformation—for example, a conversion (cf. Augustine's *Confessions*).

Furthermore, according to genre theory, all autobiography is based on the formal principle of unity. Autobiography typically fashions a clearly contoured singular experiencer—an "isolated individual" (Smith and Watson 2010: 202), whose unique life is to be described in a coherent and cohesive life story. Wayne Shumaker's (1954: 6) classic *English Autobiography: Its Emergence, Material, and Form* exemplarily shows how form and content have always been perceived as closely interwoven and to what extent both are ultimately based on the principle of well-formed unity: "Autobiography is the professedly truthful record of an individual, written by himself, and composed as a single work." He adds, "The contrast is unmistakable: an autobiography is one work, a series of entries in a diary several" (103). This short overview serves to demonstrate why autobiography as a genre has come to be identified "with master narratives of conflict resolution and development, whose hero—the overrepresented Western White Male—identifies his perspective with a God's eye view and, from that divine height, sums up his life" (Gilmore 1994: 17). Eventually, scholars of autobiography first observed and constructed and then finally expected autobiographers to "represent themselves within its limits" (17). It is because of this long-standing master narrative that fragmentary discourses that deal with and represent a discontinuous and disrupted sense of selfhood have been marginalized.

This excursion into the theory and history of autobiography shows the great overlap between autobiographical genre conventions and the "experiential narrative prototype" of personal storytelling: both rely on a bounded story (in the sense of a causal and temporal sequence) that is situated at a specific time and place, both require a moment of disruption that increases the tension and thus ensures tellability, and both require a human experiencer whose consciousness is the anchor point of the narrative.

Personal storytelling or narratives of personal experience (a model from oral story telling) have of course preceded autobiography which is regarded as "a fairly late development" (Fludernik 1996: 47), since "to write one's own life requires a sustained Augustinian effort to construct from the random succession of remembered scenes . . . that well-structured tale with teleological shape" (47). Notably, Fludernik's explanation for autobiography's late-ness, namely the effort connected to its structural and teleological coherence, takes up exactly the point which the pieces of life writing that I discuss in this article attempt to resist. While the "random succession of remembered scenes" that according to Fludernik characterizes (oral) personal storytelling have, over time, "developed into autobiographical proportions" (47), there is a trend in contemporary life writing that wants to get back to (at least the impression of) randomness. Just as we witness a new dominance of the generic conventions of traditional autobiography among storytellers in advertisement, marketing, and political campaigns (Mäkelä et al. 2021), the literary genre of autobiography, I argue, starts to reinvent itself by looking for ways to circumvent and challenge the very "experiential narrative prototype" (Herman 2009) in the production of which it was substantially involved.

Even if the generic conventions of autobiographical writing are complicit in developing this easily instrumentalized set of tools for the creation of compelling narratives, we should not forget that writers of autobiography themselves have for a long time experimented with and critically reflected on the very conventions of autobiographical writing. This self-reflexive analysis of autobiography's generic conventions has advanced as a central topic in a considerably large amount of recently published so-called meta-autobiographies (cf. Struth 2019). Works such Christine Brooke-Rose's *Remake* (1996), Dave Eggers's *A Heartbreaking Work of Staggering Genius* (2000), or J. M. Coetzee's *Summertime* (2009)[3] illuminate the methodological, epistemological, and ethical challenges of life writing as they foreground the processes of selection, the narrative process of meaning-making, and the cultural patterns and ideologies that shape the discourses of life writing.

---

3. For a discussion of J. M. Coetzee's *Summertime*, see Rüggemeier 2018; for a concise introduction to the concept of meta-autobiography, see Struth 2019.

I earlier categorized autobiographical writing around the last turn of the century as "'a gesture of refusal' against the generic conventions of autobiography" (Rüggemeier 2018: 289) and saw the generic self-reflexivity that dominated the meta-autobiographical discourses as a main trend. But I later realized that there is a new tendency in life writing that does not only engage with the generic conventions of autobiography, but also with the notion of narrative sense-making and the storification of life as such.

As for example Leigh Gilmore has shown in the *Limits of Autobiography* (2001), this is especially true for autobiographical representations of trauma. Life-writing texts that deal with trauma often rely on disruption and "gaps" (Kacandes 2008: 616) to signify "unclaimed experience" (Caruth 1995). The fragmentation and the gaps indicate that complex personal experiences of grief and loss defy narrativization because they defy comprehensibility and therefore cannot be represented through a form that stands for coherence and intelligibility.

Another recent criticism of autobiography studies' strong focus on narrative was formulated by Anna Poletti. She states that as contemporary scholars of autobiography "we must do more than focus solely on storytelling" (Poletti 2020: 6). To counter this "narrow focus on narratives" (6), Poletti draws our attention to the interconnection between life, media, and matter. She argues that "the *things* that connect us to others, and to our lived experience, play an equally powerful role in contemporary life as the telling of stories" (10). Against a long scholarly tradition that separated "mind from matter" (Hodder 2012: 15), writers such as Nelson and Kang, with their focus on colors, textures, and materialities, confirm that "the content of our so-called inner lives comes heavily freighted with material from outer sources" (Eakin 2009: 102). The turn to matter as we find it especially in the objects (rice, moon, snow, swaddling bands) that are photographed, enumerated, and written about in *The White Book* "productively challenges the focus on autobiography as a narrative act by inviting us to think differently about how autobiographers are engaged by and engage with the materiality of their lives" (Poletti 2020: 21).

It seems that while many disciplines (advertising, journalism, politics) discovered storytelling as an instrument to share and evoke certain emotions, motivations, or opinions in the later stages of the twentieth century, contemporary life writers experiment with alternative acts of "imaginative reconfiguration" (Meretoja 2018: 3). With their lists, vignettes, and enumerations, Kang and Nelson introduce alternative forms of literary representation that balance the dominance of narrative by introducing alternative reconfigurations that address the epistemic and ethical limitations of conventional forms of (life) narrative and encourage their readers to take part in the process of reimagining "the politics and ethics of form in the twenty-first century" (Vermeulen 2015: 2).

3. Maggie Nelson's *Bluets*: Fragmentation, Enumeration, and the Essaying-"I"

Maggie Nelson's *Bluets* is a generic hybrid that combines elements of memoir, essay, and philosophical meditation on themes such as grief, love, beauty, and language. It consists of 240 numbered, paragraph-length sections which are clustered around an examination of the color blue. Nelson calls them "propositions," not least to highlight her writing's relation to Ludwig Wittgenstein's *Philosophical Investigations*. Most of the paragraphs are not narrative, but rather take shape through connotation, association, or juxtaposition.

Nelson's narrator compares her project to scientific research that is based on diverse and seemingly ambivalent objects of investigation ("Over the past decade I have been given blue inks, paintings, postcards, dyes, bracelets, rocks, precious stones, water colors, pigments, paperweights, goblets, and candies" [6]). She also consults rather unusual experts: "I have been introduced to a man who had one of his front teeth replaced with lapis lazuli, . . . and to another who worships blue so devoutly that he refuses to eat blue food and grows only blue and white flowers in his garden which surround the blue ex-cathedral in which he lives" (6). She thinks of these people as her "blue correspondents" whose job it is to send her "their reports on the color blue" (6).

Strikingly, *Bluets* features all the characteristics that Ansgar Nünning and Alexander Scherr (2018: 483–84) have used recently to define the "fragmentary essay novel" which, according to the authors, is marked by "its heavy reliance on facts and references to reality, its combination of diverse discourses and heterogeneous topics; extended passages with a low degree of narrativity and a concomitant increase of discursive reflections . . . , and its fragmentary form which is underscored by what Woolf called 'the most powerful and agile leaps.'" The last passage is taken from Virginia Woolf's diary and refers to her description of the production process of her work *The Years* (1937), about which she wrote in 1932 that "its to take in everything, sex, education, life & c" (1983: 129).

There are many ways in which Woolf's fragmentary work can be seen as a reference point if not a precedent of Nelson's *Bluets*. Both texts are structured by numbers; both refuse to create coherence through narrative, and both concentrate on moments of intensely experienced states of consciousness, or, in Nelson's case, on moments of intensely experienced sensations caused by the perception of the color blue. Yet although Nelson's book (just like Woolf's) draws upon and gathers the aforementioned "diverse discourses and heterogeneous topics" (Nünning and Scherr 2018: 483) such as depression, divinity, alcohol, and desire, as well as references to Wittgenstein, Goethe, Joni Mitchell, Billy Holiday, Yves Klein, and Andy Warhol, among others, *Bluets* still resists disunity. This is not least due to the forming power of enumeration, which transforms each singular fragment to figure as part of a whole without subsuming the parts. Enumeration can be both "conjunctive" and "disjunctive" (Schumann 1945)—that is, it can add items so as to create a whole or, by contrast, itemize a whole into its parts. Enumeration thus has specific affordances as a form that narrative lacks. While narrative usually subordinates the individual elements to the coherence of the whole (though there might occur "'mutinous' nonnarrative elements that contend with the text's narrativity" [Abbott 2014: 595; paraphrasing Kermode 1983: 137]), the enumeration of individual fragments or vignettes can do both: either draw attention to the singular individual element *or* to the whole. As a framework "that holds separate and disparate items together" (Belknap 2004: 2), enumeration produces unity through form, while narratives tend to join elements by causal concatenation. Theodor W. Adorno's ([1958] 1984: 164) statement that also the essay typically "thinks in fragments just as reality is fragmented and gains its unity only by moving through the fissures, rather than by smoothing them over," echoes the sliding scale between conjunction and disjunction that fragmentary literary forms generally afford and that is specifically highlighted through the practice of enumeration.

The essay stands for trial and experiment (Nünning and Scherr 2018: 486), and for this very reason it transports at least the impression of the unfinished (even though Nelson stresses that her text is diligently constructed). *Bluets* seems undigested and raw. Yet, we might also take the opposite perspective: this text is boiled down and highly reduced. As a consequence, the binding narrative liquids evaporated, while the essential flavors remain. What Mitchum Huehls (2015: 285–86) sees as a typical feature of the "post-theory theory novel"—a genre that Nelson would later attempt with *The Argonauts* (2015)—is also true for *Bluets*: it adheres "to the mandate that texts reflexively think their own conditions of possibility and then perform the results of that thinking in and through the text itself." The very first sentence of *Bluets* exemplarily credits this poetics of the essayistic and the experimental: "1. Suppose I were to begin by saying that I had fallen in love with color. Suppose I were to speak this as though it were a confession; suppose I shredded my napkin as we spoke" (Nelson

2009: 1). While the reader actually still imagines herself in a thought experiment, the beginning of the text has already been performed. It is this very quality of immediacy and processuality that Michelle Dicinoski (2017: 2) hints at when she states that Nelson in *Bluets* creates "a sense of observing the mind of the essayist at work . . . —a method that is shaped by wild associations" (2). These "wild associations" are evoked by fragments (and often citations), but also by the white spaces between the fragments, "that invite[] the reader into those gaps, that emphasize[] what is unknown rather than the already articulated known" (Miller 2012: 237).

On the surface, *Bluets* focuses on the investigation of the color blue, while on a mostly obscured and hidden layer this is also a story about personal experiences. The relationship between the two braids can be described as an attempt to contain the unutterable in what is uttered. With this strategy, Nelson sets herself in the tradition of those who write about color in particularly fraught moments of their lives, a tradition of artists that includes filmmaker Derek Jarman, who wrote *Chroma: A Book of Color* (1994) when he was going blind and dying of AIDS (and as he created the film *Blue*), as well as Wittgenstein himself, who wrote his *Remarks on Color* (written in 1950) while dying of stomach cancer. Nelson's (2009: 10) narrator comments on the text: "He could have chosen to work on any philosophical problem under the sun. He chose to write about color. About color and pain. Much of this writing is urgent, opaque, and uncharacteristically boring." Both opacity and boredom seem to be diametrically opposed to the standards of the experiential narrative prototype (Herman 2009: 14) which typically conveys "an ordered temporal and causal sequence of events" and presents itself as a situated, particular and "compelling narrative" (Mäkelä 2021: 142) that attracts attention easily.

Charged with the reproach that *Remarks on Color* shows that he has grown "tired with thinking" (Nelson 2009: 64), Wittgenstein countered that "explanations come to an end somewhere" (quoted in Nelson 2009: 64). Nelson further quotes him when she writes "if only you do not try to utter what is unutterable then nothing gets lost. But the unutterable will be—*unutterably*—contained in what has been uttered" (67). Wittgenstein's statement reads like a poetic program of what Nelson does in *Bluets*. Suffering from severe depression ("the deepest blue" [88]), "heartache" (51), and grief for her friend who has to live with the severe consequences of an accident, Nelson refuses to form these personal experiences into a story that could—in the writing or in the reading process—be naturalized according to culturally preestablished stories or aligned with the readers own experiences and cognitive frames. Instead, she concentrates on a mediation about the color blue and trusts that in this vicarious mode of literary expression the unutterable personal experience will be contained.

4. Sabotaging Narrativity: Toward an Acceptance of the Episodic

Although there are plenty of events that disrupt the storyworld of *Bluets*, Nelson merely mentions them in passing. The narrator of *Bluets* faces the end of a relationship with "the prince of blue" (Nelson 2009: 6), an incident that seems to have triggered the process of writing: "Above all, I want to stop missing you" (4). Additionally, she is dealing with the shock and the consequences of the severe accident of a close friend. As long as we regard the end of a relationship or a severe accident as "a non-trivial change of state" (Abbott 2014: 595), as most of us would, it is clear that *Bluets* would have had the potential to be developed into a compelling narrative about personal experience, as there is a high degree of *tellability*, or, put differently, sufficient eventfulness that could make this story worth telling. Yet, Nelson refrains from narrativizing the potentially compelling stories of breakup and disruption. This decision to not focus on the "compelling" events and emotional concerns, but on the (possibly) boring and the opaque (the sensual impressions, anecdotes, and associations connected to the color blue), can be interpreted as an attempt by the writer to save her personal experiences from being narrativized by readers. Their conventionalizing scripts could eventually assimilate and channel unique literary productions that rely on singular experience into readings and interpretations that are shaped by stereotypical expectations.

For example, vignette 116 presents a moment in the text in which we come rather close to the past of the "I." It focuses on the last time she met her lover. Remarkably, however, we only get to know what happened ("We fucked for six hours straight. . . . We killed the time" [Nelson 2009: 46]) and what was said by her lover ("*I'm in love with you both in completely different ways*" [46]), and we learn about the color of his shirt ("pale blue" [46]). The passage is a report; it merely collects, in an additive way, what could objectively be observed. Notably, what is not mentioned is what the "I" feels or thinks or how she makes sense of the situation. All we get (in the following vignette) is a quotation from Goethe's Werther: "117. 'How clearly I have seen my condition, yet how childishly I have acted,' says Goethe's sorrowful young Werther" (46). And a few lines later we learn that "young Werther shoots himself in the head while he was wearing a blue coat" (47). Instead of performing the expected narrativization of tellable events, Nelson rather decides to "make art out of the not-tellable" (Ryan 2008b: 590), namely color.

As a sensory impression that depends on the interaction of external (physical) and internal (physiological) factors, "color" occurs when the photoreceptors in the retina of the eye are stimulated by the respective light particles which are then processed in the brain to a certain color impression. Nelson (2009: 20) observes, "You might even say that it is the business of the eye to make colored forms out of what is essentially shimmering." We can read this as a metalinguistic and metanarrative comment: transforming "the whole shimmering mess" (20) that "reality" actually is, into form is also the task of language or, on a different level, the task of art: giving form. In contexts of life writing we usually and (maybe too quickly) connect the notion of form-giving with notions of story and narrative. Texts such as Nelson's *Bluets* remind us that autobiographical writing actually has more possibilities than those provided by the notions of narrative and "life story."

One of these forms is the vignette. Vignettes are short impressionistic texts that focus on visual descriptions and impressions, on moments, persons, or places, rather than on action, development, or plot. As Nelson chooses vignettes instead of creating a linear, temporally ordered, and causally connecting narrative, she keeps alive the sense and the knowledge that reality is actually this "shimmering mess" of individual data. Thus, her fragmentary text is not to be understood as a challenge to the reader's narrative competence in the sense that it would "guide[] us . . . to complete the process that will achieve a story" (Scholes 1982: 60), but rather as a sabotage of the reader's very attempt at narrativity. Put differently, Nelson's decision to turn toward cataloging also puts forward the idea that the very notion of narrative competence, a notion Robert Scholes depicts as "the process by which a perceiver actively constructs a story from the fictional data provided by any narrative medium" (60), must be balanced with or include within itself the idea of what I call episodic acceptance. Eventually, depending on the readers, *Bluets* as a literary composition can either be described as an episode-based narrative or as episodes that counter narrative.

5. Choosing the Enumerative as "Civil Disobedience"

In her articulation of the promises attached to narrative and narrativization, Amy Shuman (2005: 1) states that "storytelling promises to make meaning out of raw experiences; to transcend suffering; to offer warning, advice and other guidance; to provide a means for traveling beyond the personal." Nelson refuses to make use of these "promises"—arguably, because she perceives these very promises also as dangers. She wants to keep her experiences "raw" and not simmer them in the brew of conventional narrative scripts. As she envisions a poetics of the enumerative, she decides against a mode of narrative sense-making that would suggest a mastering of experience in the sense of "putting aside and be[ing] done with" (Barton et al. 2022: 17).

To not come to terms with grief, sadness, loss or trauma contradicts the "utilitarian logic" that, according to Sujatha Fernandes (2017: 10), guides storytelling in the neoliberal era. Even (or especially) in therapeutic contexts, storytelling is by no means just a matter of understanding life through the telling of one's own story, of giving it meaning and thus experiencing it as something that can be shaped actively. Rather, therapeutic storytelling eventually turns into an act of self-improvement and self-enhancement, and thus shows the extent to which the logic of optimization has now reached not only the body but also mind and soul. Nelson interprets her refusal to narrate (and thus her not coming to terms with grief and loss) as an act of "civil disobedience" (51):

> 131. "I just don't feel like you're trying hard *enough*," one friend says to me. How can I tell her that *not trying* has become the whole point, the plan?

> 132. That is to say: I have been trying to go limp in the face of my heartache, as another friend does in the face of his anxiety. *Think of it as an act of civil disobedience, he says. Let the police peel you up.* (51)

Instead of congealing singular experiences and impressions in a bound and smooth narrative, the form of the enumerative affords to let the individual parts emerge with their detail and particularity. As the enumerative inhibits the primacy of the whole over the importance of the individual smaller details, Nelson's work offers resistance to the hierarchical subsumption of particularities under naturalizing schemata. *Bluets* opposes what Hanna Meretoja (2018: 104) has described as "an ethos of appropriation" which subsumes the singular under generalizing practices of narrativization. Instead, Nelson performs and encourages her readers to acclaim "an ethos of dialogic exploration," a form of writing and reading, in which "the singular has power to transform the general" (104).

Nelson's vignettes are numbered. And she comments on this act of sequencing, indirectly, when she writes about counting days in vignette 100: "It often happens that we count our days, as if the act of measurement made us some kind of promise" (Nelson 2009: 37). On the one hand, counting and measuring are tools and expressions of the desire to control and manage something. Nelson's speaker remembers a night when she met a doctor who wanted her to measure her pain ("on a scale from 1 to 10" [33]). She ridicules the very act of measuring experience through numbers, when she reports: "I said '6'—he said to the nurse, Write down '8,' since women always underestimate their pain" (33). Yet, on the other hand, to count and to measure are operations that work against loss, against insignificance, and also against worthlessness. As the vignettes are numbered, we would realize if one would be missing. Otherwise, the loss might stay unnoticed. The numbering also ensures unity, as the parts are thus connected through their subordination to a common whole. Sitting at her friends' bed, she states: "Often we examine parts of her body together; as if their paralysis had rendered them objects of inquiry independent of us both. . . . No matter what happens to our bodies in our lifetimes, no matter if they become like "pebbles in water," they remain ours" (Nelson 2009: 42). Although it is daring to read the grueling real experience of living in a paralyzed body as a metaphor or even as a poetological statement, there is a sense that Nelson, in this very passage, reflects upon the importance of form as an entity that allows to see the cohesion of the whole and the separation of the parts. To be formed affords an escapable unity that allows to regard the broken and the fragmentary not merely as signs of destruction, but also as affordances for the emergence of something new.

6. *The White Book* (2016) and the List: Being-in-the-Present and the Affordances of the Incomplete

After *Bluets* had moved me to think about the relevance of the enumerative with regard to its power to generate a new attitude toward narrativity among readers, Han Kang's *The White Book* (2016) seemed a relevant ground of comparison. This "fragmented autobiographical meditation" (Levy 2017) also ostensibly focuses on color, while it actually processes grief. The book deals with the autobiographical narrator's trauma that centers around the fact that she was the second child, born after the death of an unnamed baby sister who died two hours after being born. The South Korean writer is known for "dark intensity" (Kim 2020: 397) and her engagement with universal themes such as "violence, innocence, redemption and beauty" (382). These characteristics also define *The White Book*, which has been called a "mysterious text, perhaps in part a secular prayer book" (Levy 2017). Part of its mystery is already evoked when we open the book and find, after some epigraph-like Korean characters, a list:

In the spring, when I decided to write about white
things, the first thing I did was to make a list.

Swaddling bands
Newborn gown
Salt

Snow
Ice
Moon
Rice
Waves
Yulan
White bird
"Laughing whitely"
Blank paper
White dog
White hair
Shroud (Kang 2017: 5)

In the process of the first reading, readers merely understand that all these things are white or deal with some things connected to "whiteness." When we continue reading, we realize that these items must be connected to very personal experiences, as Kang notes, "With each item I wrote down, a ripple of agitation ran through me. I felt that yes, I needed to write this book, and that the process of writing it would be transformative, would itself transform, into something like white ointment applied to swelling, like gauze laid over a wound" (5–6).

The passage communicates the sense that the narrator is traumatized, wounded, and in need of healing. Yet she hesitates to actually engage with these listed words: "I sift those words through myself, sentences will shiver out, like the strange, sad shriek the bow draws from a mental string. Could I let myself hide between these sentences, veiled with white gauze? This was difficult to answer, so I left the list as it was and put off anything more" (6). Eventually, after having moved to a new place, Kang's narrator realizes that "hiding would be impossible" (6) and eventually starts to work on the book: "I step recklessly into time I have not yet lived, into this book I have not yet written" (7).

The quoted passages communicate particular hints of trauma and loss. The list's rudimentary form, namely the naturalization of omissions, gaps, and mere mentions, renders it a suitable form to confront and express her trauma (cf. Caruth 1995; Kacandes 2008), not least because it allows its writer "to stay superficial, to skip things, to avoid giving causes, effects, or explanations" (Rüggemeier 2021: 190). Seen from the reader's perspective, however, the rudimentary list form is particularly demanding: it requires that we "endure the piecework, the incomplete, the unfinished, and the incomprehensible" (190).

Lists have been conceptualized "as inherently non-narrative elements, [which] constitute 'the Other' in a literary work" (von Contzen 2016: 245).

While narratives are based on sequential or causal relationships and establish meaningful connections, lists are characterized by itemization or computationality. Yet while this list first seems like a catalog of random white things, it soon dawns on the reader that there might be a link that connects the individual items, and we start to wonder what kind of connections could be drawn between them, and to determine how they relate to one another or to the larger framework in which they are presented.

Parts of the list, especially the beginning ("Swaddling bands / Newborn gown") and the end ("White hair / Shroud") indicate that the list is representing the chronology of a life story as it seems to expand between birth and death. Based on these hints that the book at hand might allude to or take reference to a life story, the reader is supplied with a second (next to whiteness) frame which imbues the originally nonnarrative list with an "undergirding narrativity" (Abbott 2014: 591). While the terms *birth* and *death* would draw attention to the events that we connect with the beginning and the end of a life story, Kang's focus on color and material texture challenges the reader to become aware of the deeper connection between life and matter. Thus, while autobiographies offered in the medium of the book usually have a strong tendency to make sense of life as a narrative,[4] Kang's listing of white things on the very first page performs a gesture of alienation and a challenge toward our reading habits with regard to literary autobiography.

Furthermore, the sense of a possible (narrative) continuity within the usually discontinuous list form is soon disrupted. While the following nouns ("Salt / Snow / Ice / Moon / Rice / Waves") can still be integrated into the framework of the list because they share the quality of whiteness which functions as the connecting hypernym, they cannot easily be integrated into the second organizing principle, which is the notion of the life story. And the following items on the list ("Yulan / White bird / 'Laughing whitely'") further disrupt the just-gained impression that one could narrativize this list by associating it with the script of the life course. The earlier insinuation of the possible existence of a pregiven interpretive frame now strengthens the effect of the renewed defamiliarization. Thus, eventually, the list on the first page remains a challenge for readers who connect autobiographies that appear in the medium of the book with notions of "life story," coherency, and continuity. It is precisely the surprise and the bafflement that we encounter because our expectations are frustrated that might foster a humble and non-subsumptive (Meretoja 2018: 104) reading prac-

---

4. See Poletti (2020:14) for a description of how "particular media forms intersect with prevailing norms regarding subjectivity and what 'a life' is."

tice. Non-subsumptive reading describes a balance between our attempts at sense-making and narrativization—that often rely on appropriation in the sense of "assimilating new experiences into a pre-given mould" (Meretoja 2018: 105)—with an openness toward the unknown that "prompts us to look beyond our preconceptions, to be open to what we cannot control, to learn from what is new to us, and to engage with it with wonder, empathy and curiosity" (108).

As we as readers simultaneously perceive and perform the list's potential to be transformed into narrative, it becomes clear that lists and narratives are not diametrically opposed to one another. Rather, what becomes apparent is that there are degrees of narrativity which can be realized more or less fully. Lists are usually perceived as fragmentary and discontinuous forms. But lists can also serve to provide unity and order. List-making is a cognitive process that helps us "to order our surrounding world . . . putting everything into a sequence and an arrangement" (Belknap 2004: xxii). This is why, ultimately, lists must not only be seen as a formal alternative to narratives, but also as narratives in a very "diluted sense" (Zumthor 2016: 78). Though the list might refuse to "cultivate an appropriate degree of narrativity" (Leitch 1986: 35), applying the list form does not deny the capabilities of narrative. Rather, using lists in narrative discourse implies that narrative should not be seen as the only and "the universal feature of creative perception" (Abbott 2014: 598).

The White Book consists of three sections, each containing approximately a dozen brief texts whose length varies between a few lines and three pages.[5] Both the sense of incompleteness and the brevity of the discrete fragments are especially highlighted by the fact that each text is embedded in the whiteness of broad margins and empty pages (cf. especially the white empty pages after the last vignette which bears the title *All whiteness*). These white gaps hinder the fragments from fusing into each other; rather, each chapter is cut out and showcased like a precious object to look at. This presentation of the short meditative texts as something on display for close observation repeats the gesture of the outstretched hand that holds or works with and arranges white things such as feathers or rice cakes, which we see on the seven black and white photographs that are interspersed in Kang's (2016: 13, 30–31, 41, 67, 102–3, 143, 155) text.

The photographs stem from a performance by Kang, which was shot by the photographer Choi Jinhyuk (Buchanan 2017). In some of the images we see the shape of her body in a sparse white room; in others she is holding

5. Notably, the titles of these brief texts sometimes repeat the words from the list on the first page. Consequently, the list can also be made sense of as an (incomplete) table of contents.

white objects, presenting them to the camera and, eventually, also to her readers. Apart from underlining the fragility of life as she carefully holds and presents the small white things such as feathers to her readers, these photographs emphasize the perceived immediacy and sense of "being-in-the-present" which, according to Zumthor (2016: 76), "every brief form of discourse aspires to as its desired end." Zumthor's statement allows us to discern the shared effects of brevity and photography, as both are connected to "the *real time* of performance" and as such have "a tendency to lean toward what would be the pure present" (76). This notion of creating a sense of being-in-the-pure-present is of specific interest for a story-critical reading of *The White Book*, as it guides our attention away from the urge toward narrativity and allows an episodic conception of reality.

Both the multimodality and the highlighting of the white gaps further stresses the underlying idea that this is a piece in the making. Instead of undertaking a "re-cognization of a text as narrative" (Fludernik 1996: 313), *The White Book* encourages its readers to attempt a re-cognization of the text as texture, a weaving, that allows the literary work to achieve semantic unity without binding the individual elements together in a specific order, logic, or subsumptive practice of narrativization.

7. Conclusion

What connects Nelson's and Kang's texts is their exploration of the story-critical affordances of literary forms that rely on textured fragmentation, the forming devices of enumeration and list-making, and a poetics of essayistic incompleteness. Both texts highlight the opaqueness of life and ask for non-subsumptive readings (Meretoja 2018: 104). They create ambiguities and focus on the meaning that manifests itself in the moment and in the episodic impression and thereby question our idea of what a life is: the stories that we are used to perceiving and to telling, or rather the small episodes, the sensations, the impressions that appear and disappear in passing. As a consequence, they also suggest that readers must learn to formulate new expectations on the form, the content, and even the ultimate theme of life writing.

Since "stories in which nothing happens constitute massive challenges" (Vermeulen 2015: 6), as they seem to refuse the meaning-making mandate that readers continue to assign to stories of personal experience, not all readers are willing and able to read these literary artifacts that are neither compelling nor easy to follow. Nelson (2009: 107) implicitly addresses this issue of readerly expectations when she states, "Many students do not think the writing of Gertrude Stein 'means' anything. . . . They want to throw *Tender Buttons* across the room." *Bluets* is embedded in this modernist tradition that is demanding to read because it relies on fragmented forms of literary communication and focuses on the representation of sensations and associations rather than on story arcs or plot lines that would diminish and tame the richness of experience and the complexity and plurality of mental processes.

Nelson's and Kang's texts are challenging precisely because they are necessary: they challenge and oppose our demands to quickly receive accessible and compact information, our need to be entertained, and thus they also impede the dangers connected to hasty and unreflective opinion formation and quick judgments. Although, due to their brevity, both texts can be mastered in a few hours, their demand for a practice of slow reading unfolds to the extent that they make it necessary to read again and again and not to simply consume, but to contribute to the text as a dialogical product. Eventually, these texts' distinguishing feature is not to refuse narrativity, but rather to prevent and inhibit the channeling of the singularity of experience (the perception of which is already shaped by the narrative patterns we have learned to live by), which can further entrench unreflective conventions and is thus susceptible to all kinds of instrumentalization.

The texts at hand provoke us to rethink the ethics and politics of literary form. The formal experiments that have been described in this article affirm the impression that the very promises of narratives can also be seen as its dangers. They hint at the exhaustion of the form of narrative as they experiment with (more) nonnarrative forms such as vignettes, lists, and enumeration in their endeavor to essay, experiment with, and stimulate "new ethics and politics of form" (Vermeulen 2015: 12).

Nelson and Kang register and creatively respond to "the perception that the narrative mechanics which have allowed us to negotiate our being in the world, to inherit our pasts and to bequeath our accumulated wisdom to the future, have failed" (Boxall 2013: 217). As they turn toward the essayistic rather than the affirmative, the enumerative rather than the narrative, and the unity of form rather than the linear and causal cohesion of storytelling, Nelson's *Bluets* and Kang's *White Book* show their authors as deeply involved in imagining alternative acts of literary representation that exceed the scripts and protocols that are so easily activated and called up by the use of the form of narrative. However, it always remains open to what extent these potentially non-narrative texts are to be understood as either metanarrative (in the sense that they make us reflect on the possibilities and the dangers of narrative) or anti-narrative. In a time saturated with cultural as well as with (pseudo-)personal storytelling, these texts contribute to the criticism of the storytelling boom because, with their utilization of lists, enumerations, and vignettes (and also photographs and white spaces), they essay story-critical ways of literary production that engage with lived experience in ways that probe the limits of bound narrative as a means of world-making. It is to be expected that the coming decades will produce literary masterpieces that experiment with, rely on, and resist storytelling in ways that we might not be able to imagine yet. *Bluets* and *The White Book* can be seen as a promising foretaste of further experiments with non-narrative forms.

References

Abbott, Porter H. 2014. "Narrativity." In *Handbook of Narratology*, 2nd ed., edited by Peter Hühn, Jan Christoph Meister, John Pier, and Wolf Schmid, 587–607. Berlin: de Gruyter.

Adorno, Theodor W. (1958) 1984. "The Essay as Form," translated by Bob Hullot-Kentor and Frederic Will. *New German Critique*, no. 32: 151–71.

Barton, Roman Alexander, Julia Böckling, Sarah Link, and Anne Rüggemeier. 2022. "Introduction: Epistemic and Artistic List-Making." In *Forms of List-Making: Epistemic, Literary, and Visual Enumeration*, edited by Roman Alexander Barton, Julia Böckling, Sarah Link, and Anne Rüggemeier, 1–24. London: Palgrave Macmillan.

Belknap, Robert. 2004. *The List: The Uses and Pleasures of Cataloguing*. New Haven, CT: Yale University Press.

Boxall, Peter. 2013. *Twenty-First-Century Fiction: A Critical Introduction*. Cambridge: Cambridge University Press.

Brockmeier, Jens, and Donal Carbaugh. 2001. Introduction to *Narrative and Identity: Studies in Autobiography*, edited by Jens Brockmeier and Donal Carbaugh, 1–22. Amsterdam: John Benjamins.

Bruner, Jerome. 1991. "The Narrative Construction of Reality." *Critical Inquiry* 18, no. 1: 1–22.

Bruner, Jerome. 2001. "Self-Making and World-Making." In *Narrative and Identity: Studies in Autobiography*, edited by Jens Brockmeier and Donal Carbaugh, 25–37. Amsterdam: John Benjamins.

Buchanan, Rowan Hisayo. 2017. Review of *The White Book*, by Han Kang. *White Review*, November. www.thewhitereview.org/reviews/han-kangs-white-book/.

Caruth, Cathy. 1996. *Unclaimed Experience: Trauma, Narrative, and History*. Baltimore, MD: Johns Hopkins University Press.

Culler, Jonathan. 1975. *Structuralist Poetics: Structuralism, Linguistics, and the Study of Literature*. London: Routledge.

Dicinoski, Michelle. 2017. "Wild Associations: Rebecca Solnit, Maggie Nelson, and the Lyric Essay." *Text*, no. 39: 1–12.

Eakin, Paul J. 1999. *How Our Lives Become Stories: Making Selves*. Ithaca, NY: Cornell University Press.

Eakin, Paul J. 2009. *Living Autobiographically: How We Create Identity in Narrative*. Ithaca, NY: Cornell University Press.

Fernandes, Sujatha. 2017. *Curated Stories: The Uses and Misuses of Storytelling*. Oxford: Oxford University Press.

Fludernik, Monika. 1996. *Towards a "Natural" Narratology*. London: Routledge.

Gilmore, Leigh. 1994. *Autobiographics: A Feminist Theory of Women's Self-Representation*. Ithaca, NY: Cornell University Press.

Gilmore, Leigh. 2001. *The Limits of Autobiography: Trauma and Testimony.* Ithaca, NY: Cornell University Press.

Herman, David. 2009. *Basic Elements of Narrative.* Malden, MA: Wiley-Blackwell.

Herman, David, Manfred Jahn, and Marie-Laure Ryan, eds. 2008. *Routledge Encyclopedia of Narrative Theory.* New York: Routledge.

Hodder, Ian. 2012. *Entangled: An Archaeology of the Relationships between Humans and Things.* Malden, MA: John Wiley and Sons.

Huehls, Mitchum. 2015. "The Post-theory Theory Novel." *Contemporary Literature* 56, no. 2: 280–310.

Kacandes, Irene. 2008. "Trauma Theory." In Herman, Jahn, and Ryan 2008, 615–19.

Kang, Han. 2017. *The White Book*, translated by Deborah Smith. London: Portobello Books.

Kermode, Frank. 1983. *The Art of Telling: Essays on Fiction.* Cambridge, MA: Harvard University Press.

Kim, Daniel Y. 2020. "Translations and Ghostings of History." *New Literary History* 51, no. 2: 375–99.

Leitch, Thomas M. 1986. *What Stories Are: Narrative Theory and Interpretation.* University Park, PA: Pennsylvania State University Press.

Lejeune, Philippe. (1971) 1989. "The Autobiographical Pact." In *On Autobiography*, edited by Paul John Eakin, 3–28. Minneapolis: University of Minnesota Press.

Levy, Deborah. 2017. "The Fragility of Life." Review of *The White Book*, by Han Kang. *Guardian*, November 2. www.theguardian.com/books/2017/nov/02/the-white-book -by-hang-kang-review.

Mäkelä, Maria, Samuli Björninen, Laura Karttunen, Matias Nurminen, Juha Raipola, and Tytti Rantanen. 2021. "Dangers of Narrative: A Critical Approach to Narratives of Personal Experience in Contemporary Story Economy." *Narrative* 29, no. 2: 139–59.

Meretoja, Hanna. 2014. *The Narrative Turn in Fiction and Theory: The Crisis and Return of Storytelling from Robbe-Grillet to Tournier.* London: Palgrave Macmillan.

Meretoja, Hanna. 2018. "From Appropriation to Dialogic Exploration: A Non-subsumptive Model of Storytelling." In Meretoja and Davis 2018b: 101–21.

Meretoja, Hanna, and Colin Davis. 2018a. "Introduction: Intersections of Storytelling and Ethics." In Meretoja and Davis 2018b: 1–20.

Meretoja, Hanna, and Colin Davis. 2018b. *Storytelling and Ethics: Literature, Visual Arts and the Power of Narrative.* New York: Routledge.

Miller, Brenda. 2012. "A Braided Heart: Shaping the Lyric Essay." In *Tell It Slant: Creating, Refining, and Publishing Creative Nonfiction*, 2nd ed., edited by Brenda Miller and Suzanne Paola. New York: McGraw Hill.

Misch, Georg. (1907) 1950. *A History of Autobiography in Antiquity.* Vol 1. London: Routledge and Kegan Paul.

Nelson, Maggie. 2009. *Bluets.* London: Jonathan Cape.

Neumann, Birgit, and Ansgar Nünning. 2008. "Ways of Self-Making in (Fictional) Narrative: Interdisciplinary Perspectives on Narratives and Identity." In *Narrative and Identity: Theoretical Approaches and Critical Analyses*, edited by Birgit Neumann, Ansgar Nünning and Bo Pettersen. 3–22. Trier: WVT.

Nünning, Ansgar, and Alexander Scherr. 2018. "The Rise of the Fragmentary Essay-Novel: Towards a Poetics and Contextualization of an Emerging Genre in the Digital Age." *Anglia* 136, no. 3: 482–507.

Poletti, Anna. 2020. *Stories of the Self: Life Writing after the Book.* New York: New York University Press.

Ritivoi, Andreea Deciu. 2008. "Identity and Narrative." In Herman, Jahn, and Ryan 2008: 231–35.

Rüggemeier, Anne. 2018. "Auto/biographic Metafiction and Relational Lives: Antonia S. Byatt's *The Biographer's Tale* (2000) and J. M. Coetzee's *Summertime* (2009) as Paradigms of Meta-auto/biographies." In *The English Novel in the Twenty-First Century: Cultural*

Concerns—Literary Developments—Model Interpretations, edited by Ansgar Nünning and Vera Nünning, 283–96. Trier: WVT.

Rüggemeier, Anne. 2021. "Life Writing and the Poetics of List-Making: On the Manifestations, Effects, and Possible Uses of Lists in Life Writing." *a/b: Auto/Biography Studies* 36, no. 1: 183–94.

Ryan, Marie-Laure. 2008a. "Narrative." In Herman, Jahn, and Ryan 2008: 344–48.

Ryan, Marie-Laure. 2008b. "Tellability." In Herman, Jahn, and Ryan 2008: 589–91.

Sachs, Jonah. 2012. *Winning the Story Wars: Why Those Who Tell and Live the Best Stories Will Rule the Future*. Boston: Harvard Business Review Press.

Scholes, Robert. 1982. *Semiotics and Interpretation*. New Haven, CT: Yale University Press.

Schumann, Detlev W. 1945. "Conjunctive and Disjunctive Enumeration in Recent German Poetry." *Publications of the Modern Language Association of America* 60, no. 2: 517–66.

Schwalm, Helga. 2014. "Autobiography." In *Handbook of Narratology*, edited by Peter Hühn, Jan C. Meister, John Pier, and Wolf Schmid, 14–29. Berlin: de Gruyter.

Shumaker, Wayne. 1954. *English Autobiography: Its Emergence, Material, and Form*. Berkeley: University of California Press.

Shuman, Amy. 2005. *Other People's Stories: Entitlement Claims and the Critique of Empathy*. Urbana: University of Illinois Press.

Smith, Sidonie, and Julia Watson. (2001) 2010. *Reading Autobiography: A Guide for Interpreting Life Narratives*. Minneapolis: University of Minnesota Press.

Strawson, Galen. 2004. "Against Narrativity." *Ratio* 17, no. 4: 428–52.

Struth, Christiane. 2019. "Metaautobiography." In *Handbook of Autobiography/Autofiction*, edited by Martina Wagner-Egelhaaf, 636–39. Berlin: de Gruyter.

Vermeulen, Peter. 2015. *Contemporary Literature and the End of the Novel: Creature, Affect, Form*. London: Palgrave Macmillan.

von Contzen, Eva. 2016. "The Limits of Narration: Lists and Literary History." *Style* 50, no. 3: 241–61.

White, Hayden. 1981. "The Value of Narrativity in the Representation of History." In *On Narrative*, edited by W. J. T. Mitchell, 1–24. Chicago: University of Chicago Press.

Woolf, Virginia. 1982. *The Diary of Virginia Woolf*. Vol. 4, *1931–1935*, edited by Anne Olivier Bell. Harmondsworth: Penguin.

Narrative Agency and the Critical Potential of Metanarrative Reading Groups

Hanna Meretoja
University of Turku

Eevastiina Kinnunen
University of Turku

Päivi Kosonen
University of Turku

Abstract This article lays out the theoretical-analytic framework of narrative agency, three central dimensions of which are narrative awareness, narrative imagination, and narrative dialogicality, and presents a model of metanarrative reading groups, which aims at amplifying narrative agency. It argues that an important form of self-reflexivity in contemporary literary fiction is metanarrativity—self-aware reflection not only on the narratives' own narrativity but also on the significance and functions of cultural practices of narrative sense-making. It analyzes how reading together metanarrative fiction, which critically engages with the roles of cultural narrative models in contemporary society, can shape narrative agency—that is, the ability to navigate narrative environments. The article illustrates the metanarrative reading-group model through the analysis of one reading-group session, which focuses on a metanarrative excerpt from Carol Shields's *The*

This article was written in the context of the consortium project "Instrumental Narratives: The Limits of Storytelling and New Story-Critical Narrative Theory," funded by the Academy of Finland (grant no. 314769). We are thankful for helpful comments from other members of the consortium, particularly Colin Davis and Maria Mäkelä, as well as from participants of the research seminar of literary studies at the University of Turku.

Poetics Today 43:2 (June 2022) DOI 10.1215/03335372-9642679

Stone Diaries. The article suggests that a creative, dialogical space of a metanarrative reading group forms a productive environment for exploring the affordances, limitations, and power of narratives. It argues that working with narrative agency has the potential to help participants gain critical awareness of—and thereby more agentic power over—their narrative environments, and to engage with them in more critical and creative ways.

Keywords   narrative agency, metanarrative fiction, reading groups, Carol Shields, *The Stone Diaries*

Recent years have witnessed heated debates both on the health benefits of fiction and on the value and dangers of narratives. Because these two debates have remained largely separate from one another, there is a need to bring them into closer dialogue. The first debate, on whether literature is good for us, often draws on a rather narrow conception of well-being, understood in terms of individual psychology and individuals' feelings and moods. Well-being in a broader sense, however, is linked to implicitly social experiences: a sense of meaningfulness and agency that involves being part of dialogical relationships in which one is heard and seen.[1] The second debate has been notably polarized, divided between antinarrativist views of narrative form as inherently problematic (for example, because narratives allegedly impose a false sense of order on inherently incoherent and discontinuous stream of experiences) and narrativist views according to which narratives are in themselves good for us (for example, because narratives allegedly help us develop a sense of direction and purpose).[2] We aim to contribute to these debates by arguing that metanarrative fiction has the potential to enhance our narrative agency through its critical engagement with culturally dominant narrative models, and that such potential can be productively actualized in metanarrative reading groups. Our approach sees culturally mediated narratives as important to agency, and a fortiori to well-being in a broad sense, but does not take narratives to be inherently harmful or beneficial for us. Rather, we consider the meanings of narratives to be always contextual—formed in processes of interpretation and interaction—and hence the evaluation of narrative practices should be context-sensitive, attentive to how narratives function in spe-

---

1. Arguments on the health benefits of fiction are presented in diverse fields ranging from empirical psychology (see, e.g., Kidd and Castano 2013; for critical discussion see Mäkelä and Meretoja, in this special issue, and Meretoja 2018) to sociologically informed research on reading for well-being (see, e.g., Brewster 2018a; Billington 2016). On the importance of the experience of meaningfulness for well-being, see, e.g., Antonovsky 1990.
2. Examples of extreme antinarrativist and narrativist positions include, respectively, Strawson 2004 and MacIntyre 1984. On this polarized debate, see Meretoja 2014, 2018.

cific situations (Meretoja 2018: 170). In this article, we present a pilot study which examines how reading together metanarrative fiction, which critically engages with the roles of narratives in our lives and in contemporary society, can amplify our narrative agency—that is, our ability to navigate our narrative environments.

In the context of the current storytelling boom, narratives have acquired an increasingly prominent role in virtually all areas of our lives.[3] The notion of finding one's own narrative has pervaded culture at large, and it has been put to extensive commercial use. While recent story-critical discussions have highlighted problems of the current story economy in which emotionally appealing stories of personal experience distract us from structural problems in society, some strands of this discussion may have created the impression that narratives that focus on individual experience are inherently problematic.[4] However, there are also (individual-centered) narratives that offer complex critical reflections on the significance of narratives for the lives of individuals and communities, and arguably contemporary narrative fiction is a particularly rich domain of such reflections. So far, little attention has been paid to the ways in which contemporary fiction is responding to the storytelling boom through its critical engagement with the problematic aspects of the roles of narratives in our lives. While metafiction (Hutcheon 1980; Waugh 1984; Currie 2014) was a key characteristic of postmodernist literature, in the current age of storytelling, an important form of self-reflexivity in literary fiction is metanarrativity, which we define (following Meretoja 2014, 2018, 2022a) as self-aware reflection not only on the narratives' own narrativity but also on the significance and functions of cultural practices of narrative sense-making in our lives. There is a need for sustained research on how such metanarrative fiction participates, through its specific fictional means, in critical discussion on narratives. The critical potential of fiction, however, is only actualized in the process of reading. This centrality of reading prompts the question: what kind of reading could simultaneously foster critical awareness of problematic uses of narrative and acknowledge the specificity of fiction in dealing with the ways in which our being in the world is entangled with stories? What kind of potential for critical engagement with the storytelling boom does reading together in reading groups open up?

3. On the storytelling boom, see Salmon 2010; Fernandes 2017; Meretoja 2018; Mäkelä et al. 2021.
4. The most fervent antinarrativist positions usually draw on Galen Strawson's (2004: 447) polemical arguments (e.g., that narrative "almost always does more harm than good"); Maria Mäkelä and her coauthors present the more nuanced argument that "the prototypical story of personal experience and its potential for virality in social media networks" is inherently problematic (Mäkelä et al. 2021: 143).

In our research project Narratives, Reading, and Well-Being, we have explored ways in which metanarrative reading groups can contribute to a critical engagement with the current storytelling boom.[5] It is our hypothesis that reading together metanarrative fiction in reading groups can amplify the participants' narrative agency in ways that facilitate critical engagement with dominant cultural narrative models, and that this allows the participants to have more agentic power over their narrative environments. The project studies whether reading together metanarrative fiction can enhance different aspects of narrative agency: our awareness of cultural narratives that surround us, our ability to imagine different life trajectories, and our ability to engage in narratively mediated dialogical relationships with others. In this article, we present our new metanarrative reading-group model, and illustrate it through the analysis of one reading-group session. This is a pilot study that tests our theoretical-methodological approach through the example of a group that convened biweekly in the fall of 2019 and which, in the session we analyze, discussed a metanarrative excerpt from Carol Shields's *The Stone Diaries*.

Narrative Agency and Metanarrativity

Our theoretical-methodological approach is narrative hermeneutics, which Hanna Meretoja has developed in her earlier work and in collaboration with the narrative psychologist Jens Brockmeier (Meretoja 2014, 2018; Brockmeier and Meretoja 2014).[6] Whereas in dominant forms of narratology narrative is seen as a textual representation of a series of events (as in structuralist narratology) or as a universal, ahistorical cognitive model (as in cognitive narratology), narrative hermeneutics understands narratives as cultural practices of sense-making that provide interpretations of being in the world. Meretoja (2018: 48) defines narrative as "an interpretative activity of cultural sense-making in which experiences are presented to someone from a certain perspective (or perspectives) as part of a mean-

5. In the project, we have analyzed group sessions and interviews conducted with the participants before and after their participation in the reading groups. The group sessions were recorded, and the participants gave the research project texts written during the group sessions. The facilitators kept a facilitation diary. The participants also filled in the Ryff well-being scale (Ryff and Keyes 1995) and a questionnaire on narrative agency (designed by ourselves). The project, led by Hanna Meretoja, is part of the research consortium "Instrumental Narratives: Limits of Storytelling and Contemporary Story-Critical Narrative Theory" (Academy of Finland, 2018–22).
6. Narrative hermeneutics draws on and further develops the Ricoeurean line of narrative studies (see Ricoeur 1983–85). See also Brockmeier 2016; Freeman 2015; Korthals Altes and Meretoja 2018.

ingful, connected account; it has a dialogical and a performative dimension and is relevant for our understanding of human possibilities." This approach draws attention to the existential significance of narratives: narratives are crucial to how we understand our possibilities in the world. It is hence integral to our agency, which we practice by navigating the narrative environments that shape how we perceive our possibilities—by following or challenging narrative models that are culturally available to us.

In addition to *explicit narratives* (narrative artifacts with a concrete textual form), there are *implicit narratives* that function as models of sense-making, and which underlie specific narratives but may not be anywhere available in a material form. These implicit narratives must be constructed by interpreters of explicit narratives; they are embedded within explicit narratives as what the latter resist or reinforce (Meretoja 2021, 2022b).[7] There are certain culturally dominant patterns of narrating different aspects of life. Such implicit cultural narratives provide models of what it means, for example, to live a good life, to be a good mother, or to go through illness or loss. They are models that largely affect us without our awareness but which nevertheless shape our actions, attitudes, and sense of what is possible for us as individuals and communities. In other words, our agency is narratively mediated: models of sense-making that are culturally available to us affect how we orient ourselves to the world and understand our place in it—that is, our sense of who we are and could be (Meretoja 2018: 11–21).

Meretoja's (2018, 2022a, 2022b) concept of narrative agency refers to our ability to navigate our narrative environments: to use, (re)interpret, and engage with narratives that are culturally available to us, to analyze and challenge them, and to practice agential choice over which narratives we use and how we narrate our lives, relationships, and the world around us. Previously, the notion has been used, particularly in philosophy, to foreground the role of narrative self-interpretation in bringing about "integration of the self over time"—a process that is "dynamic, provisional and open to change and revision" (Mackenzie 2008: 11–12).[8] However, the narrative dimension is arguably more broadly a constitutive aspect of our agency as we navigate our narrative environments and participate in narrative practices that perpetuate and challenge social structures. The concept of narrative agency signals that culturally mediated narrative interpretations play an important role in constituting us as subjects capable of

7. While Matti Hyvärinen (2021: 20) suggests that "possibly (most) master-narratives are not narratives at all," Meretoja's concept of implicit narrative aims to articulate in what sense they are narratives (i.e., in the sense of functioning as narrative models of sense-making).
8. Narratologists, in contrast, have traditionally referred to narrative agency in the context of the agency of narrators, not with reference to the agency of real-world subjects.

action, while simultaneously alerting us to the ways in which our narrative agency is socially conditioned. Narrative agency can be amplified or
diminished, and agentic power is unevenly distributed both within societies and across the globe (Meretoja 2018: 11–12). Amplified narrative agency
can manifest itself, for example, as enhanced awareness of one's possibilities of action, affect, and thought in relation to one's narrative environments, and as an ability to imagine different modes of living a fulfilling life.

In Meretoja's (2022a, 2022b) model, narrative agency has three central
dimensions: narrative awareness, narrative imagination, and narrative
dialogicality.[9]

1. *Narrative awareness* means awareness of culturally available narratives
   that shape people's lives by functioning as models of sense-making.
   Cultural narrative models affect us whether we like it or not, and
   bringing them to the level of conscious reflection allows us to evaluate those narratives critically. Narrative awareness includes *self-
   understanding* with regard to the kinds of narratives we use in making
   sense of our lives, and *perspective awareness*, which entails awareness of
   how each narrative is told from a certain perspective and involves
   interpretation, selectivity, and meaning-giving. It is awareness of how
   each story can be told differently—from someone else's perspective,
   interpreted by someone else (Meretoja 2018: 98–107; 125–32).

2. *Narrative imagination* refers to our ability to imagine beyond what
   appears to be self-evident in the present, to creatively and critically
   engage with cultural narrative models, and to imagine different narrative trajectories for oneself, one's community, humankind, and the
   planet more broadly. The notion of narrative imagination has been
   discussed by several narrative scholars, from Jens Brockmeier (2009:
   227), who links it to a creative "what if" dimension of our everyday
   practical actions, to Molly Andrews (2014: 7, 10), who describes imagination as a "social faculty" at work when "we think about our lives
   as they have been lived, and as they might be led." Mark Freeman
   (2014) associates narrative imagination with narrative reflection on
   the goals and objectives that direct one's actions, and with imagining one's future self—a self that will be or should be. For us, a central
   aspect of narrative imagination is our ability to cultivate our *sense of the
   possible* (Meretoja 2018: 90–97)—that is, our sense of how things could

---

9. Meretoja has developed this model on the basis of her earlier work on the six evaluative
continua of the ethically relevant aspects of narratives (see Meretoja 2018, 2021; also briefly
presented in Mäkelä and Meretoja, in this special issue).

be otherwise as well as our sense of how different worlds function as spaces of possibility in which certain experiences, affects, thoughts, and actions are possible and others impossible or unlikely. Narrative imagination also involves the ability to engage in explorative *ethical inquiry* (Meretoja 2018: 133–42) about basic existential issues (e.g., of what good life might mean), issues that lack definitive answers but are crucial to how we orient ourselves in the world.

3. *Narrative dialogicality* refers to the narratively mediated process of how we become who we are in relation to other agents in the world—in a fundamentally dialogical and relational way. It means our ability to enter into a narratively mediated dialogue with others and their stories as well as with cultural narrative models. Critical engagement with normative cultural narratives of relationships and communities, which often draw problematic lines of division between "us" and "them," can open up new possibilities of relationality. The ability to enter into a genuine dialogue with others requires fundamental openness and responsiveness, as well as the courage to be exposed to the other and to let the other challenge one's preconceptions (Gadamer [1960] 1997: 362–75). Some narratives are particularly dialogical in that they invite us to understand the singularity of others' experience by functioning *non-subsumptively* (Meretoja 2018: 107–16): instead of subsuming the other under a pregiven mold, they function in an explorative mode to foster openness to what is unfamiliar, new, and unique in the experience of the other. Narrative dialogicality also involves the ability to participate in creating new *narrative in-betweens* (Meretoja 2018: 117–25), intersubjective spaces that make it possible for us to imagine new relationships and communities, and thus to create conditions for solidarity and social change.

While the model of narrative agency can be used to analyze any narrative, we are here particularly interested in the potential of metanarrative fiction to amplify our narrative agency, and we mean to explore the ways in which such potential can be actualized in metanarrative reading groups. To date, metanarratives have been studied from two perspectives that differ from ours. First, the term *metanarrative* is used in critical theory, particularly in connection to postmodernism, predominantly with reference to what Jean-François Lyotard (1979) called grand narratives (*grands récits*). In this context, it refers to master narratives that seek to offer legitimation through the anticipated completion of a master idea (typical examples are the narratives of Marxism and the Enlightenment). It is misleading, however, to call the Lyotardian master narratives "metanarratives" because the prefix *meta-* suggests that they are narratives about narratives—that is, narratives that make narratives their theme.[10] Master narratives, in contrast, do not thematize their narrativity but, rather, mask it. Second, metanarrativity (or metanarrative commentary) within the context of narratology is understood as a phenomenon in which narrators reflect on their own process of narration (Fludernik 1996, 2003; Neumann and Nünning 2012; Macrae 2019).

These approaches to metanarrativity leave out two aspects of self-reflexive storytelling that we consider crucial. Metanarrativity is characterized by reflection, first, on the significance of cultural narrative practices for individuals and communities, and, second, on the functions of narrative processes in our social reality. Metanarrative fiction self-reflexively makes narrative its theme by reflecting not only on its own nature as a narrative but also, more broadly, on narrativity as a cultural phenomenon, on the significance and functions of narratives in our lives, and on the nature and conditions of narrative agency. It can provide critical insights with regard to dominant cultural narrative models that are imposed on us—on their normative and limiting aspects—and new resources for imagining different life courses as well as personal and collective futures.

There are many ways in which metanarrative fiction can be relevant to narrative agency. Such fiction can contribute to *narrative awareness* by encouraging us to critically reflect on the kinds of cultural narrative models that dominate in society. It can contribute to *narrative imagination* by helping us take critical distance from culturally available repertoire of narrative models and to find alternative ways of imagining different life trajectories and collective futures. It can contribute to *narrative dialogicality* by developing our ability to engage in a dialogue with others, to encounter other people as unique subjects, and to participate in constructing intersubjective narrative in-betweens that make possible new relationships and forms of solidarity.[11]

Whether and how the transformative potential of metanarrative fiction is actualized, however, depends on what happens in the encounters between readers and texts. In the discussions on the well-being benefits of literature, reading is usually understood as a largely solitary practice. Sociological and cultural studies-oriented approaches, however, have for some time observed changes in the reading culture. New forms of reading

10. On narrative as theme in French fiction, see Prince 1992 (which focuses on issues of truth) and Meretoja 2014 (which focuses on the crisis and return of storytelling and their philosophical underpinnings).
11. For examples of how metanarrative (auto)fiction can contribute to these three dimensions of narrative agency, see Meretoja 2022a.

together have complemented solitary reading. There is now empirical evidence of how reading groups can contribute to the well-being of the participants, particularly in relation to the British Shared Reading method,[12] but no study of reading groups prior to ours has engaged with issues of narrative agency. Our research aims to establish a new dialogue between reading research, narrative studies, and the study of well-being, as well as between the theoretical model of narrative agency and its practical applications.[13] While the model provides a theoretical ground for reading-group practices, the empirical findings can help to further develop and fine-tune the theoretical model. Similarly, theory and practice ideally inform one another when the model is used as an analytic lens in literary analysis.

Reading Metanarrative Fiction: Carol Shields's *The Stone Diaries*

We will now briefly demonstrate how the model of narrative agency can be used in the analysis of metanarrative fiction. Our example is Carol Shields's (1993) novel *The Stone Diaries*, which tells the story of a character called Daisy Goodwill Hoad, from her birth to death, predominantly in the third person, but as the narrative progresses it becomes obvious that the narrator is Daisy herself. The narrator uses the third-person mode to gain distance from her own life and to perceive and evaluate it from the perspectives of multiple persons. Hence, although the narrative explores the role of the individual subject in narrativizing her life ("You can make of your lives one thing or the other" [116]), it makes clear that the individual does not carve her life into stories all by herself but does so in dialogue with others and in relation to the cultural narrative models that surround her. Our brief analysis of the novel here is meant to illustrate not only how the model of narrative agency can be used as an analytic lens for reading metanarrative fiction but also how metanarrative fiction provides insights relevant to the three aspects of narrative agency.

First, the novel promotes *narrative awareness* in multiple ways. The narrator-protagonist, Daisy Goodwill, is surrounded by narratives that limit her, particularly gossipy narratives that naturalize a certain story about her. She is aware of how narrative models that shape us are culture-specific and gendered: "Men, it seemed to me in those days, were uniquely honored by

---

12. See, e.g., Hodge, Robinson, and Davis 2007; Longden et al. 2015; Gray et al. 2016; Pettersson 2018; Robinson et al. 2019. On the growing evidence base for using fiction as therapy and on the need for further research, see Brewster 2018a.
13. Our reading-group model is meant to be widely applicable in libraries, schools, and other educational institutions, in the healthcare sector, and in bibliotherapeutic contexts.

the stories that erupted in their lives, whereas women were more likely to be smothered by theirs" (121). While narrative models culturally available to men often open possibilities for them, the ones available to women tend to leave less room for the unique individuality of women as persons: "The stories that happen to women blow themselves up as big as balloons and cover over the day-to-day measure of their lives, swelling and pressing with such fierceness that even the plain and simple separations of time—hours, weeks, months—get lost from view" (121–22). The narrator questions this injustice and asks, "Why should men be allowed to strut under the privilege of their life adventures, wearing them like a breastful of medals, while women went all gray and silent beneath the weight of theirs?" (121).

The narrator mentions examples of cases in which women have been reduced to a simple story. For example, "the famous Dionne quintuplets, born to an ordinary Canadian farm," have turned into "a story so potent and compelling that the little girls themselves are lost, and will always be lost, that's my opinion, inside its convolutions" (122). The narrator reflects on the unfairness of such a tendency to see women through a simple, shocking, emotionally charged storyline: "The unfairness of this—that a single dramatic episode can shave the fine thistles from a woman's life" (123). The novel as a whole promotes the readers' narrative awareness: it enhances our self-understanding by drawing attention to the culturally dominant narratives (e.g., linked to gender) that impose normative power on our lives, and it suggests that becoming aware of them can help us break free from some of those pregiven narratives. The novel also contributes to the readers' perspective awareness by drawing attention to the tension between (third-person) gossipy narratives and the complexity of (first-person) lived experience.

Second, with regard to *narrative imagination*, the novel emphasizes the role of gossip in shaping collective narrative imagination. The narrator conveys the idea that the social power of gossip is not just a women's issue, but concerns, rather, the more general problem that people have a tendency to reduce the complexity of an individual life to a simple, sentimental storyline. Through gossipy storytelling, Daisy is reduced to an anecdote about two dramatic episodes in her life: her birth process, during which her mother died, and her honeymoon, during which her husband died: "still living in the hurt of her first story, a mother dead of childbirth, and then a ghastly second chapter, a husband killed on his honeymoon" (122). The narrative template of a tragic loss of a loved one leads people to assume that she is traumatized or at least heartbroken: "Her poor heart must be broken, people say, but it isn't true" (122). The narrative of being traumatized by tragic loss diminishes her sense of the possible: "Yet wherever she goes, her story marches ahead of her. Announces her. Declares and cancels her true self. Oh, she did so want to be happy, but what choice did she have, stepping to the beat of that ragbag history of hers?" (122).

The novel shows how Daisy feels smothered by being reduced to a simple story, but at the same time it makes clear that she is much more than her "story": "You might like to believe that Daisy has no gaiety left in her, but this is not true, since she lives outside her story as well as inside. . . . She's becoming more and more detached from her story's ripples and echoes and variations. Still, they persist. 'Isn't she the one who—?'" (123–24). Daisy dislikes the story but recognizes her own complicity in it. She has stored in her stomach grief—not for her husband but "for what she allowed. For the great story she let rise up and swamp her" (125). This awareness, however, makes it possible for her to imagine other stories for herself, to envision a different life in which she is not defined by a limiting story and has a range of possibilities open for her. She embraces imagination as a mode of claiming agentic power over her own life: "She understood that if she was going to hold on to her life at all, she would have to rescue it by a primary act of imagination, supplementing, modifying, summoning up the necessary connections" (76). Eventually, the ability to exercise her narrative imagination prompts her to flee to a town where no one "knew her story" (133).

The narrator's narrative imagination significantly manifests itself in her ability to change the perspective, to observe herself both in the first and third persons, as a unique subject of experience but also from the outside, as a member of a broader community. This mode of narration engages readers in an open-ended ethical inquiry. Our narrative imagination, as readers, expands as the text invites us to reflect on the narratives that shape our lives and to consider how we might imagine our lives differently. The novel as a whole cultivates our sense of the possible by showing how the choices we make lead us to different life trajectories and how the ways we narrate our lives open and close possibilities for us.

Third, *narrative dialogicality* is a central aspect of the novel. Within the novel, gossipy oral storytelling, in particular, is a salient mode of social interaction. It functions as a form of social glue that does not foster an openness to the uniqueness of each individual, but rather excludes as much as promotes social cohesion. In this regard, Shields's novel has a story-critical dimension. Even though the text originally appeared in 1993, the way it thematizes the functioning of gossipy narratives affords critical insights relevant to the current storytelling boom, as it is precisely such easily shareable and tellable narratives, reducing individuals to anecdotes, that dominate in social media. At the same time, however, the novel shows how it is ultimately only through telling one's life story in one's own terms, as Daisy does, that an individual can position herself in a critical dialogical relationship with socially dominant narratives (such as the constraining gossipy narratives) and thereby take the role of an active agent. While the dominant collective narratives lock Daisy within a story that separates her from others, the novel also affords Daisy the power to tell her own story. She does so in the third person, by looking at herself both from the perspective of her lived experience and from the perspective of the community, and thus succeeds in viewing herself as a character in the life of the community. The novel makes clear how narrative is ultimately a crucial means for us to tell others who we are. As the narrator renders to the readers Daisy's life story in its incompleteness, full of imaginings and fantasies, she notes: "Still, hers is the only account there is, written on air, written with imagination's invisible ink" (149). Telling the narrative of her life in all its ordinariness contributes to a *narrative in-between* that has the potential to make us more compassionate to the others' stories, more alive to their everyday struggles, hopes, and anxieties.

The form of Shields's novel is also saliently dialogical. Narrating Daisy's life in the third person provides the narrator with wider possibilities than would be afforded by a traditional autobiography to explore the multiple ways in which the life of an individual is entangled with the lives and stories of others, as well as within wider cultural narrative webs. Daisy's story is constantly in dialogue with other voices, reflections, and stories. Thereby the novel expands, through its form—that is, through different shifting narrative positions (including those of letters and photographs interspersed with the narrative)—into a reflection on the possibilities and limits of narrating life. In its kaleidoscopic, protean narrativity, it gestures toward the possibility to retell each life story from ever-new perspectives. *The Stone Diaries* thus can be seen as a reflecting stone mosaic that sheds light, in a multifaceted way, on the different aspects of narrative agency. It contributes to a narrative in-between characterized by critical awareness of the dangers of diminishing others through gossipy narratives and by a non-subsumptive aspiration to be open to the unique complexity of one another's storied experiences.

As we have seen, *The Stone Diaries* has a rich metanarrative dimension. This is why it was chosen as one of the texts discussed in the metanarrative reading groups. This highly self-reflexive novel invites readers to reflect on the relationship between life and narrative, on the significance and functions of narratives for individuals and communities, and on how individuals negotiate their lives in relation to cultural narrative models and collectively shared narratives. Metanarrative reading groups aim to create a dialogical space in which the text's metanarrative potential can be actualized through a process of cointerpretation.

The Metanarrative Reading-Group Model

Our metanarrative reading-group model is based on the theoretical-analytic framework that we articulated above, principles of creative reading, and a specific structure of sessions that focus on a shared discussion on metanarrative fiction. The following creative reading-group guidelines have been modeled on creative group practices (see, e.g., Bolton 1999; Hunt 2013) and on creative and interactive bibliotherapeutic practices (see, e.g., Mazza 2017; Gray et al. 2016; Kosonen 2019b).

1. The structure of the reading group is set up in order to secure a safe and creative space for participants and facilitators;

2. the focus is on metanarrative fiction, which functions as an instrument and mediator for sharing reading experiences and is, due to its self-reflexivity, particularly well suited to discuss issues of narrative agency;

3. creative writing exercises support the participants' creative engagement with issues of narrative agency;

4. participants' individual experiences and personal agency are valued;

5. the sessions nurture a dialogical ethos that creates an accepting, affirmative atmosphere of togetherness;

6. the reading groups have the potential for change, but there is no pressure for change: rather than on accomplishing something, the focus is on evocative and meaningful experiences of reading that have the potential to cultivate our "sense of the possible" (see Meretoja 2018).

Creative reading groups are neither text analysis groups nor therapeutic groups, but rather structured reading groups in which participants share their reading experiences in facilitated group sessions that involve creative writing exercises. The creative space allows the participants to enter into a dialogue with the text, to allow themselves be affected by its evocative potential, and to verbalize how the events of the storyworld resonate with their individual life experiences, in dialogue with the experiences and responses of others. Focusing on literature, rather than directly on the participants' experiences, gives participants a medium in relation to which they can safely reflect on and process their experiences. The facilitator tries to nurture the participants' sense of the possible in relation to the possibilities and new directions opened up by the discussed metanarrative text.

Our research project studies how two different kinds of reading groups—basic creative reading groups and metanarrative creative reading groups—shape the participants' narrative agency. In both reading-group models, the creative reading principles and the structure of the sessions were alike.[14] In the first stage of the research, the main element differentiating the groups was the reading material: in basic creative reading groups, participants read narrative fiction, and in metanarrative reading groups, participants read metanarrative fiction. Moreover, in metanarrative reading groups, the facilitator not only took care of the creative space and the group dynamics but also gently directed the discussion toward issues relevant to narrative agency. At this stage of the research project the vocabulary of narrative agency was not used in the groups, as our starting-point was to draw on the critical potential of the texts themselves. However, as we will see, not only the discussed texts but also the group process and facilitating have turned out to be significant.

The creative reading-group sessions have the following structure: with the guidance of the facilitator, the participants tune into the creative space, work on and around the text, engage in a creative writing exercise, and participate in final reflection in which they write down and share meaningful moments of the meeting. In the tuning-in phase, the moment of settling down becomes a transitional ritual that creates safety. The tuning in (e.g., a writing exercise) helps participants to transition from everyday life into the creative, playful dialogical space of the reading group. For some sessions, literature (e.g., a whole novel) is read at home, while in some sessions a short story or an excerpt from a novel is read aloud by the participants, by taking turns, a practice which makes the text alive and present for the group.[15] In both models, the focus is on close and deep reading in which participants both pay detailed attention to the text and engage with it in ways that involve relating the text to their own personal experiences.[16] In the metanarrative creative reading groups, specifically metanarrative

14. In the research project, we organized ten reading groups. Half of the groups were basic groups and the other half metanarrative groups. In forthcoming publications, we will compare how the two types of reading groups shape the narrative agency of the participants. This comparison is beyond the scope of the current article.

15. The novels that the participants read at home included Jeanette Winterson's *Lighthousekeeping* and Siri Hustvedt's *A Summer Without Men*; the short stories and excerpts that were read aloud during the session included, in addition to the Shields excerpt, Lucia Berlin's "Point of View" and "Another Pamuk" from Orhan Pamuk's *Istanbul: Memories and the City*. Reading together aloud has been researched in Shared Reading studies (e.g., Longden et al. 2015).

16. On deep reading, see Billington 2016. Close reading is also integral to narrative medicine; see Charon 2006.

questions are explored in the creative space of the groups, such as issues of how different cultural narrative models limit the characters or open up new possibilities for them. The idea is that metanarrative fiction critically engages with cultural narratives, and the facilitator draws attention to them and deepens the processing of these questions. In our metanarrative reading-group model, structured creative writing exercises provide an additional way to critically engage with cultural narratives and to widen and deepen the discussions that otherwise might focus exclusively on the themes of the discussed text.

At the end of the creative reading-group meetings, participants articulate, in a few words, what have been for them "meaningful moments" of the session. These moments might include, for example, affective aspects of the experience of participating in the reading group, or new insights about the possibilities or limits of narratives. We have observed that the participants tend to present their account of the meaningful moments in ways that foreground potential for change: they often bring up something that has provided them with new perspectives or insights, indicating some kind of change in thinking, mood, or orientation to certain aspects of their lives. There is no pressure to focus upon change in particular, but the collective creative process also has transformative potential,[17] including the potential to shape narrative agency, which we will next demonstrate through the discussion of a case study.

A Case Study: A Metanarrative Reading-Group Session

We will now briefly analyze one metanarrative reading-group session, in which the participants read aloud a fragment from Carol Shields's *The Stone Diaries,* from the chapter "Love, 1936," which has a particularly rich metanarrative dimension.[18] While we earlier presented a literary analysis of Shields's novel, the analysis of a group session, in contrast, must also take into account the social dimension of the reading group. The example group consists of four health-care professionals (medical doctors and nurses); the group met seven times during the fall of 2019.[19] In the second

17. On the transformative potential of reading literature, see Ihanus 2019; Kosonen 2019a, 2019b; Meretoja 2018; Tangerås 2018.
18. The group read Shields in Finnish translation, and the group discussions were in Finnish.
19. The participants were volunteers who wanted to participate in a reading group. We recruited participants from different organizations, including through student health care, cafes, a yoga studio, etc., and the groups took place in different settings. All the groups were open to adults regardless of age or gender. Some of the groups were directed to university

session, which we will analyze here, three out of the four members of the group and the facilitator were present. The two-hour session followed the reading-group model we outlined above.

As the group meets after a workday, the initial exercise ritual—in this session a writing exercise called "I today, on October 1, 2019"—helps the participants transition to the shared creative, dialogical space of the reading group. After this tuning in, the group reads the fragment from Shields by taking turns: the facilitator begins, the others continue. The facilitator first takes care to ensure that the group keep up with what is happening in the narrative. The text is not previously known to the participants, but it sparks a lively discussion right from the beginning, and the participants quickly begin to link the text's metanarrative reflections to their own experiences of narratives, life events, and their interconnections. The group consists of women, and they readily pick up the narrator's idea about the specificity of women's stories. Helena voices her experience of recognition, and she begins to reflect on how the text relates to her own life: "It's interesting. [She quotes:] 'The stories that happen to women blow themselves up as big as balloons. . . .' Somehow I recognize here myself, how I was married and had that everyday life, a small child and everything, and somehow it feels like it was just that kind of achievement-oriented life, no friends to share that with, and so it was a bit lonely too."[20] The group validates Helena's comment by mumbling approval. Then Janika returns to the text and picks up the question of Daisy's agency: "I don't know if this is connected to that or not, but I kind of thought about this first story [i.e., Daisy's mother's death] and that second chapter [i.e., Daisy's husband's death], so they are both the kind of things that are linked to other people and not to the protagonist herself, so, you know, *she* hasn't done anything but things have happened *to her*." The comment gestures toward the communal, dialogical way in which narratives take shape: we do not build our narratives autonomously and self-sufficiently; instead, they emerge in an intersubjective process in which contingent events and other people's interpretations of them play an important role. Translating the comment into the vocabulary of narrative agency, we can say that it reflects awareness of the *limits* of narrative agency. Pia, in turn, draws attention to all the "losses around Daisy." In this manner, the participants go back and forth between the text and what it evokes in them.

---

students, and some were open to everyone interested, regardless of educational background. The group analyzed in this article was the only group of health-care professionals.
20. The participants' names have been changed. We have permission from all the participants to conduct this study and to publish this article. The quotations from the participants were originally in Finnish.

The facilitator searches for a balance between a free-floating discussion and a more directed kind of facilitating. At times, she asks about issues of narrativity directly and draws the group's attention to cultural narrative models, in the text and beyond it. For example, she asks about the anecdotal stories embedded within the main text:

> Facilitator: But what are they examples of? . . . Why are we being told the example of the Dionne quintuplets, and why does the narrator tell the incomprehensible story of Bessie Trumble? . . . What are they examples of?
>
> Janika: Well, I thought that it must be about the way people are so easily condensed into kind of one thing—like okay, they were the quintuplets, or okay she's that woman who lost a leg and she's the woman whose husband died. . . .
>
> Facilitator: Yes. . . .
>
> Janika: That's what we all do quite a bit, we talk about such and such a patient who has this and that, that they are that kind of type.

The direct facilitation works, and the group comes up with more examples of "narratives that define individuals," as Janika aptly puts it. The participants remember individuals whose lives have been condensed around a single event or chain of events: Anneli Auer (a Finnish woman who was charged with the murder of her husband), a survivor of the Estonia ferry disaster of 1994, the rap artist Cheek, Nelson Mandela. The group shows awareness of the power aspect linked to telling tragic narratives, and it engages in a long discussion on gossiping. Thereby the complex narrative pattern of the discussed text begins to unravel: that the narrator constantly brings "counter-light" to the dramatic narrative by interweaving it with other perspectives. Pia now points to the relativity of the truth of Daisy's story and to different possibilities of interpretation depending on who is telling: "Or is it gossip, that this is how people want to see it? But the truth can be different." The group also raises the question: can we ultimately ever fully know anyone? Janika disentangles from the narrator's discourse an alternative narrative model of survival:

> I haven't encountered exactly this kind of dramatic cases in my patients, but there are people who have gone through a terrible crisis and then it's clear that she will nevertheless make it, that she will get back on her feet. . . . It's precisely that, the way it's evident, just minutes after a crisis, that I will get through this, and so on, it's something like that, realizing that people do get through real tough things.

In Janika's account, the narrative of survival is cross-illuminated from many different directions. First, the individual story of survival is woven together with a witness narrative of a health-care professional: "it's clear that she will nevertheless make it." The comment involves shifts of meaning that are interesting from the point of view of narrative dialogicality, in particular by way of a nuanced repositioning of the speaker's own narrative identity. Janika first aligns herself with the narrator's perspective and then shifts her perspective to her own life and to patients whose struggle through various crises she witnesses in her work: "She will get back on her feet." Janika uses indirect discourse and then moves for a moment in a personal register: "That I will get through this." In the end, Janika concludes with the generalization: "people do get through real tough things."

After the discussion, the session continues with a writing exercise: "Squashed by a narrative." It focuses on the quotation that we already discussed: "Yet wherever she goes, her story marches ahead of her. Announces her. Declares and cancels her true self" (Shields 1993: 122). First, the facilitator asks the participants to create a mental image of a real or fictional person in front of whom a narrative marches, and to write about that. In the second step, she asks the participants to imagine that the chosen character breaks free from the confines of the narrative. In the final step, the participants end their story.

After the writing process, the participants share experiences of the writing exercise. Two participants have chosen a public figure: Helena writes about Cheek, and Pia about Nelson Mandela. This leads the group to reflect on the relationship between a celebrity's public story and their private, personal stories. Janika writes about an anonymous patient who may say about their diagnosis: "This doesn't define me, I have much more." Janika's example takes the discussion in a personal direction. The participants indicate that this is an experience they share. Pia verbalizes it: "It must be like that, that each one of us has a story that presses us."

Overall, the participants engage in a rich discussion on issues relevant to narrative agency. Their narrative awareness and imagination manifest themselves through their understanding of the multiple perspectives from which things can be told. They also verbalize how imagining others' perspectives and not reducing others to mere "cases" are of utmost importance in their work as health-care professionals. Such understanding is also important in narrative medicine, but there is scope for it to expand in the direction of critical engagement with cultural narrative models, reflection not only on how narratives enable understanding but also on how they can limit or diminish us.[21] Narrative medicine operates with the con-

---

21. See, e.g., Charon 2006; Brewster 2018b.

cept of narrative competence, which overlaps with our notion of narrative agency, but the concept of narrative competence lays the emphasis on analytic skills (i.e., the ability to analyze narratives), and hence it has the air of a certain detachment from the object of analysis, whereas narrative agency explicitly emphasizes relationality, engagement and involvement in the social world, acting in the world with others. We suggest that these concepts complement one another and that the model of narrative agency could be used to develop narrative medicine in new directions.

The Question of Definitional Power in the Dialogical Space of the Group Process

Toward the end of the session, the discussion of Daisy's story leads the group to a situation that makes visible certain challenges in reading-group facilitation. While it would appear that the group has advanced in its narrative awareness, and we might thus be tempted to draw the conclusion that the narrative agency of the participants has developed during the session, things turn out to be more complicated.

In addition to the gendered aspects of stories, the group discussed generational and age-specific experiences. The temporal marker in the chapter's title, "Love, 1936," invites such consideration. Daisy's story is narrated by a fictional autobiographical narrator, Daisy as an adult, who places her current perspective above that of her past self—"a young Bloomington widow" (Shields 1993: 122)—and underlines how young Daisy was and how limited her understanding. The narrator refers to (gendered) attitudes that prevailed "back in the year 1936" (121) and suggests they have now changed. In the group discussion, Daisy's "young age" is foregrounded, linked to her limited perspective. The participants characterize her as "really young," a "twenty-year-old." When the meanings of youth are discussed, the group refers to progressiveness but also to thoughtlessness. They also mention the narrator's conception of a mistake that Daisy made as a young woman. Toward the end of the session, Janika insists on the issue of age:

> To be honest, I have to confess that I didn't think of this person [Daisy] as young and ignorant, [laughs] because somehow I just don't think about people in that way. . . . Because I'm myself in that situation, so I don't . . . I find it funny, somehow funny to hear what other people think, what young people are like and so on . . . because I can't think like that myself, that other young people are like that. . .

Janika is herself young in the reading group of middle-aged women, and her comment foregrounds the difference of her own way of thinking from that of the other group members. She has not interpreted Daisy's love story as a "youthful mistake," and feels as if the other participants are reducing Daisy to one story, linked to her youth: "So that she's young in that way and that's the kind of things the young do . . . that they can't know what they do—oh, okay, really?" Janika criticizes the group in a gentle tone, but at the same time asserts her desire to defend herself against the definitional authority of the group: "Something this dramatic happens to few of us, having this clear a story, but then in the end there's still something that others take to be a factor that defines me, even when I don't necessarily know myself what it is." She thus applies the analytic lens of narrative agency to the group process by drawing attention to the way narrative power works and how it takes place in the group too; it is something she experiences right here and now. The tendency to reduce people to a single story easily happens without anyone even noticing it.

At the end of the session, in the "meaningful moments" exercise, Janika returns to the issue of categorizing people: "I think this awakened in me a kind of compassion or something like that, that I should remember that there's no need to assume or judge, to lock up people in boxes, and perhaps we should just let them tell their own stories and then go with that." At this stage, the facilitator feels a need to validate Janika's generational perspective more emphatically and to apologize that Janika ended up feeling that the group defined her one-dimensionally as just a young person.

The issue is resolved in the group discussion, but it reminds us of how fragile creative reading-group dynamics can be in their situated, shifting now-time. It also demonstrates how reading-group activity builds narrative dialogicality on a practical level so that, in the group, the issue of how narratives define us emerges as a concrete question that applies to the group's own dynamics as well. Hence, narrative agency is not only about the text but also about the dialogical relations among the participants.

Final Reflections on Navigating Narrative Environments

At the end of the session, the facilitator guides the participants through a final writing exercise that provides them a chance to reflect on how the discussion has affected the way they think about the role of narratives in their lives. Afterward, group members share their thoughts. They all bring up, in different variations, the idea that they now think differently about narratives: Pia says, "I have never really thought that they [narratives] have such a determining role . . . that they even define your person. . . . They have quite a major significance. . . . In a way people are a bundle of different narratives." Others feel that Pia's remark encapsulates their experience too: Janika says, "You managed to say what I couldn't put in words"; "Mine were just vague formulations, but what Pia said is just so true," adds Helena. This interchange demonstrates how shared interpretations take shape in a dialogue in which sharing experiences can help individual participants verbalize their own experiences.

In the final round, the participants also articulate a sense of agency and empowerment that they associate with the effects of the creative group process (without specifically linking it to aspects of narrativity). Janika, for example, expresses a sense of moving from feeling "tense," burdened by "everything I should do," to feeling affirmative about carrying out the things she wants to do. Helena says: "I have really missed something like this," and she refers to "a space of peace" in the group and to how she now feels "invigorated like after a singing lesson." Pia notes how "writing and concentration, after initial difficulties, somehow just take off": "It's surprising how it just takes off." Discussing the group process is itself part of the process of practicing narrative agency in dialogue with others—narrating what happened and what it means. Such a practice also works to build a narrative in-between in which it is possible to continue discussing issues of narrativity in a safe, creative space.

After the reading group finished, the participants were interviewed in semi-structured interviews in which they were asked about the reading-group experience, whether it changed anything in their lives or about the way they think about narratives. The final interviews show that after participating in the reading group the participants reflect, from new perspectives, on issues of narrative agency.

In comparison to the initial interviews, the participants express more nuanced *narrative awareness*, particularly about different kinds of narratives, their affordances and risks. They go through different types of narratives: Helena says, "There are so many different kinds of stories. There are stories in which you are thrown by chance, there are stories of development, there are adventure stories." Janika draws a distinction between the dominant cultural model of a "survival story," which is told from a perspective defined by a happy end, and stories of "real people" who post—for example, as YouTube videos—alternative "coping stories," in which "not everything has to be like this is over now but they can be about what's going on right now, that it's difficult now. . . . That has made it easier to tell unpleasant stories, too, that it doesn't have to be just survival stories so that now [all the difficulties are] over and my life is better than ever, but they are really the kind of stories that now it's hard and please try to understand." Pia says that attending the reading group made her more aware of the stories she encounters in her work: "I'm surrounded by sad stories."

She has found, however, a new approach to that sadness, not just being horrified by it but trying to see how they can work on it together through a reparative approach: "Bad things have happened and they can't be taken away, but much can be done, repaired."

In terms of *narrative imagination*, all the participants express the idea that narratives can help imagine others' experiences and new possibilities. Janika reflects on how reading helps understand that "there is not just one truth, there are different possibilities and perspectives. . . . One does not need to experience everything by oneself in order to understand." She mentions specifically the "exchange of perspectives" as valuable, as something that helps gain distance from one's own life and imagine different experiences, and she asserts that narratives can function as "a means of understanding the self and others." Helena reflects on how different life stages and personal experiences offer different perspectives on the same text: "That's precisely the brilliance of it." Pia suggests that medical doctors should read more fiction because it helps imagine situations different from one's own: "it opens up the world in quite a different way. They [literary narratives] can function as a mediator of feelings, like this is how I would feel, it can verbalize those feelings and situations." Interestingly, two of the participants also draw attention to the *limits* of agency in envisioning new directions for one's life. Pia reflects on how we can affect our life stories to some extent with our own actions even as there remain limits to such control: "It's also the case that things just happen to us, and that's what's difficult: when you can't control everything. In a way it's best not to try to control everything—what comes, comes, and we have to take it." Helena ponders whether her work is what she wants to do for the rest of her life, and continues: "On the other hand, it's life, whatever will happen. You can't control life, can you."

Most empathically, however, the participants voice insights linked to the aspect of *narrative dialogicality*. All of the participants emphasize the significance of reading together, togetherness—"a sense of community," as Pia says. Helena feels that "unraveling the text together" created a sense of the multifacetedness of it and ignited in her a desire to reread it (she refers particularly to Jeanette Winterson's *Lighthousekeeping*). The interviewer never directly asks about the perceived well-being benefits of the reading group, but interestingly all the participants nevertheless connect it to well-being, which they link to the experience of sharing reading experiences.[22] It is

---

22. Further research is needed to establish whether the perceived well-being (such as feeling reinvigorated) emerges from the participation in reading groups in general, or whether it is linked to metanarrative groups in particular. Our initial analysis suggests the former, but it

possible that this well-being perspective emerges from their background in the health-care sector. Janika compares the reading group as a hobby to yoga: for her, "it goes in the same well-being category" in its ability to help the participants take a pause and connect with themselves. When asked whether the group changed anything for her, Janika says, "Of course I hope that I have grown as a person and am now much smarter and better, but perhaps I'll just say that I'm now reinvigorated." Helena compares the reading group to singing in a choir: it has similar changes of rhythm; it is "lively and feels real." She says it has "opened up some emotional locks" for her. Pia considers reading together "a kind of spiritual sports" and emphasizes the significance of "commonality," "togetherness."

The interviews suggest that metanarrative fiction provides critical resources for engagement with the current storytelling boom. As we observed above, many of the metanarrative insights of *The Stone Diaries* are relevant for analyzing problems in the twenty-first-century storytelling boom, characterized by gossipy narratives that circulate in the social media and reduce individuals to easily shareable and tellable anecdotes. Both Janika and Helena explicitly reflect on social media narratives, raising questions about what kind of stories people share and how these platforms affect us. Janika, for example, analyzes commercially motivated stories that people share in social media and which "do not create any sense of conflict." She reflects on the tension between the way news stories portray the world as heading toward annihilation and the way social media is full of stories like "Look at my new high-heels." Such reflections express the participants' awareness of the types of narratives that impede our ability to imagine the complexity of real everyday experience, and it problematizes the kind of narrative in-between that commercially driven social media creates.

Overall, our initial analysis of the whole reading-group data indicates that most participants of the metanarrative reading groups have become more aware of the roles of cultural narratives in their lives. This narrative awareness aspect of narrative agency emerges most readily from the final interviews, whereas the two other aspects of narrative agency raise more questions of interpretation. Thus, metanarrative reading groups seem to have a particularly significant potential to amplify the participants' narrative awareness but can be seen to contribute to the other two aspects as well. The enhancement of the latter two can be seen, for example, as we saw in the analysis of our case study, in the participants' tendency to

---

also suggests that metanarrative groups significantly contribute to well-being, understood in the broader sense that our notion of narrative agency articulates.

emphasize the ways in which listening to others' points of view and attending to the facilitators' questions that guided the discussions toward issues of narrativity enriched their own reading experiences and their sense of different possible perspectives on the discussed themes. This interestingly raises the question of how the different aspects of narrative agency lend themselves to observation and interpretation through different research methods.[23] Overall, our analysis suggests that while each of the metanarrative reading groups has its specific group process, the data consistently supports the conclusion that narrative agency is shaped, and can be enhanced, through the dialogical group process, and that metanarrative facilitation plays an important role in contributing to the amplification of the three dimensions of narrative agency.

Conclusion

In this article, we have laid out the theoretical-analytic model of narrative agency, shown how it can be used in the analysis of metanarrative fiction, and discussed the potential of metanarrative reading groups to shape the narrative agency of the participants. While metanarrative fiction in itself draws attention to issues relevant to narrative agency, these issues gain meaning through a process of interpretation, which is a fundamentally dialogical process. In the groups, the richness of the discussion relevant to narrative agency depends not only on the text but also on the modes of facilitation and on factors specific to each group, such as group dynamics and how each session unfolds through the interaction of the participants.

Our analysis suggests that metanarrative fiction provides significant critical resources for engagement with the current storytelling boom. The example of *The Stone Diaries* highlights how gossipy narratives can diminish an individual to a simple anecdote. The pressure to mold our lives into easily shareable, tellable, and sellable stories can be seen as a key characteristic of the current storytelling boom; hence, the novel's insights on problematic forms of narrative relationality are valuable for our critical engagement with our current cultural condition. The novel also shows how multidimensionally metanarrative fiction can deal with the significance of narratives for individuals. It presents individuals' critical engagements with their narrative environments as ambivalent, fragile, lifelong processes in which situations and perspectives constantly shift.

---

23. We will return to this question and report more detailed results from the whole research project in later publications.

This pilot study has suggested that a creative, dialogical space of a metanarrative reading group forms a productive environment for exploring the affordances, limitations, and power of narratives. It allows a critical approach to the narrative environments in which the participants find themselves without losing sight of personal engagement with the lively presence of literature that moves them and matters to them. This is the challenge and subtlety of the model: how to foster personal engagement and interpretative freedom while at the same time encouraging critical engagement with problematic aspects of narratives in the current cultural moment. Our research on the reading groups suggests that this kind of combination of critique and personal engagement can foster shared verbalization of interpretations in ways that have the potential to contribute to narrative agency in a multifaceted way, in a shared space of critique, creativeness, and relationality—that is, in relation to awareness, imagination, and dialogicality.

Our understanding of how metanarrative reading groups can shape narrative agency will develop further as our research project moves on to compare the various groups with one another. Much work remains to be done before our findings can be established conclusively; for example, they need to be tested with a broader range of reading groups involving participants from more diverse backgrounds. Although it is not possible to draw wide-ranging conclusions from one session, there are certain elements in the session that can be interpreted as signs of strengthening narrative agency. Our analysis suggests that working with narrative agency has the potential to help participants gain critical awareness of—and thereby more agentic power over—their narrative environments, and to engage with them more creatively through critical dialogue. We have indicated how critical reflection and creative engagement can come together in a group process that can support critical engagement with problematic aspects of the storytelling boom and strengthen the participants' narrative agency—that is, their ability to navigate their narrative environments in more critical and creative ways. The model of narrative agency allows approaching well-being in broader terms, with an emphasis on experiences of meaningfulness, a sense of one's possibilities, and the relationality of our being.

This article has highlighted one of our main research findings so far: the importance of facilitating in order to open up the metanarrative dimensions of the texts for the participants. In the analyzed session, the facilitator did not explicitly use the vocabulary of narrative agency, because our idea was that the facilitator should only gently draw attention to the ways in which metanarrative fiction itself critically engages with practices of narrativizing lives. During the research process, however, we have come to think that the theoretical model of narrative agency could be used as an explicit analytic lens that can contribute to the participants' narrative agency: providing them with this vocabulary could itself increase their self-reflexive abilities and give them tools to reflect on the various dimensions of their narrative agency. In line with this insight, we have developed the metanarrative reading-group model toward a narrative-agency reading group that involves explicitly working on the three dimensions of narrative agency. Further research is needed, but we believe that this opens one meaningful direction for narrative studies in the era of the current storytelling boom: to provide tools and vocabularies that have the potential to amplify, in dialogical processes of cointerpretation, the critical potential of narrative fiction in its engagement with the affordances and risks of various narrative practices.

References

Andrews, Molly. 2014. *Narrative Imagination and Everyday Life*. Oxford: Oxford University Press.

Antonovsky, Aaron. 1990. *Pathways Leading to Successful Coping and Health*. New York: Springer.

Billington, Josie. 2016. *Is Literature Healthy? The Literary Agenda*. Oxford: Oxford University Press.

Bolton, Gillie. 1999. *The Therapeutic Potential of Creative Writing: Writing Myself*. London: Jessica Kingsley.

Brewster, Liz. 2018a. "Bibliotherapy: A Critical History." In *Bibliotherapy*, edited by Sarah McNicol and Liz Brewster, 3–22. London: Facet.

Brewster, Liz. 2018b. "Bibliotherapy, Illness Narratives, and Narrative Medicine." In *Bibliotherapy*, edited by Sarah McNicol and Liz Brewster, 41–57. London: Facet.

Brockmeier, Jens. 2009. "Reaching for Meaning: Human Agency and the Narrative Imagination." *Theory and Psychology* 19, no. 2: 213–33.

Brockmeier, Jens, ed. 2016. "Narrative Hermeneutics." Special issue, *Storyworlds* 8, no. 1.

Brockmeier, Jens, and Hanna Meretoja. 2014. "Understanding Narrative Hermeneutics." *Storyworlds* 6, no. 2: 1–27.

Charon, Rita. 2006. *Narrative Medicine: Honoring the Stories of Illness*. Oxford: Oxford University Press.

Currie, Mark. 2014. *Metafiction*. London: Routledge.

Fernandes, Sujatha. 2017. *Curated Stories: The Political Uses and Misuses of Storytelling*. Oxford: Oxford University Press.

Fludernik, Monika. 1996. *Towards a "Natural" Narratology*. London: Routledge.

Fludernik, Monika. 2003. "Metanarrative and Metafictional Commentary: From Metadiscursivity to Metanarration and Metafiction." *Poetica* 35, no. 1–2: 1–39.

Freeman, Mark. 2014. "Narrative, Ethics, and the Development of Identity." *Narrative Works* 4, no. 2: 8–27.

Freeman, Mark. 2015. "Narrative Hermeneutics." In *The Wiley Handbook of Theoretical and Philosophical Psychology*, edited by Jack Martin, Jeff Sugarman, and Kathleen L. Slaney, 234–47. Malden, MA: Wiley Blackwell.

Gadamer, Hans-Georg. (1960) 1997. *Truth and Method*, translated by Joel Weinsheimer and Donald G. Marshall. New York: Continuum.

Gray, Ellie, Gundi Kiemle, Philip Davis, and Josie Billington. 2016. "Making Sense of Mental Health Difficulties through Live Reading: An Interpretative Phenomenological Analysis of the Experience of Being in a Reader Group." *Arts and Health* 8, no. 3: 248–61.

Hodge, Suzanne, Jude Robinson, and Philip Davis. 2007. "Reading between the Lines: The Experience of Taking Part in a Community Reading Project." *Medical Humanities* 33, no. 1: 100–4.

Hunt, Celia. 2013. *Transformative Learning through Creative Life Writing.* London: Routledge.

Hutcheon, Linda. 1980. *Narcissistic Narrative: The Metafictional Paradox.* Waterloo: Wilfrid Laurier University Press.

Hyvärinen, Matti. 2021. "Toward a Theory of Counter-narratives: Narrative Contestation, Cultural Canonicity, and Tellability." In *The Routledge Handbook of Counter-narratives,* edited by Marianne Wolff Lundholt and Klarissa Lueg, 17–29. London: Routledge.

Ihanus, Juhani. 2019. *Transformative Words: Writing Otherness and Identities.* New York: Nova Science.

Kidd, David Comer, and Emanuele Castano. 2013. "Reading Literary Fiction Improves Theory of Mind." *Science* 342, no. 6156: 377–80.

Korthals Altes, Liesbeth, and Hanna Meretoja. 2018. "Ethics and Literature." In *The Palgrave Handbook of Philosophy and Literature,* edited by Barry Stocker and Michael Mack, 601–21. London: Palgrave Macmillan.

Kosonen, Päivi. 2019a. "The Interactive Process of Reading." Pt. 2 of "Towards Therapeutic Reading." *Scriptum* 6, no. 1: 17–39.

Kosonen, Päivi. 2019b. "Forms of Shared Reading." Pt. 3 of "Towards Therapeutic Reading." *Scriptum* 6, no. 2: 43–56.

Longden, Eleanor, Philip Davis, Josie Billington, Sofia Lampropoulou, Grace Farrington, Fiona Magee, Erin Walsh, and Rhiannon Corcoran. 2015. "Shared Reading: Assessing the Intrinsic Value of a Literature-Based Health Intervention." *Medical Humanities* 41, no. 2: 113–20.

Lyotard, Jean-François. 1979. *La condition postmoderne: Rapport sur la savoir.* Paris: Minuit.

MacIntyre, Alasdair. 1984. *After Virtue: A Study in Moral Theory.* Notre Dame, IN: University of Notre Dame Press.

Mackenzie, Catriona. 2008. "Introduction: Practical Identity and Narrative Agency." In *Practical Identity and Narrative Agency,* edited by Kim Atkins and Catriona Mackenzie, 1–28. London: Routledge.

Macrae, Andrea. 2019. *Discourse Deixis in Metafiction: The Language of Metanarration, Metalepsis, and Disnarration.* London: Routledge.

Mäkelä, Maria, Samuli Björninen, Laura Karttunen, Matias Nurminen, Juha Raipola, and Tytti Rantanen. 2021. "Dangers of Narrative: A Critical Approach to Narratives of Personal Experience in Contemporary Story Economy." *Narrative* 28, no. 2: 139–59.

Mazza, Nicholas. 2017. *Poetry Therapy: Theory and Practice.* 2nd ed. New York: Routledge.

Meretoja, Hanna. 2014. *The Narrative Turn in Fiction and Theory: The Crisis and Return of Storytelling from Robbe-Grillet to Tournier.* New York: Palgrave Macmillan.

Meretoja, Hanna. 2018. *The Ethics of Storytelling: Narrative Hermeneutics, History, and the Possible.* Oxford: Oxford University Press.

Meretoja, Hanna. 2021. "A Dialogics of Counter-narratives." In *The Routledge Handbook of Counter-narratives,* edited by Marianne Wolff Lundholt and Klarissa Lueg, 30–42. London: Routledge.

Meretoja, Hanna. 2022a. "Metanarrative Autofiction: Critical Engagement with Cultural Narrative Models." In *The Autofictional: Approaches, Affordances, Forms,* edited by Alexandra Effe and Hannie Lawlor, 121–40. London: Palgrave Macmillan.

Meretoja, Hanna. 2022b. "Implicit Narratives and Narrative Agency: Evaluating Pandemic Storytelling." *Narrative Inquiry,* Online First, https://doi.org/10.1075/ni.21076.mer.

Neumann, Birgit, and Ansgar Nünning. 2012. "Metanarration and Metafiction." In *The*

Living Handbook of Narratology, edited by Peter Hühn, Jan Christoph Meister, John Pier, and Wolf Schmid, 344–52. Hamburg: Hamburg University Press.

Pettersson, Cecilia. 2018. "Psychological Well-Being, Improved Self-Confidence, and Social Capacity: Bibliotherapy from a User Perspective." *Journal of Poetry Therapy* 31, no. 2: 124–34.

Prince, Gerald. 1992. *Narrative as Theme*. Lincoln: University of Nebraska Press.

Ricoeur, Paul. 1983–85. *Temps et récit*. 3 vols. Paris: Seuil.

Robinson, Jude, Josie Billington, Ellie Gray, and Melissa Chapple. 2019. "Qualitative Methodologies 1: Using Established Qualitative Methods in Research on Reading and Health." In *Reading and Mental Health*, edited by Josie Billington, 155–90. Cham: Palgrave Macmillan.

Ryff, Carol. D., and Corel M. Keyes. 1995. "The Structure of Psychological Well-Being Revisited." *Journal of Personality and Social Psychology* 69, no. 4: 719–27.

Salmon, Christian. 2010. *Storytelling: Bewitching the Modern Mind*, translated by David Macey. London: Verso Books.

Shields, Carol. 1993. *The Stone Diaries*. Toronto: Random House.

Strawson, Galen. 2004. "Against Narrativity." *Ratio* 17, no. 4: 428–52.

Tangerås, Thor Magnus. 2018. "'How Literature Changed My Life': A Hermeneutically Oriented Narrative Inquiry into Transformative Experiences of Reading Imaginative Literature." PhD diss., Oslo Metropolitan University.

Waugh, Patricia. 1984. *Metafiction: The Theory and Practice of Self-Conscious Fiction*. London: Methuen.

Book Reviews

Erin James and Eric Morel, eds., *Environment and Narrative: New Directions in Econarratology*. Columbus: Ohio State University Press, 2020. x + 224 pp.

The past decade has seen a proliferation of publications that consider the relationship between the humanities and a rapidly changing environment. This development has in part been shaped by paradigm shifts such as the recent materialist, affective, and posthuman turns. *Environment and Narrative*, edited by Erin James and Eric Morel, adds to this burgeoning body of work by examining the contribution that narrative approaches make to our understanding of the environment. Continuing James's (2015) earlier work on econarratology, as set out in *The Storyworld Accord*, the edited volume *Environment and Narrative* is structured around three prominent directions in econarratology: representation of the nonhuman; narrative ethics, with an understanding of narrative "as a multisided ethical interaction" (8); and cognitive narratology and readerly interaction with narrated storyworlds. Econarratology, as it takes shape in this volume, is understood as "the paired consideration of material environments and their representations and narrative forms of understanding" (1), and situates itself within the broader field of the environmental humanities, with close links to ecocriticism and to literary studies of the Anthropocene.

Considering the ongoing existential environmental and ecological crises, and the growing consensus that these are bound up with a profound crisis of the imagination, this volume is not only an important but indeed a necessary book, which speaks to the most urgent questions of our times. Before outlining the strengths of *Environment and Narrative*, I will first note several

Poetics Today 43:2 (June 2022)

somewhat contradictory features, which this book shares with a range of other recent publications that look at literature and the environment (e.g., Timothy Clark's [2019] *The Value of Ecocriticism*). Noting these contradictions may help clarify the important contributions made by the individual chapters, and will also, I hope, shed light on some of the ways in which future research within the environmental humanities may interact with the arguments that are made in this book. First, while the authors foreground the importance of different literary traditions and narrative modes and acknowledge that "environmental ethos is also culturally coded and dependent upon local contexts" (13), *Environment and Narrative* focuses almost exclusively on a small set of contemporary novels written in English; texts (by, among others, Jeff VanderMeer, Richard Powers, Barbara Kingsolver, Ian McEwan, and Nathaniel Rich) that have quickly become Anthropocene classics of sorts. Second, these are for the most part texts in which questions of the weather and the environment are writ large, rather than visible in more tangential or symbolical ways. Such a corpus in turn invites referential readings, rather than symbolical or allegorical ones. Third, there is a notable element of prescriptiveness in how the poetics of the Anthropocene are conceived: one of the key premises of the collection is to propose alternatives for the kinds of stories we tell about the environment, and there is the suggestion that some texts or genres are "environmentally more sound than others" (169). There is only limited explicit consideration, however, of how this ethos can be squared with the more descriptive practices prevalent in literary studies and the humanities. Fourth, and related to this somewhat prescriptive stance, the authors take a keen interest in how "narratives might affect real-world attitudes and behaviors" (1). This remains largely hypothetical, however, since the volume does not present examples of empirical research to underpin such interests.

Despite the contradictory features of the general framework described above, it is important to note that within the individual chapters, the authors effectively complicate this framework by drawing attention to the complexity and profound discrepancies of such underlying choices and alignments. Markku Lehtimäki, for example, in his analysis of Ian McEwan's *Solar*, questions ecocritical tendencies toward referential reading (101); Greg Garrard, in a chapter on Richard Powers's *Gain*, notes the lack of empirical research by ecocritics (108) and problematizes tendencies toward prescriptive aesthetics (109). In his insightful reading of Mark Twain's *The American Claimant*, Eric Morel critiques the tendency to draw on a limited corpus for making wide-ranging claims (83), and then goes on to remind the reader of the importance of rhetorical (rather than referential) readings of the weather. One of the rewards of this volume lies in how the individual contributions refuse to instrumentalize either literary texts or narrative methodologies, and instead unpack the complexities of the chosen material by way of rigorous analysis, drawing attention to the heteroglossia and contradictions in literature.

The introduction to *Environment and Narrative* promises insights from ecocriticism and the environmental humanities to promote a narratological vocabulary that could help "environmental scholars better account for the formal aspects of representations of environment in various types of narratives" (20). While the introduction could perhaps have spelled out in more explicit terms what specific concepts, methods, and narrative patterns it considers central in such a vocabulary for the Anthropocene, the individual chapters deliver on the promise by productively applying a selection of existing concepts to diverse econarratological readings. Marco Carraciolo showcases the importance of "material anchors," which are active in "making manifest and at the same time *grounding* at the diegetic level the abstract pattern of plot" (51) in object-oriented plotting; Alexa Weik von Mossner draws on the notions of "qualia" in her exploration of character empathy; Astrid Bracke and Erin James demonstrate the applicability of the "principle of minimal departure" and narrative structures such as the "we-narrator," respectively, for the narrative understanding of material environments and their narrative representations.

In addition to providing a toolbox of narrative concepts for environmental studies, *Environment and Narrative* does an excellent job introducing and contextualizing the key questions of the developing fields within which it operates, from econarratology to the broader environmental humanities. The introduction by Erin James and Eric Morel will surely find its way to the reading lists of graduate and undergraduate seminars within the environmental humanities. John Hegglund's chapter on unnatural narratology and weird realism elegantly brings together recent discussions in postclassical narratology with paradigm shifts in ecocriticism and environmental humanities. And in her afterword, Ursula Heise, one of the leading thinkers in the environmental humanities, takes stock of the rewards of this volume and looks forward to future directions. In short, *Environment and Narrative* outlines econarratology as a stimulating field of inquiry that examines material environments and their narrative forms; it establishes a distinct vocabulary of concepts for environmental scholars interested in the formal aspects of representations of environment; and it presents important and necessary avenues for further research.

Lieven Ameel
Tampere University
DOI 10.1215/03335372-9642693

References

Clark, Timothy. 2019. *The Value of Ecocriticism*. Cambridge: Cambridge University Press.
James, Erin. 2015. *The Storyworld Accord: Econarratology and Postcolonial Narratives*. Lincoln: University of Nebraska Press.

Natalya Bekhta, *We-Narratives: Collective Storytelling in Contemporary Fiction*. Columbus: Ohio State University Press, 2020. 230 pp.

Natalya Bekhta's monograph on first-person plural narrative is the first book-length account of this innovative form of writing. The study is based on Bekhta's (2016) PhD thesis at the University of Giessen. She has published a series of essays on the topic (Bekhta 2017a, 2017b) and a special issue of *Style* (Bekhta 2020). In her essays, Bekhta takes exception to earlier work on we-narratives, claiming that only texts with a communal we-voice can properly be called we-narratives. The heavily revised monograph continues to give the communal voice a special status of what she calls "performative" we-narrative, but acknowledges the existence of "indicative" we-narration, in which an "I" narrates the story as spokesperson for a group. Indicative we-narratives are defined as providing "a statement about a certain group," while performative we-narratives "construct[] a collective subject" (60). In addition, the study under review draws attention to texts in which we-sections or chapters alternate with third- (or second-)person narrative or first-person singular accounts. It also focuses extensively on the way in which the plural *we* is split into subgroups and individuals, an aspect of group representation that I have myself discussed (see Fludernik 2014, 2018): "Rather than voicing a fully homogeneous group, 'we' move between general statements that are true for all group members . . . and particularizations true for parts of the group" (62). Bekhta's book was unfortunately completed before Gibbons and Macrae 2018 appeared, in which quite a few essays concern first-person plural texts.

Bekhta's monograph is based on insights from the work of Uri Margolin (1996, 2000, 2001), Brian Richardson (1994, 2006, 2011, 2015), myself (Fludernik 2011, 2017, 2018), and Amit Marcus (2008) on we-narrative, and on a combination of influences from James Phelan (2005) and F. K. Stanzel (1984). Her main critical thrust is directed against the basic assumption of a first-person speaker in we-narratives. Instead, she proposes the existence of a collective voice as narrator ("group character narrator" [61]—unfortunately always in the singular, which undermines the illusion of that voice's communal quality). Since such joint narration is not realistically possible (only in chorus-like situations of utterance [41]), one would have expected her to espouse the paradigm of unnatural narrative of Jan Alber, Brian Richardson, and others. However, in her reviews of publications on unnatural narratives (Bekhta 2013, 2019) and in an essay coauthored with Ansgar Nünning (Bekhta and Nünning 2016), she has positioned herself against this paradigm, and in this study, too, she rejects the label for we-narratives (17), arguing for a mimetic interpretation of we-narration despite the fact that the joint utterance or writing of a we-narrative is a fiction, or (as she calls it) "artificial," or a "collective artefact" (Tuomela 1995): "I talk about ascriptions of mental states to we-narrators, rather than suggesting that group characters construct a literal (fictional) mind" (Bekhta 12–13). Taking her cue from Richard Walsh's (2007) *The Rhetoric of Fictionality*, Bekhta sees the author rhetorically constructing the we-narrative, "and the we-narrator, consequently, does not have to bear the role of an 'impossible narrator'" (75).

The book consists of a theoretical section (the introduction and chapters 1–2), three interpretative chapters that illustrate variants of we-narration, and two concluding chapters that summarize and extend her insights into thematically and politically relevant contexts.

In the first section, Bekhta criticizes previous studies on we-narrative on two counts: for their imprecise inclusion of texts that, for her, are not "proper" we-narratives in the corpus of first-person plural texts, and, more particularly, for taking first-person singular stories that utilize a number of we pronouns to be legitimate we-narratives. She is perhaps a little uncharitable in criticizing the pioneers of we-narrative, who were primarily interested in collecting examples—that is, providing the corpus on the basis of which more detailed distinctions could be made. Bekhta's approach deviates from the standard method of classifying "pronominal" categories of narrative. In the opposition between first-person and third-person narratives, the crucial factor is that in the former the (main) *protagonist* is referred to by the first-person pronoun—this homodiegesis stands out because in third-person texts the textual "I" (where it exists) belongs to the narrator on the extradiegetic level. Likewise, for second-person fiction, what makes such fiction second-person narratives is the reference to the main protagonist as "you" (using the address pronoun). Along these lines, the main criterion for we-narratives is the existence of a collective protagonist on the *diegetic* level, with an open choice of narrator: covert, an "I," or a collective I+she/he/they or I+you (cf. Fludernik 2011, 2015). In fact, Bekhta sees herself straddling the divide between homo- and heterodiegesis: "even when the we-narrator seems to be outside the storyworld, the characters it speaks about are still part *of itself*, and if it is inside the storyworld, its transpersonal and transgenerational potential renders insignificant the restrictions typically associated with homodiegetic narration" (122).

For Bekhta, the *we* is located primarily on the *narratorial* level: it is the teller-we that interests her. This perspective has significant consequences for the way in which one looks at actual texts of the corpus of narratives utilizing the we-form. Bekhta is, of course, correct in positing the existence of a homodiegetic *we* as equivalent to a we-narrational utterance on the level of *narration* and a collective we-protagonist on the level of the *histoire*—this conjunction will be entirely homodiegetic (plural homodiegesis). However, as she herself acknowledges, many "indicative" we-texts are first-person narratives in which the narrator ("I") serves as a spokesperson for a group—this is the variant of we-narrative that prevails in factual we-narratives such as soldiers' accounts of their war experience, pupils' stories about their time at school or at college, or one person's narrative of the holiday trip with the family, and so on. In oral situations of storytelling, the experiences of the group (a couple, for instance) may also be told in alternation. Susan Sontag's short story "Baby" (1978), which Bekhta discusses in chapter 3, seems to belong to such a format—the husband and wife telling the psychoanalyst about their experiences with the child individually at different sessions; however—unlike oral storytellers—they never employ an "I"; there is also no indication when it is the wife's and when the husband's dramatic monologue to the therapist. Despite Bekhta's insistence on collective narration for we-narratives, she does acknowledge the existence of "borderline cases" (65) and shifts between indicative and performative we-narration. A certain inconsistency exists in her summary on pages 180–81 when the first point of her definition of we-narrative stipulates that no "concealed/postulated I-reference is recognizable," but acknowledges that "an I-reference" may occur "at some point," whose "significance should be assessed interpretatively" (181).

Bekhta's chapter 3 also contains an analysis of Julie Otsuka's *The Buddha in the Attic* (2011), a tour de force which narrates the experiences of Japanese picture brides in the United States. Bekhta utilizes Phelan's (2005) notion of lyric progression to explain the curiously static effect of the narrative. The novel is also emblematic of we-narrative's common strategy of balancing an overall communal identity with individual experiences of subgroups and even specific persons. Since the narratorial *we* cannot be in several places at once and look into different people's minds, the telling is artificial or nonnatural: there is no realistic standpoint from which the we-narration could be conducted—the we-perspective is an extrapolation from the ethnic experience, which is only imaginatively a common one given the actual diversity of individual circumstances.

Another important theoretical intervention on the part of Bekhta is her introduction of the notion of communal focalization in chapter 5. In her text, focalization consists in "perception orient[ing] the narration" (132). Many we-texts concentrate on a particular village or town perspective from which the events are being presented. The narration reflects prejudices and viewpoints on the part of the group. However, as Bekhta illustrates, in many texts we are nevertheless given insights into individuals' minds—which is quite unrealistic from a logical perspective (how could the community know?). These insights are at least partially explained by the workings of gossip, since in such communities everybody knows everything about everybody else. This constellation is particularly strongly present in Zakes Mda's *Ways of Dying* (1995), discussed in chapter 5. In this novel, the village *we* keeps making brief one-sentence appearances in longer passages in which the story is presented from the reflectoral perspective of Noria or Toloki. This combination of internal focalization (reflector mode narrative in Stanzel's paradigm) and communal knowledge is striking. There are clear we-sections in the novel (in which *we* and *our* occur in almost every sentence), but when the focus is on Noria and Toloki, the return to "our" and "we" seems odd, particularly because of the present-tense form of the narrative in these reflectoral sections. More generally, Bekhta's examples demonstrate the pervasive use of free indirect discourse in we-narratives, though her explicit exemplum ("we thought moving to India might be better" [62]) is psychonarration rather than FID.

While Bekhta in chapter 5 is concerned with the unreliability of we-narration, what obtrudes on my narratological mind is rather the recurring use of *peripheral* we-narratives. The village folk in Mda's novel are witnesses to the love between the protagonists, yet little happens in their own lives. From Stanzel's narrative theory we are familiar with the first-person peripheral narrator (Nick in *The Great Gatsby* or Serenus Zeitblom in Thomas Mann's *Doctor Faustus*). Jeffrey Eugenides's *The Virgin Suicides* could likewise be treated as a peripheral first-person plural text, even though the boys are much more involved with the Lisbon sisters than the village is in the story of Noria and Toloki in Mda's tale.

Bekhta's monograph makes a convincing case for the ideological significance of we-narratives (see also Fludernik 2020), though she gestures toward it rather than devoting a full chapter to the question. Thus, in a brief discussion of *deadkidsongs* by Toby Litt, she demonstrates how processes of inclusion and exclusion work in we-narration. More postcolonial we-writing could have profitably been discussed (see Richardson 2011; Fludernik 2012). Owing to her choice of examples (the book only discusses a fraction of we-narratives that have been collected by Richardson and others), her remarks focus especially on the positive and negative feelings of the group toward one of their community. She also highlights the fact that a first-person narrator who is part of a group or its spokesperson occupies a different ideological position than a joint we-narrator (179), though I would contend that is not always the case. Bekhta sees her book as part of the comparative project "of the forms of contemporary fiction, which include, at least, first-person, authorial, figural, second-person, and, independently, first-person plural narrative situations" (184). This list betrays an imprecision in her conceptualization of we-narrative as a "narrative situation" in Stanzel's framework, mixing up perspective and person as narratological categories. Nonetheless, the study makes an important point about the fictionality of literary we-narratives with a communal narrative voice and is apt to inspire more work on different forms of we-narration, their range, history, and contrast with factual we-narratives.

Monika Fludernik

University of Freiburg

DOI 10.1215/03335372-9642707

References

Bekhta, Natalya. 2013. Review of *Unnatural Narratives—Unnatural Narratology*, edited by Jan Alber and Rüdiger Heinze. *Germanisch-Romanische Monatsschrift* 63, no. 1: 166–68.

Bekhta, Natalya. 2016. "We-Narratives and Multiperson Narration: Untypical Pronominal Organisation of Narrative in Contemporary Fiction." PhD diss., University of Giessen.

Bekhta, Natalya. 2017a. "Emerging Narrative Situations: A Definition of We-Narrative Proper." In *Emerging Vectors of Narratology*, edited by Per Krogh Hansen, John Pier, Philippe Roussin, and Wolf Schmid, 101–26. Narratologia 57. Berlin: de Gruyter.

Bekhta, Natalya. 2017b. "We-Narratives: The Distinctiveness of Collective Narration." *Narrative* 25, no. 2: 164–81.

Bekhta, Natalya. 2019. Review of *Unnatural Narrative: Impossible Worlds in Fiction and Drama*, by Jan Alber. *Zeitschrift für Anglistik und Amerikanistik* 67, no. 1: 91–6.

Bekhta, Natalya, ed. 2020. "We-Narratives and We-Discourses across Genres." Special issue, *Style* 54, no. 1.

Bekhta, Natalya, and Ansgar Nünning. 2016. "'Unnatural' or 'Fictional'?: A Partial Critique of Unnatural Narrative and Its Discontents." *Style* 50, no. 4: 419–24.

Fludernik, Monika. 2011. "The Category of 'Person' in Fiction: You and We Narrative-Multiplicity and Indeterminacy of Reference." In *Current Trends in Narratology*, edited by Greta Olson and Monika Fludernik, 100–41. Narratologia 27. Berlin: de Gruyter.

Fludernik, Monika. 2012. "The Narrative Forms of Postcolonial Fiction." In *The Cambridge History of Postcolonial Literature*, edited by Ato Quayson, 903–37. Cambridge: Cambridge University Press.

Fludernik, Monika. 2014. "Collective Minds in Fact and Fiction: Intermental Thought and Group Consciousness in Early Modern Narrative." In "Theoretical Approaches to the Early Modern: Beyond New Historicism?" Special issue, *Poetics Today* 35, no. 4: 689–730.

Fludernik, Monika. 2015. "Collective Consciousness in Drama: A Cognitive Approach." In *Dramatic Minds: Performance, Cognition, and the Representation of Interiority; Essays in Honour of Margarete Rubik*, edited by Werner Huber, Elke Mettinger, and Eva Zettelmann, 21–41. Frankfurt: Lang.

Fludernik, Monika. 2017. "The Many in Action and Thought: Towards a Poetics of the Collective in Narrative." *Narrative* 25, no. 2: 139–63.

Fludernik, Monika. 2018. "Let Us Tell You Our Story: We Narration and Its Pronominal Peculiarities." In Gibbons and Macrae 2018: 171–92.

Fludernik, Monika. 2020. "The Politics of We-Narration: The One vs. the Many." In Bekhta 2020: 98–110.

Gibbons, Alison, and Andrea Macrae, eds. 2018. *Pronouns in Literature: Positions and Perspectives in Language.* Basingstoke: Palgrave Macmillan.

Marcus, Amit. 2008. "*We* are *You*: The Plural and the Dual in 'We' Fictional Narratives." *Journal of Literary Semantics* 37, no. 1: 1–21.

Margolin, Uri. 1996. "Telling Our Story: On 'We' Literary Narratives." *Language and Literature* 5, no. 2: 115–33.

Margolin, Uri. 2000. "Telling in the Plural: From Grammar to Ideology." *Poetics Today* 21, no. 3: 591–618.

Margolin, Uri. 2001. "Collective Perspective, Individual Perspective, and the Speaker in Between: On 'We' Literary Narratives." In *New Perspectives on Narrative Perspective*, edited by Willie van Peer and Seymour Chatman, 241–53. Albany: State University of New York Press.

Phelan, James. 2005. *Living to Tell about It.* Columbus: Ohio State University Press.

Richardson, Brian. 1994. "I etcetera: On the Poetics and Ideology of Multipersoned Narratives." *Style* 28, no. 3: 312–28.

Richardson, Brian. 2006. *Unnatural Voices: Extreme Narration in Modern and Postmodern Contemporary Fiction.* Columbus: Ohio State University Press.

Richardson, Brian. 2011. "U.S. Ethnic and Postcolonial Fiction: Toward a Poetics of Collective Narratives." In *Analyzing World Fiction: New Horizons in Narrative Theory*, edited by Frederick Luis Aldama, 3–16. Austin: University of Texas Press.

Richardson, Brian. 2015. "Representing Social Minds: 'We' and 'They' Narratives, Natural and Unnatural." *Narrative* 23, no. 2: 200–12.

Stanzel, F. K. 1984. *A Theory of Narrative.* Cambridge: Cambridge University Press.

Tuomela, Raimo. 1995. *The Importance of Us: A Philosophical Study of Basic Social Notions.* Stanford, CA: Stanford University Press.

Walsh, Richard. 2007. *The Rhetoric of Fictionality.* Columbus: Ohio State University Press.

Notes on Contributors

Lieven Ameel is senior lecturer in comparative literature at Tampere University, Finland. He holds a PhD in Finnish literature and comparative literature from the University of Helsinki and the Justus Liebig University, Giessen, Germany. He has published widely on literary experiences of space, narrative planning, and urban futures. His books include *Helsinki in Early Twentieth-Century Literature* (2014), *The Narrative Turn in Urban Planning* (2020), and the coedited volumes *Literature and the Peripheral City* (2015), *Literary Second Cities* (2017), *The Materiality of Literary Narratives in Urban History* (2019), and *Literatures of Urban Possibility* (2021).

Monika Fludernik is professor of English literature at the University of Freiburg, Germany. She is also the director of the graduate school Factual and Fictional Narration (GRK 1767). Her major research interests include narratology; linguistic approaches to literature, especially metaphor studies; law and literature; postcolonial studies; and eighteenth-century aesthetics. She is the author of *The Fictions of Language and the Languages of Fiction* (1993), the award-winning *Towards a "Natural" Narratology* (1996), and *Metaphors of Confinement: The Prison in Fact, Fiction, and Fantasy* (2019). Among her several (co)edited volumes are *Hybridity and Postcolonialism* (1998), *In the Grip of the Law* (2004), *Idleness, Indolence, and Leisure in English Literature* (2014), and *Narrative Factuality: A Handbook* (2019).

Alex Georgakopoulou is professor of discourse analysis and sociolinguistics at King's College London. She has developed small stories research, a paradigm for studying identities in everyday life stories. Her latest publications include *Quantified Storytelling: A Narrative Analysis of Metrics on Social Media* (with Stefan Iversen and Carsten Stage, 2020) and *The Cambridge Handbook*

Poetics Today 43:2 (June 2022) DOI 10.1215/03335372-9642721

of Discourse Studies (coedited with Anna De Fina, 2020). She is the coeditor of the Routledge Research in Narrative, Interaction, and Discourse series.

Korina Giaxoglou is senior lecturer in applied linguistics and English language at the Open University, UK. Her research focuses on narrative, affect, and sharing in digital contexts, and her work has appeared in edited volumes, handbooks, and peer-reviewed journals. She has published a research monograph entitled *A Narrative Approach to Social Media Mourning: Small Stories and Affective Positioning* (2021). Her public engagement work includes an Open Learn interactive experience, in which users are invited to reflect on how social media technologies have changed how we share grief.

Eevastiina Kinnunen, MA, is a PhD candidate in the Doctoral Programme in History, Culture, and Arts Studies at the University of Turku. She is interested in the potential of collective creative reading and in the connections between reading, writing, and well-being. Kinnunen is currently writing her PhD thesis on reading groups, creative reading practices, and narrative well-being. She also works as a bibliotherapy facilitator and creative writing instructor.

Päivi Kosonen, PhD, is senior researcher in comparative literature and member of SELMA: Centre for the Study of Storytelling, Experientiality, and Memory at the University of Turku, adjunct professor of comparative literature at the University of Helsinki, and trained bibliotherapist and bibliotherapeutic educator (Finnish Association of Biblio/Poetry Therapy). She specializes in autobiographical literature, bibliotherapeutic writing and reading methods, and the therapeutic potential of reading groups. Her recent publications include a series of three articles on therapeutic reading published in *Scriptum: Creative Writing Research Journal*: "Identity Work: Growth and Development through Reading" (2018), "The Interactive Process of Reading" (2019), and "Forms of Shared Reading" (2019).

Andrea Macrae is principal lecturer at Oxford Brookes University. She specializes in cognitive poetics and narratology. She is the author of *Discourse Deixis in Metafiction: The Language of Metanarration, Metalepsis, and Disnarration* (2019) and various chapters and articles, and is the coeditor of *Pronouns in Literature: Positions and Perspectives in Language* (2018).

Maria Mäkelä, PhD, is senior lecturer in comparative literature and former director (2016–20) of Narrare: Centre for Interdisciplinary Narrative Studies at Tampere University, Finland. Currently she heads two research projects: the Instrumental Narratives consortium (2018–22) and Storytelling in Information Systems Development (2019–22). Her latest publications include *The Routledge Companion for Narrative Theory* (coedited with Paul Dawson, 2022), and a "story-critical" manual in Finnish entitled *Kertomuksen vaarat (Dangers of Narrative,* forthcoming), coedited with her research team and written in collaboration with thirty-two professionals coming from other research disciplines and outside the academia: journalism, politics, business, the arts, healthcare, and the police.

Hanna Meretoja is professor of comparative literature and director of SELMA: Centre for the Study of Storytelling, Experientiality, and Memory at the University of Turku, Finland, and principal investigator in the Academy of Finland research consortium "Instrumental Narratives: The Limits of Storytelling and New Story-Critical Narrative Theory" (2018–22). Her monographs include *The Ethics of Storytelling: Narrative Hermeneutics, History, and the Possible* (2018) and *The Narrative Turn in Fiction and Theory* (2014), and she has coedited, with Colin Davis, *The Routledge Companion to Literature and Trauma* (2020) and *Storytelling and Ethics: Literature, Visual Arts, and the Power of Narrative* (2018).

Matias Nurminen, MA, is a doctoral student in comparative literature at Tampere University. In his ongoing PhD project "Narrative Warfare: Strategic Narratives in the Antifeminist Manosphere," Nurminen maps out how radical masculinity movements utilize narratives, counternarratives, and fictional works to promote their worldview. Nurminen specializes in interdisciplinary narrative studies and applying narratology in analyzing real-world storytelling contexts. His has had recent articles published in *Narrative Inquiry* (2019) and *The Routledge Handbook of Counter-narratives* (2020).

Laura Piippo, PhD, is a postdoctoral researcher at Narrare: Centre for Interdiscplinary Narrative Studies at Tampere University, Finland. Her current research focuses on the places, forms, and value of a book (codex) in digital environments. The topic of Piippo's doctoral thesis (2020) was the experimental poetics of the contemporary Finnish novel *Neuromaani*, by Jaakko Yli-Juonikas, especially the materiality and paratextuality of the book. Her peer-reviewed articles, edited volumes, and special issues on these topics have been published (or are forthcoming) both in English and in Finnish.

Hanna-Riikka Roine has a PhD in literary studies and works as a postdoctoral research fellow funded by the Academy of Finland at the Tampere University and as an affiliated researcher in the consortium *Instrumental Narratives.* Her current research explores the ways in which our entanglement with digital media affects, guides, and shapes our engagement with the possible. Roine is a coeditor of the book *The Ethos of Digital Environments:*

Technology, Literary Theory, and Philosophy (2021) and has published articles, for instance, on the ways in which narratological inquiry may be extended toward the machines of computational media.

Anne Rüggemeier is postdoctoral research fellow at the Freiburg Institute for Advanced Studies (FRIAS), Germany. As a member of the ERC-funded project Lists in Literature and Culture, she investigates the multiple ways in which lists in illness narratives renegotiate the power effects of science and administration. She has published extensively on the poetics of list-making, life writing, relationality, and graphic narratives, and in the field of medical humanities. Her work appeared in the *Journal of Comics and Graphic Novels*, the *European Journal of Life Writing*, and *a/b: Autobiography Studies*. She coedited the volume titled *Forms of List-Making: Epistemic, Literary, and Visual Enumeration* (2022) and authored the monograph *Die relationale Autobiographie* (2014). She is also the Principal Investigator of the project "A Literary History of Isolation" (seventeenth- to twenty-first-century English literature), funded by the German-Research Council (DFG). She teaches English literature at the University of Freiburg.

Kristiana Willsey has a PhD in folklore and is currently a lecturer in anthropology at the University of Southern California. Previously, she was a visiting scholar at the American Academy of Arts and Sciences in Cambridge. She has published research on personal narrative, folk and fairy tales, and popular culture in the *Journal of American Folklore, Humanities*, and various edited scholarly volumes.